Sex Differences in Depression

Susan Nolen-Hoeksema

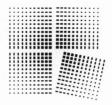

Sex Differences in Depression

STANFORD UNIVERSITY PRESS, Stanford, California

Stanford University Press
Stanford, California
© 1990 by the Board of Trustees of the
Leland Stanford Junior University
Printed in the United States of America

CIP data appear at the end of the book

Original printing 1990

Last figure below indicates year of this printing:
02 01 00 99 98 97 96 95 94 93

Preface

My interest in women's depressions began when I was an under-graduate, reading the poetry of Charlotte Perkins Gilman. Gilman wrote of endless days of mental fatigue, despair, self-hate. I soon discovered that many women poets, writers, and leaders have lost days, weeks, even years, to the pain of depression. Indeed, women in all walks of life seemed to be more likely to be depressed than men. I wanted to know why. I began to investigate the theories of women's vulnerability to depression, and the studies done to test these theories. They ranged from biological theories about the role of hormones in women's moods to social theories about the effects of oppression on women's mental health to psychological theories about the influence of women's personality traits on their vulnera-bility to depression. Time and time again, I found that plausible theories either had not been tested adequately or had been tested and not supported. Yet they seem to be accepted as fact in much of the psychological and popular literature. Women are being advised how to run their lives on the basis of these theories.

It is ten years since I first read Gilman's poetry and began to collect information on depression in women. Some of my own research in those years has been dedicated to testing possible sources of women's vulnerability to depression (see Chapter 7). In writing this book, I have compiled many studies of women and depression into a critical review of each of the major theories of why women are more prone to depression than men. My primary goal was to assess the current knowledge of sex differences in depression. My hope is that this review will challenge many researchers to direct their talents and energies toward understanding women's vulnerability to depression. Toward that end, I have commented throughout the book on methodological problems in existing studies that have precluded my drawing firm conclusions about the evidence for a theory, and I have suggested how studies should have been done. In Chapter 9, I outline ten questions I believe should be addressed in future research, and offer suggestions for carrying out relevant studies. I also hope that the critiques of existing theories presented here will lead clinicians and others who give advice to women to temper their advice with a caution that, as yet, we do not fully understand why women are prone to depression.

This book was written to be accessible to many groups of interested readers. It can be used as a text for advanced undergraduate or graduate courses in psychopathology, women's studies, or research methods. It can serve as a resource for social science researchers and mental health professionals. Finally, I have attempted to omit jargon and to present just enough research to enable people without training in the social sciences to understand the work that has been done and its implications. Throughout, I have worked hard to be balanced and objective in my reviews of the literature. I urge readers to open their minds and challenge their assumptions about women and depression.

Over the years I have been writing this book, I have received a tremendous amount of intellectual guidance and personal support from Martin Seligman of the University of Pennsylvania, with whom I worked as a graduate student and now continue to collaborate. Marty taught me how to take a scholarly approach to critiquing a literature, and also helped me to maintain my motivation for this topic by reminding me frequently how important it is. Christopher Peterson, of the University of Michigan, has also provided insightful comments on both the content and the writing style of this book, and I am very grateful. Much of the most recent information on the effects of hormones on moods was provided by Jean Hamilton, of the Institute for Research on Women's Health. Jean's comments on the chapter on biological explanations helped me to understand where the research on hormones and moods may be going in the future. I also wish to thank the students who have contributed to my thinking on sex differences in depression and to research on the topic, particularly Jannay Morrow, Tomi-Ann Roberts, and Barbara Fredrickson, all of Stanford University.

Muriel Bell, my editor at Stanford University Press, has supported the idea of a scholarly review of the literature presented here since she learned of the project, and has facilitated the project in many ways over the last few years. Neil Channing Hughes has provided excellent advice on how to make the text both scholarly and comprehensible to the reader.

My thanks for moral support during the writing of this book go to many people: my husband, Richard, my parents, Catherine and John Nolen, my late aunt Bonnie Behner, my parents-in-law, Marjorie and Renze Hoeksema, and several other friends and relatives. Their confidence in me has been tremendous. Every woman should have such support.

S.N.-H.

Contents

Sex Differences in Depression

CHAPTER ONE

The Dark Cloud: Definitions and Explanations of Depression

"A sort of gray fog drifted across my mind, a cloud that grew and darkened."
—Charlotte Perkins Gilman

We have all had periods when we feel depressed or unhappy, when we have no motivation, find it difficult to concentrate, and become passive and have no energy. Survey studies have found that at any given time, approximately one out of six adult Americans reports moderate to severe levels of depression (Eaton & Kessler, 1981). For most of us these episodes last only a few hours or a few days and do not interfere with our day-to-day functioning. However, nearly 8 percent of all Americans have at some time in their lives experienced an episode of severe depression that has left them incapacitated for a period of weeks or months (Robins et al., 1984). Depression is a common experience, then. It is more common among women than among men, however. Women are about twice as likely as men to develop both moderate and severe depressions (Nolen-Hoeksema, 1987; Weissman & Klerman, 1977). This book explores why depression is so much more common in women than in men.

Many explanations for the sex differences in depression have been proposed over the years. In the nineteenth century and before, depression and anxiety in women were usually viewed either as inevitable consequences of women's inferior anatomy or as the consequences of shirking the "natural" feminine role (Ehrenreich & English, 1978). For example, the clinician who treated Charlotte Perkins Gilman for the depression she describes in the epigraph to this chapter thought that Gilman's depression resulted in part from her "manly" habit of writing books. He recommended that Gilman "live as domestic a life as possible. Have your child with you at all times. Lie down an hour after every meal. Have but two hours intellectual life every day. And never touch a pen, brush or pencil as long as you live" (Gilman, 1975, p. 96). Gilman followed the doctor's orders and soon had a "nervous breakdown." Later Gilman became an influential feminist who spoke out against nineteenth-century modes of treatment for women's emotional and physical problems.

It would be easy to dismiss nineteenth-century attitudes about emotional health as uninformed and no longer relevant. Yet these attitudes still affect the present-day view of women's emotional health. For example, the notion that women are predestined to fulfill certain roles in life if they are to be emotionally healthy remains with us in psychodynamic theories of women and depression. Moreover, the notion that women's emotional health is strongly influenced by biological changes associated with their reproductive organs remains with us in some of the biological explanations for sex differences in depression. That these notions date from the nineteenth century and before does not mean they are wrong. It means only that many of our current perspectives on women's health are rooted in some very old presumptions about females. The history of theories of depression in women is reviewed later in this chapter.

The focus of this book, however, is contemporary explanations for sex differences in depression. The purpose of the book is to evaluate the evidence for each theory critically, and to reach some conclusions about what we do and do not know about sex differences in depression. There is much we do not know: the data supporting most of the commonly believed explanations for sex differences in depression prove to be meager. Often the crucial studies for testing these explanations have yet to be carried out, and the studies that exist have often been inconclusive. In fact it is remarkable how little attention empiricists have given to such an important phenomenon as sex differences in depression. Another purpose of this book is therefore to suggest directions for new research on sex differences in depression. Studies that are needed are described intermittently throughout the chapters. The final chapter highlights ten important but unanswered questions that should guide future research.

Definitions of Depression

Common symptoms of depression include loss of motivation, sadness, low self-esteem, physical aches and pains, and difficulty concentrating. The depressed person often talks about "not caring any more" and shows decreased interest in the activities she used to enjoy. She may lose her appetite, or she may begin eating more. She may have trouble sleeping, or she may want to sleep all the time. Depressed people are slowed down in movement, in speech, and in thought. Very common to depression are thoughts of worthlessness and guilt. And some depressed people attempt or commit suicide.

The opposite of depression is mania. Manic symptoms include greatly increased energy, racing thoughts, pressured speech, wild and extravagant behaviors, and grandiosity. A manic person may sell all his worldly goods in one afternoon in order to raise money to run for president of the United States. One person I know gets married or divorced during manic episodes, which occur every few years. People who suffer manic episodes typically also suffer, at other periods in their lives, from episodes of depression.

Unipolar Disorders Versus Bipolar Disorders

Empirical studies (e.g., Andreasen et al., 1987) have indicated that people who suffer only from episodes of depression and people who suffer from alternating episodes of mania and depression have two distinct types of disorders. People who suffer only from depression are said to have a *unipolar depressive disorder*, and those who suffer from both depression and mania are said to have a *bipolar disorder* (American Psychiatric Association, 1987). People with unipolar depressive disorder have different genetic histories, different biochemical abnormalities, and different reactions to drugs from people with bipolar disorders.

To date, almost all the discussion of sex differences in depression has been concerned with sex differences in unipolar depression. It has been generally assumed that there are no sex differences in bipolar disorder (e.g., Boyd & Weissman, 1981; Weissman & Klerman, 1977). Yet in a review of the literature on bipolar disorder, Clayton (1981) showed that both bipolar disorder and unipolar depression are more prevalent among women than among men. The only explanation that has been offered for sex differences in bipolar disorder is the suggestion of Winokur and colleagues (see Cadoret & Winokur, 1974; Gershon & Bunney, 1976) that both bipolar disorder and unipolar depression are associated with genetic abnormalities linked to the female chromosomes. I will discuss this explanation in reviewing biological explanations in general. Since all other explanations of sex differences in depression to be reviewed refer only to sex differences in unipolar depression, I will be dealing primarily with studies of unipolar depression.

Depressive Disorders Versus Depressive Symptoms

I have been referring to depressive *disorders* thus far. But how do we know when an episode of depression qualifies as a disorder? To diagnose psychological disorders, clinicians in the United States use the criteria in the *Diagnostic and Statistical Manual of the American Psychiatric Association*, known as DSM (American Psychiatric Association, 1987). The DSM lists nine symptoms of depression: (1) a depressed mood, (2) a diminished interest or pleasure in most activities, (3) significant weight loss or weight gain that is unintentional, or a decrease or an increase in appetite, (4) insomnia or hypersomnia, (5) psychomotor agitation or retardation, (6) fatigue or loss of energy, (7) feelings of worthlessness or excessive or inappropriate guilt, (8) diminished ability to think or concentrate, or indecisiveness, and (9) recurrent thoughts of death or suicide attempts. To be diagnosed as having a major depressive episode, a person must show at least five of these symptoms (at least one of which must be a depressed mood or a diminished interest or pleasure) for two or more weeks. These symptoms must also represent a change from the individual's previous functioning.*

But what about people whose depressive symptoms do not meet these criteria? Are they not truly depressed? The question whether depressive disorders are discrete and distinguishable from "subclinical" depressive symptoms is debated by clinicians and researchers

---

*A major depressive episode is *not* diagnosed, however, if the disturbance is a normal reaction to the death of a loved one, or if it is established that an organic factor initiated and maintained the disturbance. It also is not diagnosed if the person has experienced hallucinations or delusions in the absence of mood symptoms or if the person already has a diagnosis of schizophrenia, schizophreniform disorder, or delusional disorder.

alike. There are clearly some people whose depressions "feel" like a disorder to those observing them, much as multiple sclerosis and epilepsy feel like disorders. For these people, depressive episodes often seem to come on without warning or obvious cause. Some people even become psychotic during an episode of depression. But do these depressions differ in kind or only in degree from the subclinical depressions we all experience occasionally?

There is no definitive answer to this question. The line between subclinical and clinical levels of depression is blurry at best (Hirschfeld & Cross, 1982). Subclinical depressions are usually assessed by asking subjects to complete questionnaires. Cut-off scores are designated for the level of symptoms representing "severe" depression. About 60 percent of persons scoring in the "severe" ranges of depression questionnaires are diagnosed by DSM criteria as having a depressive disorder (Weissman & Myers, 1978). But the cut-off scores for the "severe" ranges of depression questionnaires are made arbitrarily, and it would probably not be too difficult to make the cut-off score such that 100 percent of the people who scored above it would be diagnosed as depressed by DSM criteria. The DSM criteria for depression are themselves arbitrary to some extent. They were derived by agreement among a number of clinicians and represent compromises between those clinicians' differing points of view about the defining characteristics of depression.

I would argue, moreover, that we do a disservice to people whose depressions do not quite meet diagnostic criteria by discounting their depressions as "only normal." Even moderate levels of depression appear to significantly impair functioning in work and school settings and in social situations (e.g., Hirschfeld & Cross, 1982; Kandel & Davies, 1986; Masters, Barden & Ford, 1979). If a moderately depressed person is having problems keeping up at work or at school, such problems can have lasting effects. For example, a college student who is moderately depressed during final exam week may be more likely to fail one or more exams, lowering her grade-point average and perhaps hurting her chances of being accepted by a graduate or professional school.

It is also important to examine rates of depressive symptoms, and not just rates of diagnosed depressive disorders, because several factors affect whether a person seeks medical treatment from health professionals and thus is diagnosed as having a depressive disorder.

The effects of a person's socioeconomic status, geographic setting (for example, urban versus rural residence), and age on help-seeking appear to be substantial (Wing, 1976). Usually, only a person willing and able to be treated by mental professionals is given a diagnosis. Thus it is important to survey all sectors of the general population, asking about the experience of depressive symptoms, in order to obtain accurate estimates of the rates of depression in the population.

The review of the data on sex differences in depression presented in Chapter 2 will cover studies of people who were depressed enough to seek treatment, and studies in which cut-off scores from depression questionnaires were used to define depression. As we shall see in that chapter, no matter how you define depression, after puberty women show more depression than men.

The History of Theories of Depression

In ancient times, depression and mania, like all abnormalities, were thought to result from possession by demons or from punishment by the gods. Treatments usually involved exorcism by shamans or priests, or having the victim sleep in religious temples in the expectation of relief from the gods. In the fifth century B.C., however, the Greek physician Hippocrates argued that it was not demons or gods that caused psychological disorders, but abnormalities in physiology. Hippocrates classified mental disorders into three categories: melancholia, mania, and "brain fever." The label *melancholia* was applied to the syndrome we now call depression. Hippocrates considered melancholia a physical disorder, caused by an excess of black bile, one of the four basic body "humors" or fluids. (The term *melancholia* is from the Greek *melan* for "black" and *cholē* for "bile.") Hippocrates' prescribed treatment for melancholia was quietness, abstinence from alcohol and sexual activity, and a careful diet (Davison & Neale, 1982).

The word *mania* comes from the Greek *mainesthai*, which means "to be mad." Hippocrates and his students also considered mania, and other forms of behavior and thought that seemed completely out of touch with reality, to be the result of biological factors. Later, in the second century B.C., Aretaeus, another Greek physician, argued that at least some mental disorders were simply exaggerations in normal personalities. He suggested that persons who were naturally irritable and often became elated were prone to mania (Davison & Neale, 1982). In turn, people who were naturally serious were prone to melancholia. Thus Aretaeus proposed one of the earliest personality theories of the affective disorders. He also noted that people could switch back and forth between episodes of mania and melancholia.

From about the third century to the twelfth century A.D., the care of the sick, including the care of the mentally ill, was often left to monks. Many people who had lost touch with reality were simply abandoned, however, and allowed to roam the countryside. There was essentially no progress in theorizing about mental disorders or treatment for them during the Dark Ages. From about the twelfth century, the mentally ill were often the victims of witch-hunts. In a crusade that reached its peak in the seventeenth and eighteenth century, the Church sent forth its inquisitors in search of heretics and witches, to extract confessions from them, by torture if necessary, and usually to execute them by burning at the stake. In 1486 two inquisitors named Heinrich Kraemer and Johann Sprenger published a guide to witch-hunting called the *Malleus Maleficarum* or *The Witches' Hammer*. This practical guide gave tips on how to recognize witches. Birthmarks were considered indications that a person had been touched by the devil. Another sign of demonic possession was a sudden loss of reason (Davison & Neale, 1982). Indeed, some historians have argued that many people suffering from mania, schizophrenia, or psychotic depression were charged as witches and burned at the stake during the Middle Ages (see Zilboorg & Henry, 1941); others argue that only a small proportion of those burned at the stake were insane (see Davison & Neale, 1982; Ehrenreich & English, 1978). It is well established that over 85 percent of those burned at the stake were female. Over 100,000 women, along with many thousands of men, were executed over the three centuries of witch-hunts. According to the *Malleus Maleficarum*, women were particularly likely to become possessed by the devil because their insatiable lust led them to submit to intercourse even with devils.

Following the witch-hunts, asylums became the repositories both for the mentally ill and for beggars. Patients who made a nuisance of themselves (for instance, those showing symptoms like those of mania and schizophrenia) were chained to walls and floors for years, put in straitjackets, restrained in chairs, and sometimes locked in small coffinlike boxes. The large, cold stone rooms in which inmates stayed were unsanitary, with rats roaming freely. Not until the late eighteenth and early nineteenth century did people begin to question the idea that the insane were no better than animals and could be treated as such. Reformers such as Philippe Pinel and William Tuke argued for more humane treatment of the insane and, despite much public resistance, won freedom and care for many inmates of asylums (Foucault, 1965).

Finally, late in the nineteenth century, Emil Kraepelin suggested one of the first systems for distinguishing and classifying different types of mental disorders. The development of a classificatory system was a breakthrough that was necessary before research could be done on the causes and cures of disorders. Kraepelin proposed that there were two major groups of severe mental disorders: manic-depressive psychosis and dementia praecox (later called schizophrenia). Kraepelin argued that manic-depressive psychosis was caused by metabolic irregularities and that schizophrenia was caused by chemical imbalances.

About the same time, a young Viennese neurologist named Sigmund Freud began to study with Jean Charcot, a famous French neurologist who was using hypnosis to help cure women suffering from hysteria. Hysteria was an exceptionally common disorder among middle- and upper-class women of the Victorian period. It was characterized by headaches, muscular aches, weakness, indigestion, depression, and sometimes complete loss of functioning in some part of the body (for example, paralysis of a limb) with no apparent physical cause. In dramatic presentations before other physicians and medical students, Charcot supposedly would hypnotize such patients and give them the suggestion that their symptoms would remit. Sometimes he would have them try to recount, under hypnosis, any traumatic event they thought was connected to their disorder. Charcot believed that the emotional release, or catharsis, of recounting a traumatic event, along with his hypnotic suggestions, produced the cures that seemed to occur during his presentations. In reality, Charcot's medical students were coaching the patients to fake hypnosis and to overcome or deny their symptoms during Charcot's presentations.

Although it is questionable whether Charcot's patients benefited from the presentations, Sigmund Freud certainly did. Charcot's theories of catharsis and his apparent ability to tap hidden regions of the mind through hypnosis contributed to Freud's developing theory of the unconscious. From his time with Charcot in the 1880's until his death in 1939, Freud developed his ideas of the unconscious and its role in psychological disorders into what became known as psychoanalysis. One of Freud's best-known theories of a psychological disorder is his theory of melancholia (Freud, 1917). Freud first pointed to the similarities between melancholia and grief: in both the sufferer feels sad, alone, unmotivated, and lethargic. But, Freud noted, the grieving person has a reason to feel this way, because she has lost a loved one, whereas the melancholic has not. Further, the melancholic displays a much greater degree of self-blame and self-hatred than the grieving person—indeed, melancholic people appear to be punishing themselves. Freud argued that the melancholic has experienced a loss as tragic as the loss of the grieving person, at least in the melancholic's mind. That is, the melancholic has perceived the loss of some important object of her love—perhaps in a rejection by another person or in a failure at work. As is normal, the melancholic feels some anger as a result of such a loss. But what distinguishes a person who becomes melancholic from one who does not is that the melancholic turns that anger in on herself. Thus the melancholic appears to be punishing herself as well as experiencing the symptoms of grief. This is Freud's "introjected hostility" theory of melancholia. Contemporary psychoanalysts have revised Freud's theory substantially, but the notion that introjected hostility is the cause of melancholia remains one of the most common theories of depression held by laypeople.

Psychoanalysis was the predominant theoretical framework in psychiatry and clinical psychology through the first half of the twentieth century. It was severely criticized, however, by proponents of behaviorism, or learning theory, a school of psychology that became increasingly popular in the 1960's and early 1970's. For example, Peter Lewinsohn (1974) proposed that depression resulted from a reduction in positive events, or reinforcers. The obvious treatment for depression, then, was to increase the positive reinforcers in the depressive's life. Just having good things happen wasn't enough to cure depression, however. Depressives needed to believe they caused the good things. Lewinsohn suggested that people become depressed when they do not act in ways designed to bring about good events, and thus experience few "response-contingent positive reinforcers." That is, they become depressed because they fail to exhibit responses that bring about good events (and prevent bad events). The appropriate therapy for depression, according to this new theory, was to increase depressives' skills in obtaining positive reinforcers through their own responses.

A similar idea underlies the learned helplessness theory of depression, namely, the idea that people who cannot control their environment lose motivation and look depressed. Martin Seligman and his colleagues carried out experiments in the 1960's in which dogs were given either a controllable or an uncontrollable shock (Overmier & Seligman, 1967; Seligman & Maier, 1967). The dogs in the "controllable shock" group could turn off the shock by jumping a short barrier, and they quickly learned how to do so. The dogs in the "uncontrollable shock" group could not turn off or otherwise escape the shock. Remarkably, when these dogs were put into a situation where they could control the shock, they seemed unable to learn how to do so. They would just sit in the box, passive and whimpering, until the shock went off. Even when these dogs were dragged across the barrier by the experimenter, in an attempt to teach them how to turn off the shock, the dogs did not learn the response. Seligman and his colleagues called the phenomenon they witnessed in the dogs in the uncontrollable shock group "learned helplessness." They identified a cluster of problems that characterized the response of organisms to uncontrollable situations. These problems included decreased motivation, an inability to learn new responses to control the environment, passivity, and, in humans, sadness. These symptoms are similar to those of human depression.

The generalization of learned helplessness theory to human depression, however, did not come about fully until 1975, with the appearance of Seligman's book *Helplessness: On Depression, Development, and Death*. Here Seligman pointed out the similarities between the symptoms, causes, and cures of human depression and helplessness deficits and argued that at least some depressions might be caused by the expectation that one cannot control important outcomes in one's environment. Learned helplessness theory described the process by which unfortunate life circumstances, such as poverty and social oppression, could lead to the psychological disorder called depression, and it quickly attracted the attention of those interested in depression in economically and socially deprived groups, such as blacks, the unemployed, and women.

A major problem with the behavioral theories of depression was that they could not explain why some people who are confronted by uncontrollable circumstances become depressed and some do not.* That is, different people react to the same event in different ways. To account for these differences in reactions, most theoreticians began to look for differences in the way people appraised and interpreted events. An early proponent of such a cognitive theory was Aaron Beck (Beck, 1967). Beck began to notice that certain errors were consistently made by depressed patients in the interpretations and conclusions they drew from information. Depressed patients often overgeneralized from one negative experience, concluding, for instance, that they had no ability in math after failing one math exam. They also personalized circumstances inappropriately, perhaps concluding that their child's failure in a math exam was their fault. Beck hypothesized that depressed people have a negative view of the world, of themselves, and of the future, which leads them into errors in logic such as overgeneralization and personalization. In turn, these errors maintain and exacerbate the depressed person's negative perspective. Beck developed a cognitive therapy for depression (Beck et al., 1979) that is designed to correct the illogical thinking of a depressed person. The therapy has proved very effective (Kovacs et al., 1981; Rush et al., 1977).

Only three years after the publication of *Helplessness*, Seligman, along with Lynn Abramson and John Teasdale, published a reformulation of the learned helplessness theory (Abramson, Seligman & Teasdale, 1978) that also focused on thinking styles that lead to depression. They proposed that people's attributions or explanations of an event influence their helplessness deficits (depressive symptoms) in reaction to the event. People who tend to attribute bad events to

---

* Lewinsohn (1974) and Seligman (1975) did argue that a person's learning history —that is, her experiences with controlling the environment and obtaining positive reinforcers in the past—can influence her susceptibility to a depressive reaction to a particular event. In other words, people who have experienced little controllability and few positive reinforcers will have a greater tendency to become helpless and depressed in response to a new uncontrollable event. Because this behavioral account of individual differences in susceptibility to depressive reactions to events proved more difficult to test than the cognitive account, the cognitive account became more widely accepted.

causes that influence many areas of their lives (global causes), instead of to causes that influence only one area (specific causes), will expect to be helpless in many areas of their lives and thus will show deficits in many areas. People who attribute bad events to causes that are long-lasting rather than short-lived will expect to be helpless in the future, and thus their helplessness will be long-term. People who blame themselves instead of others for bad events will experience a loss of self-esteem. So, according to Abramson, Seligman, and Teasdale, people who habitually tend to explain bad events in terms of causes that are internal, stable, and global (and good events in terms of external, unstable, and specific causes) will expect many bad events (and few good events) to recur, will blame themselves for bad events, and will thus be more vulnerable to depression than people with the opposite style. For example, suppose that on a given day both Joan and Terri had fights with their lovers and had articles accepted for publication. Joan attributes her fight with her lover to the fact that he did not sleep well the night before and attributes her paper's acceptance for publication to her skill as a researcher. Such attributions will lead Joan to be happy, have high self-esteem, and expect better interaction with her lover when she arrives at home in the evening. On the other hand, Terri attributes her fight with her lover to her tendency to nag him and assumes that her paper was accepted for publication because the journal's editor doesn't know anything about Terri's field of research and therefore couldn't see the errors in her methodology. Terri is likely to be depressed and to lack hope at the end of the day—and frequently throughout her life. To some extent, Joan and Terri may both have judged events accurately. That is, Joan's lover may indeed have slept poorly, and Terri may indeed have a tendency to nag. But most events have multiple causes. Some people habitually focus on optimistic causes, whereas other people habitually focus on pessimistic causes. According to the reformulated helplessness theory, people who tend to make pessimistic attributions are more prone to depression than those who tend to make optimistic attributions. Many studies conducted with adults and the few studies conducted with children have supported this prediction (for reviews see Peterson & Seligman, 1984; Sweeney, Anderson & Bailey, 1986).

While most psychologists were developing psychosocial theories of depression, many psychiatrists and some psychologists searched for biological causes of depression. In the late 1960's and early 1970's, one hypothesis about the biological origins of depression began to gain prominence: the "amine hypothesis of depression" (see Baldessarini, 1986). Amines are one type of neurotransmitter, a biochemical that facilitates transmission of impulses from one neuron to another. Amines appear to play an important role in the transmission of information between neurons in the limbic system, a part of the brain that seems to influence emotion. The amine hypothesis of depression states that the loss of drive and the negative emotions that characterize depression result from the depletion of amines in the limbic system.

The amine hypothesis of depression was based initially on chance discoveries. In the 1950's one drug commonly used to treat hypertension was reserpine. Physicians noted that reserpine induced serious depressions in approximately 15 percent of the patients who took it. Laboratory studies indicated that reserpine led to the depletion of two of the amine neurotransmitters, norepinephrine and serotonin, in the synapses between neurons in the central nervous system (Bunney & Davis, 1982). This discovery led some investigators to propose that naturally occurring depressions resulted from a depletion of these amines. Additional evidence for the amine hypothesis also came about accidentally: clinicians who were testing an antituberculosis drug called iproniazid observed that subjects experienced a relief from any depressive symptoms, and some even experienced euphoria. Iproniazid is an inhibitor of the enzyme monoamine oxidase, or MAO. In the nervous system, MAO chemically breaks down and depletes amines in the synapses. Thus iproniazid appeared to have antidepressant effects because it inhibited MAO, in turn preventing the breakdown and depletion of amines in the synapses. When investigators purposely gave MAO inhibitors to depressed patients, many patients showed relief of their symptoms. In the intervening decades there have been hundreds of studies attempting to test more directly the hypothesis that depression is caused by a depletion of amines (particularly norepinephrine and serotonin). Some of these studies are discussed in Chapter 3. Support for the amine hypothesis has been mixed (see Baldessarini, 1986; Thase, Frank & Kupfer, 1985), but it remains one of the most frequently researched biological theories of depression.

Historical Views of Women's Depression

Until about the nineteenth century, Eve's role in the fall from grace was considered an adequate explanation for any pains women might be more likely than men to suffer (Williams, 1979). With the passion for science that emerged in the nineteenth century, however, a more scientific explanation of the differences between women and men began to be sought. Physical differences between men and women were assumed to cause differences in men's and women's psychological functioning, temperament, abilities, and intellect (Shields, 1975). Nineteenth-century scientists sought to determine which biological differences between men and women accounted for the "obvious" and profound differences in the psychology of men and women. More generally, the question was why women are different from men—the so-called Woman Question.

One of the most frequent topics of discussion among physicians in the nineteenth century was the epidemic of "nervous disorders" in women, particularly middle- and upper-class women. S. Weir Mitchell, a leading nineteenth-century American physician, described these disorders as follows: "The woman grows pale and thin, eats little, or if she eats does not profit by it. Everything wearies her—to sew, to write, to read, to walk—and by and by the sofa or the bed is her only comfort. Every effort is paid for dearly, and she describes herself as aching and sore, as sleeping ill, and as needing constant stimulus and endless tonics. . . . If such a person is emotional, she does not fail to become more so, and even the firmest women lose self-control at last under incessant feebleness" (quoted in Ehrenreich & English, 1978, pp. 103–4). This syndrome, which had many of the features of depression, was often chronic. Many prominent women suffered from this disorder. For example, Alice James suffered from this disorder from age 19 until her death of breast cancer at age 43.

Ehrenreich and English (1978) argue that the outbreak of nervous disorders in women and scientists' obsession with the Woman Question resulted from the cataclysmic changes in the daily lives of women and men during the Industrial Revolution. Prior to this revolution, a woman's role was recognized as extremely important: she ground corn, baked bread, spun cotton and wove cloth, made candles, preserved food, and clothed her family. In short, she was indispensable to the family's survival. During the Industrial Revolution, however, many of the essential domestic tasks performed by women were taken over by factories. The centuries-old patterns of interaction between wife and husband, between mother and children, were broken forever by the industrialization of women's work and the mass migration of people into the cities to find paid work. One aspect of the Woman Question, argue Ehrenreich and English, was the question of what to do with women now that their traditional role in the family had been usurped by the factories.

One solution suggested by early feminists was to give women fully equal status in the new industrial society (Gilman, 1975). Instead, the society chose to romanticize women, to define them as the exact opposites of men and therefore the perfect complements to men (Ehrenreich & English, 1978). Whereas men were aggressive and self-interested, women were nurturant and sacrificing. Men were stoic; women were emotional. Men were rational; women were irrational and intuitive. Women and the home should be the opposite of men and the marketplace, providing respite for men from the rigors of work. Women (at least middle- and upper-class women) were expected to devote all their energies to family and home, even though much of the skilled labor of homemaking was now done in factories.

The favorite cure for nervous disorders, called the "rest cure," was based on this romantic view of women. The patient was to engage in absolutely no intellectual activity and was to throw herself completely into the care and nurturing of her children and husband. Charlotte Perkins Gilman was prescribed such a "rest cure" by S. Weir Mitchell, her doctor. Indeed, the result of this cure was nearly tragic for Gilman: "[I] came perilously close to losing my mind. The mental agony grew so unbearable that I would sit blankly moving my head from side to side. . . . I would crawl into remote closets and under beds—to hide from the grinding pressure of that distress" (Gilman, 1975, p. 96). Gilman recovered, but only after she rejected the rest cure, left her husband, and started a career as a writer and feminist activist. She was convinced that her "nervous disorder" was the result of being forced to remain at home caring for her child and ignoring her desires for an independent career.

The notion that women were inferior to men in their personality and abilities, and that a quiet, secluded life as wife and mother best fit their natures, remained the predominant view of the time. Physicians and scientists began to seek biological differences between men and women that would account for women's inferiority. Women's greatest weakness was said to be their emotionality, which predisposed them to nervous disorders. Some physicians attributed this emotionality to a more excitable nervous system. For example, G. T. W. Patrick wrote: "One of the most marked differences between man and woman is the greater excitability of the nerve centers in the latter. Woman possesses in a higher degree than man the fundamental property of all nervous tissue, irritability, or response to any stimulus. The vasomotor system is particularly excitable, and this fact is in immediate connection with her emotional life. That woman is more emotional than man is only another way of stating the same fact" (Patrick, 1895/1979, p. 7).

A more vague though firmly held belief was that a woman's reproductive system "overpowered" her brain, that her intellectual powers were controlled by her ovaries and uterus. For example, Dr. F. Hollick wrote, "The uterus, it must be remembered, is the controlling organ in the female body, being the most excitable of all, and so intimately connected by the ramifications of its numerous nerves, with every other part" (Hollick, 1849, quoted in Ehrenreich & English, 1978, p. 120). All abnormalities, including insanity, were traced to diseased reproductive systems. During menstruation, women were thought to be nearly psychotic. The brain and reproductive organs were said to compete for blood: menstruation took blood away from the brain and therefore diminished intellectual power. Physicians recommended complete bed rest during menstruation to preserve the woman's sanity; the psychologist Granville Stanley Hall wrote in 1916: "All heavy exercise should be omitted during the menstrual week. . . . [A] girl should not only retire earlier at this time, but ought to stay out of school from one to three days as the case may be, resting the mind and taking extra hours of rest and sleep" (quoted in Ehrenreich & English, 1978, p. 111).

Another biological explanation for women's greater emotionality was "maternal instinct." Shields (1975) argues that the notion of maternal instinct, although it had been around for centuries, gained credence among nineteenth-century academicians because of the growing popularity of evolutionary theory, with its emphasis on the biological foundations of temperament. Necessary components of the maternal instinct were thought to be an unselfish devotion to others and a greater degree of emotionality (McDougall, 1921; Spencer, 1891; Thorndike, 1911). It was argued, however, that the gift of great emotional feeling was at the same time a woman's curse, making her more prone to nervous disorders. Although little reputable evidence was provided to support most of these claims, they were staunchly believed by both the scientific and the lay communities of the nineteenth and early twentieth century.

While many were trying to find biological or sociological causes of women's apparent greater emotionality and vulnerability to depression, Freud and his colleagues were providing a psychoanalytic explanation. Freud (1925, 1931) argued, as did the biologists of his time, that females tended to be more self-punishing, even more masochistic, than males. But he gave a completely different explanation for this phenomenon from his contemporaries. He argued that the tendency toward masochism developed because little girls realize that they are inferior biologically to boys, particularly with regard to their sexual organs. Freud also argued that a tendency toward masochism was necessary if a female was to enjoy the "passive and painful" role she naturally had to take in sexual intercourse. A masochistic personality in turn predisposes females to introject hostility and thus to suffer from melancholia.

Even some of Freud's followers challenged his contention that females are more masochistic because of penis envy or because the female role in intercourse is necessarily submissive and painful. In particular, Karen Horney (1935) argued that women's tendency toward masochism and passivity resulted from their oppression as the inferior sex and their missed opportunities for psychological growth. But the very notion that women are more masochistic than men was not challenged by Horney or in any significant way by other psychoanalysts of that era. The development of psychoanalytic theories of women's depression is discussed in more depth in Chapter 5.

Contemporary Views of Women's Depression

There are two types of modern biological theories of sex differences in depression. The first harks back to the belief that women are particularly prone to emotionality and depression during certain phases of the menstrual cycle. Modern biologists do not believe that menstrual bleeding saps energy from a woman's brain. Rather, they argue that the hormonal changes during the menstrual cycle can affect some women's moods negatively. To bolster this argument, proponents note that women sometimes experience increased levels of depression during the postpartum period and during menopause, periods when levels of certain hormones change dramatically. Hormones may affect moods by altering the functioning of amines. The second type of biological explanation for women's greater tendency toward depression is a genetic explanation: the genetic mutation that "causes" depression is said to be linked to the chromosomes determining gender such that women have greater predisposition for depression. Both explanations are discussed in Chapter 3.

Feminist writers such as Gilman offered a sociological explanation for women's nervous problems. They argued that women become depressed because they are undervalued by society and often find the job of full-time homemaker unstimulating and unsatisfying. In *The Feminine Mystique*, a treatise against the romantic view of women, Betty Friedan (1963) described the "housewife malady," or sense of boredom, undervaluation, and hopelessness felt by many women who were full-time homemakers. Poet Adrienne Rich gave voice to the terrible conflict many women felt between their tender love for their children and their resentment of the unstimulating, isolated life they were living: "My children cause me the most exquisite suffering of which I have any experience. It is the suffering of ambivalence: the murderous alternation between bitter resentment and raw-edged nerves, and blissful gratification and tenderness" (Rich, 1976, p. 21).

In the last two decades, fewer and fewer women have taken the role of full-time mothers and homemakers. Instead, women have moved into full-time paid work, with more and more women entering formerly male-dominated professions such as medicine and law. Many women are waiting until their mid-30's to marry, or deciding to not marry at all. Thus the position of a housewife "stuck in suburbia" is not nearly as common as it was 25 years ago. Yet women are still twice as likely as men to become depressed. One possible explanation is the fact that they have not yet achieved equality with men in most fields. They are paid less than men for the same work. They face sex discrimination in hiring and promotion decisions. Women who have families and a job are usually the ones who do all the housework and cleaning, in essence holding down two full-time jobs (Gerson, 1985). Outside the workplace, many women experience more severe and frequent victimization in the form of domestic violence and rape. Radloff and Monroe (1978) suggest that these obstacles and threats, because they create learned helplessness in women, can lead to women's greater vulnerability to depression. (See also LeUnes, Nation & Turley, 1980.) Girls and women come to expect that they will have little control over the events at work, at home, and in relationships. As a result they show lowered motivation and self-esteem—in other words, helplessness and depression.

Other sociologists have argued that, in addition to the boring nature of housework and the undervaluation of the housewife role, being a full-time homemaker provides a woman with only one source of gratification. When the home does not provide enough gratification, a homemaker has no other source to which to turn, as her husband does. The absence of multiple sources of gratification may predispose women to depression and other psychological disorders (e.g., Gove & Tudor, 1973). On the other hand, other social-role theories of depression in women focus on the conflicting sets of expectations placed upon women who work: they must be nurturant and passive to attract men, but assertive and selfish to succeed in their career (e.g., Kohn et al., 1965). The conflict between these two roles may cause despair and depression. These social-role perspectives are discussed in Chapter 4.

There is a set of explanations of women's depressions that attributes these depressions not to the social conditions they face, but to their personalities. Many modern-day psychologists have rejected Freud's theories of female development and personality. In explaining women's greater vulnerability to depression, they have focused instead on differences in the ways girls and boys are socialized to think about their opportunities and their talents as sources of self-esteem and motivation. A number of studies have shown that females tend to have a lower sense of their own competence, to interpret events more negatively, to evaluate themselves more harshly, to set lower goals for themselves, and to rely more on external feedback in making judgments about themselves than do males (e.g., Dweck & Elliott, 1983; Eccles, Adler & Meece, 1984; Roberts & Nolen-Hoeksema, 1990). Such negative thinking styles have been associated with problems in motivation, achievement, and self-esteem, as well as with a tendency toward depression. The possibility that women's vulnerability to depression can be attributed to maladaptive self-concepts and thinking styles is discussed in Chapter 6.

The great variety of explanations for depression in women is indicative of the compelling nature of the problem. Millions of women are troubled, even incapacitated, by depression each year. There seems to be no single, simple explanation for women's greater tendency toward depression. Biological and social and psychological factors all seem to play a role.

In the next chapter I examine the epidemiology of sex differences in depression. The epidemiology of a disorder is important because it can provide clues about the causes of a disorder. If we know that one group of people has higher rates of a disorder than most other groups, we can begin to investigate what experiences or characteristics of the high-risk group may account for the higher rates. Similarly, if we can determine that there are no sex differences in depression in certain socioeconomic or cultural groups, then we can try to isolate experiences or characteristics of the men and women in that group that might explain the absence of sex differences in depression. Such information can also be used to test existing theories of sex differences in depression.

CHAPTER TWO

The Evidence for Sex Differences in Depression

How pervasive are sex differences in depression? Are females more likely than males to be depressed in all age groups? In all cultures? In all socioeconomic classes? In this chapter I review the epidemiology of sex differences in depression, examining both the rates of depressive symptoms and the rates of depressive disorders in males and females from different age groups and sociocultural backgrounds.* I examine sex differences in symptoms and in disorders separately because many psychologists and psychiatrists believe that these two types of depression are quite different.

Sex Differences in Depressive Symptoms

Most studies of the rates of depressive symptoms in different groups use questionnaires to assess depression. Typically, the ques-

*Portions of this chapter appeared originally in Nolen-Hoeksema (1988). The number of studies examining sex differences in depression, or the characteristics of women's depressions, in ethnic minority groups, lower socioeconomic classes, and groups defined by sexual orientation is very small. Generally, the rates of depression in groups with relatively low social status are higher than those in the dominant culture. Studies providing data on sex differences in depression in special groups that are pertinent to the theories discussed in Chapters 3–8 will be reviewed in this book, but the reader is referred to the Report of the Task Force on Women and Depression (American Psychological Association, 1989) for further examination of depression in special populations.

tions describe symptoms of depression, and respondents are asked to indicate how often in the last week or two they have experienced such symptoms. Cut-off scores are used to categorize a person's score on a depression questionnaire as in the not depressed, moderately depressed, or severely depressed range. Questionnaires are easy to administer and thus allow a researcher to gather data from a large number of people efficiently. But because they rely on respondents to be honest and accurate in reporting their symptoms, questionnaires can be biased by respondents' level of self-awareness and by their willingness to report depression. This problem can be particularly significant in studies of children. Even so, questionnaire studies of depressive symptoms have provided us with most of the existing data on rates of depression in different sociocultural groups.

Depressive Symptoms in Children

Depression in children was rarely studied before the 1970's. Proponents of the traditional psychoanalytic theory of depression once argued that children cannot become depressed because they are too immature psychologically to engage in the complex unconscious processes that cause depression (see Rie, 1966). Others argued that if children do become depressed, they will not show "adult" symptoms of depression but will instead mask their depression with aggressive behavior, hypochondriasis, anxiety, or one of a large number of other nonnormative behaviors (see Kovacs & Beck, 1977). In the last two decades, however, evidence has accumulated showing that children as young as age 6 show adult symptoms of depression such as guilt, self-hate, pessimism, and sadness (Puig-Antich, 1986).

Much less is known about the characteristics and prevalence of depression in preschool children, in large part because it is difficult to study depression in preschoolers. They cannot read or complete questionnaires, and their language skills are not sufficiently developed for them to describe how they feel. The few existing studies of depression in preschoolers have relied on parents' and teachers' ratings of preschoolers' moods. For example, Kashani, Holcomb, and Orvaschel (1986) asked the parents and teachers of 109 preschool children (54 boys and 55 girls, average age 4) to rate the tendency of each child to show the symptoms of depression described in the *Diagnostic and Statistical Manual* (American Psychiatric Association, 1980). Approximately 9 percent of the boys and 7 percent of the girls in this study showed moderate to severe levels of sadness, guilt, self-hate, lethargy, and other depressive symptoms. (Although the boys appeared slightly more prone to depression in this preschool group, this sex difference was not statistically significant.) The researchers in this study did not examine possible sociocultural differences in rates of depressive symptoms. The parents of the more depressed children, however, were more likely than the parents of the nondepressed children to report that there had been major negative events (for example, divorce of the parents) in these children's lives.

We find similar results in elementary school children. Once children reach about age 7, they can begin to verbalize their feelings and respond to questionnaires. A number of questionnaires are used to assess depression in elementary school children. One of the most commonly used is the Children's Depression Inventory (Kovacs, 1980). This inventory includes 27 items, each containing three sentences that describe a level of a given depressive symptom. For example, the three sentences in item 1 are "I am sad once in a while," "I am sad much of the time," and "I am sad all the time." Children are asked to indicate which sentence describes how they have been feeling in the last two weeks.

In one of the largest studies of self-reported depressive symptoms in elementary school children, 2,790 children between third and ninth grades in rural Pennsylvania completed the Children's Depression Inventory (Smucker, 1982). In all grade levels about 15 percent of the children scored in the moderately to severely depressed range of this questionnaire. There were no differences in either the percentage of boys and girls who were depressed or the mean scores of the boys and girls. Other studies of depressive symptoms in preadolescent children have found either no sex differences or a slight propensity for boys to be more depressed than girls (e.g., Pearce, 1978). In a study of Children's Depression Inventory scores in 352 third-grade boys and girls (Nolen-Hoeksema et al., in press), my colleagues and I found a slight tendency for boys to have a higher mean score than girls, suggesting that the average level of depression in boys was greater than in girls. In prepubescent children, then, girls do not appear more likely to report depression than boys—in fact, boys may be slightly more likely to report depression than girls.

One might question the validity of children's self-reports of depression. Do children have an exaggerated sense of their feelings or tend to choose the most extreme answers? Would it be better to continue to ask parents and teachers about children's symptoms, rather than asking the children themselves? There are a few studies comparing children's self-reports of depressive symptoms both to psychiatrists' ratings of the children's symptoms and to parents' and teachers' ratings (Carlson & Cantwell, 1980; Kazdin et al., 1983; Moretti et al., 1985). In general, psychiatrists' ratings of the children's moods correlate well with children's self-ratings but do not correlate well at all with parents' or teachers' ratings. (Parents seem to be particularly bad at accurately reporting their children's moods.) In other words, children's self-ratings are more valid than the ratings of parents and teachers. Although we would not want to diagnose a child as having a severe depressive disorder merely on the basis of self-report, self-ratings do appear to be reasonably valid indicators of a child's level of depression.

Depressive Symptoms in Adolescents

Adolescence has traditionally been considered a period in which most young people go through distressing self-analysis and experience frequent periods of anxiety and depression. Most studies find that the rates of depressive symptoms rise substantially from childhood into adolescence (e.g., Albert & Beck, 1975; Kaplan, Hong & Weinhold, 1984). For example, Kandel and Davies (1986) found that 21 percent of a group of 762 adolescents age 15 or 16 scored in the depressed range on a questionnaire. This figure is substantially higher than the 15 percent of preadolescent subjects who scored in the depressed range of the Children's Depression Inventory in the Smucker (1982) study. In addition, the rate of suicide among adolescents is enormously higher than among children (see Nolen-Hoeksema, 1988). Because a large majority of people who commit suicide are depressed, these data on suicide also suggest that the rates of depression rise substantially in adolescence.

Sometime during adolescence females begin to be much more likely to report depression than males. Some studies find that this sex difference begins to emerge in early adolescence. For example, one study of children averaging around age 13 found that 57 percent of the girls but only 23 percent of the boys reported levels of depression in the moderate to severe range of the Beck Depression

Inventory, a widely used depression questionnaire (Albert & Beck, 1975). These data are somewhat suspect, however, because only 63 subjects were tested. By contrast, Smucker (1982) found no sex differences in rates of depression in children as old as age 14 in his very large study. A number of studies (e.g., Simmons & Blyth, 1987) suggest that sex differences in depression are consistently found in subjects starting about age 15. Kandel and Davies (1986) found that 23 percent of girls age 15 or 16 reported levels of depression in the moderate to severe range on their depression questionnaire, whereas only 10 percent of boys that age reported such levels. Similarly, in a study of 150 subjects age 14 to 16, Kashani and colleagues (1987) found that 29 percent of the girls and 15 percent of the boys reported depressive symptoms of at least moderate severity. This switch in the ratio of depressed girls to depressed boys during adolescence is examined in greater detail in Chapter 8.

How do depressed male and female adolescents fare over the long run? Kandel and Davies (1986) have carried out a nine-year prospective study of the levels of depression in a large sample, beginning at age 15 or 16 and continuing into early adulthood. Subjects who scored in the depressed range of the depression questionnaire as adolescents were significantly more likely to be depressed at age 24 or 25 than were subjects who were not depressed as adolescents. In addition, female subjects who were depressed in adolescence were more likely to have consulted with mental health professionals and to have been hospitalized for a mental disorder over the nine years of the study than were subjects who were not depressed as adolescents. For both males and females, those who had been depressed in adolescence reported more health problems, more work days lost, and poorer interpersonal relationships over the nine years than those who had not been depressed in adolescence. These data indicate that adolescents with moderate to severe levels of depression have problems with psychological illnesses and social and occupational functioning throughout adolescence and into early adulthood. The data also indicate that depressed females are more likely to consult a mental health professional than are depressed males. These consultations apparently do not lead to decreased rates of depression in females over the years, however.

Depressive Symptoms in Adults

The age range with the highest rates of depressive symptoms is 18 to 24 (see Nolen-Hoeksema, 1988). In one very large study almost 30 percent of the subjects in this age group scored in the depressed range on the Center for Epidemiological Studies Depression Scale (CESD), a widely used self-report inventory for depression (Comstock & Helsing, 1976). In this study, 3,845 adults age 18 and older completed the CESD. The rates of moderate to severe depression were substantially lower in all groups older than 18 to 24. Specifically, 19 percent of the subjects age 25 to 44, 15 percent of those age 45 to 64, and 15 percent of those age 65 or older scored in the depressed range. Across all age groups in the Comstock and Helsing study, women reported significantly more depressive symptoms than men. Several other studies have found similar results (for a review, see Nolen-Hoeksema, 1987). There are, however, some groups in which we do not see greater levels of depression in women than in men. Several studies have failed to find any sex differences in depression among college students. A questionnaire study of over a thousand UCLA undergraduates, for example, found no sex differences in the mean depression scores of men and women (Hammen & Padesky, 1977).

One possible explanation for the absence of sex differences in depression in college students is that only women with exceptionally good mental health (that is, those who are not depressed) go to college. On the other hand, men who go to college may be more representative of the mental health of men in general, perhaps because men are expected to go to college more than women are. This hypothesis is supported by data from a study by Radloff (1975), who compared the CESD scores of 62 men and 109 women age 18 to 24 who were not attending college. She found that the women's average score was significantly higher than the men's, indicating more depression in the women. Something about being in college—or the factors that determine who goes to college—seems to diminish the sex differences in depression found in people of this age group.

Another factor that appears to affect sex differences in depression is marital status. Radloff (1975) found that women were more depressed than men among those who were married, divorced, or separated. But among the widowed, men were more depressed than women. There were no sex differences in depression in those who had never been married (see Table 1). Married men showed particularly low levels of depression, whereas in two of the three nonmarried groups (never married and widowed) either there were no sex differences or men showed more depression than women. These data suggest that marriage has a more positive effect on men's mental health than on women's.

Other studies have found that the death of a spouse is associated with as great a tendency toward depression in men as in women. For example, Bornstein and colleagues (1973) used standardized criteria (Feighner et al., 1972) to diagnose depression in a sample of 65 women and 27 men recently widowed. One month after their spouse's death, 33 percent of the men and 35 percent of the women met the criteria for depression. One year later, 19 percent of the men and 17 percent of the women continued to be depressed. In a review of the literature on physical and mental health of widowed men and women, Stroebe and Stroebe (1983) concluded that women show less decline in physical and mental health than men do after the death of a spouse. Stroebe and Stroebe suggest that since women have a longer life expectancy than men, they expect their spouse to die before them, whereas men do not. Thus the death of a spouse may not be as much of a shock for women as for men. Some studies of depression in older adults find no sex differences (Blazer & Williams, 1980; Ensel, 1982). Since many older people lose a spouse, the tendency for men to become depressed when they are widowed may, in part, account for the absence of sex differences in depression in older adults. Men may also have more problems adjusting to re-

TABLE 1   *Sex Differences in Depression Across Marital Groups*

	Mean depression scores	
Marital status	Male (n = 679)	Female (n = 958)
Married	7.33	9.26
Divorced/separated	8.51	14.19
Never married	10.05	10.20
Widowed	11.28	10.46

SOURCE: Adopted from Radloff (1975). Subjects completed the Center for Epidemiological Studies Depression Scale (CESD).

tirement or to declining health than women. These hypotheses and others are discussed in Chapter 4.

Summary of Data on Depressive Symptoms

The rates of depressive symptoms appear to be extremely low in preschool children but appear to rise substantially throughout childhood and adolescence. Among preschool children and elementary school children, some studies find that boys and girls report equal levels of depressive symptoms, whereas other studies find that boys report more symptoms than girls. Starting at around age 14, girls begin to report symptoms of depression much more often than boys do. The tendency of females to have depressive symptoms more often than males thus appears to emerge sometime in early adolescence. In addition, depression in adolescent girls is associated with a tendency to seek psychiatric consultations and hospitalization during the adolescent and early adult years. Among adults, women report significantly more depression than men across most age groups and income levels. There is a tendency, however, for studies to find no sex differences in depression among college students and among some samples of people age 65 or older. Among the recently widowed, men report more depression than women.

Sex Differences in Depressive Disorders

We can draw from two types of data to determine the rates of depressive disorders in men and women of different ages. The first type is records of persons *treated* for depressive disorders by mental health professionals. The second type is information taken from structured clinical interviews designed to assess disorders in people in the general population. As mentioned in Chapter 1, the criteria currently used in the United States to diagnose mental disorders come from the *Diagnostic and Statistical Manual of the American Psychiatric Association* or DSM (American Psychiatric Association, 1987). The criteria for the diagnosis of a depressive episode are given in Table 2. The DSM divides unipolar depression into major depressive disorder and dysthymic disorder. To qualify for a diagnosis of major depressive disorder, a person must show a depressive episode, as defined by the criteria in Table 2, for at least two weeks. The

TABLE 2   *Diagnostic Criteria from the* Diagnostic and Statistical Manual *for a Depressive Episode*

A. At least five of the following symptoms have been present during the same two-week period and represent a change from previous functioning. At least one of the symptoms is either depressed mood, or loss of interest of pleasure:

1. depressed mood;
2. loss of interest of pleasure in all, or almost all activities;
3. poor appetite, significant weight loss, increased appetite, or significant weight gain;
4. insomnia or hypersomnia;
5. psychomotor agitation or retardation;
6. fatigue or loss of energy;
7. feelings of worthlessness, self-reproach, or excessive or inappropriate guilt;
8. complaints or evidence of diminished ability to think or concentrate; indecisiveness;
9. recurrent thoughts of death, suicidal ideation, wishes to be dead, or suicide attempt.

B. Neither preoccupation with a mood-incongruent delusion or hallucination nor bizarre behavior dominates the clinical picture when an affective syndrome is not present.

C. Not superimposed on either schizophrenia, schizophreniform disorder, or paranoid disorder.

D. Not due to organic mental disorder or uncomplicated bereavement.

---

diagnosis of dysthymic disorder is given to people whose symptoms of depression are not quite as severe as those of major depressive disorder but have been chronic for at least two years. People who show episodes of both depression and mania are diagnosed with bipolar disorder. One important advantage of basing estimates of rates of depression on diagnoses of people seeking treatment is that such diagnoses are made by professionals who know what questions to ask a patient and do not rely on a patient's ability to accurately assess her own condition. And because the patient sought treatment, it is clear that her symptoms are relatively severe and should be of concern. There are some disadvantages to using records of treated cases, however. Socioeconomic status, geographical setting (rural versus urban residence), and age, among other factors, affect whether someone seeks psychiatric help. Some people do not have the money to seek psychiatric counseling, and some people are not comfortable doing so. In addition, in many areas mental health facilities simply are not available. Often only the most severe cases of a disorder, or those persons most disruptive to a society, will be treated (see Wing, 1976). Thus not all persons with depressive disorders receive treatment. Another problem with using diagnoses made in mental health facilities to estimate rates of depression is that different clinicians apply diagnostic criteria in different ways (Mazer, 1967). For example, since "everyone knows" that women frequently are depressed, some clinicians may be biased to diagnose a woman's problem as depression rather than as some other disorder, thus inflating the estimates of depression in women.

Researchers have tried to overcome these problems by using *structured clinical interviews*. These interviews are conducted by researchers trained to ask respondents, in an unbiased manner, for information needed to make diagnoses. The information from these interviews is compared to standard diagnostic criteria, such as those in the DSM. The most frequently used structured interview is the Diagnostic Interview Schedule, or DIS (Robins et al., 1981). From a respondent's answers to the DIS questions, trained coders can assign diagnoses of DSM mental disorders where warranted. There are thus two advantages of using data from a structured interview rather than from treated cases. First, diagnoses made on the basis of interviews are less affected by the idiosyncratic application of diagnostic criteria; second, interviews can be conducted across the general population in order to overcome the self-selection inherent in the sample of people who seek psychiatric help.

Depressive Disorders in Children and Adolescents

In one of the few existing studies of depression in preschool children receiving psychiatric treatment, only 9 of the 1,000 preschoolers interviewed met the criteria for a major depressive disorder, and no children received the diagnosis of dysthymic disorder (Kashani & Carlson, 1987). Of these nine children, six were boys and three were girls. Thus the rate of serious depression is extremely low even among preschoolers receiving psychiatric treatment. In this study, depression appeared to be more common in boys than in girls. The numbers of children who were depressed were so small, however, that we cannot draw conclusions about sex differences with confidence.

The rates of depressive disorders in elementary school children referred for psychiatric treatment are much higher than among preschoolers referred for treatment. In a study of 100 elementary school children admitted to a child psychiatry ward of a hospital, 15 percent of the boys and 8 percent of the girls were diagnosed as suffering from a major depressive disorder (Kashani et al., 1982). This suggests a greater tendency toward depression in boys than in girls, although the small numbers of children diagnosed as depressed (11/75 boys and 2/25 girls) again preclude firm conclusions.

It is probably even more unwise to rely on treatment statistics for information about the rates of depression in children than to rely on such statistics for information on depression in adults, however. As mentioned earlier, parents appear to be bad at detecting or acknowledging depression in children. In addition, there appear to be very strong biases against taking children for psychiatric treatment. For example, one large study of children in the general population found that only 29 percent of those qualifying for some type of DSM diagnosis had ever been taken by their parents to a teacher or mental health professional for help (Anderson et al., 1987). Thus it is particularly important to base our estimates of the rates of depression in children on studies of children in the general population.

The only existing study of depressive disorders in preschoolers in the general population is the study described earlier, by Kashani, Holcomb, and Orvaschel (1986), in which parents and teachers were asked to rate levels of depression in 54 boys and 55 girls with an average age of 4 years. After obtaining these parent and teacher ratings, the researchers interviewed the 5 boys and 4 girls rated as moderately to severely depressed in order to assess whether these children met the criteria for a DSM diagnosis of major depressive disorder or dysthymic disorder. Only one child, a boy, met the criteria for a major depressive disorder, and no child met the criteria for a dysthymic disorder. The fact that only 1 of 109 children met the diagnosis for a depressive disorder indicates that the rates of such disorders are very low in preschool children. Again, because the rates are so low, little can be said about the possible sex differences in depression in preschoolers.

Rates of depressive disorders in the general population of ele-

TABLE 3   *Rates of Depressive Disorders in the
General Population Diagnosed Through Structured
Clinical Interviews*

Age group	Percent females	Percent males
Elementary school children[a]	0.5	2.5
Adolescents[b]	13.3	2.7
18–24 years[c]	6.9	3.8
25–44 years[c]	10.8	4.8
45–64 years[c]	7.8	3.3
65+ years[c]	3.2	1.2

SOURCES: (a) from Anderson et al. (1987); (b) from Kashani et al. (1987); (c) from Myers et al. (1984).

mentary school children were obtained by Anderson and colleagues (1987). These researchers administered the Diagnostic Interview Schedule for Children, or DIS-C, to 792 children age 11. They found that 2.5 percent of the boys, but only 0.5 percent of the girls, met the criteria for a major depressive disorder or dysthymic disorder (see Table 3). These data, together with the data on depression in children taken to clinics, clearly indicate that the rates of depressive disorders are much higher in boys than in girls before puberty. After puberty, however, the sex differences in depression switch dramatically, and adolescent girls are much more likely to be seriously depressed than adolescent boys. The rates of depressive disorders in adolescents shown in Table 3 are from a study by Kashani and colleagues (1987). These researchers administered the Diagnostic Interview Schedule for Children and Adolescents to 150 adolescents age 14 to 16 and found that 13.3 percent of the girls and 2.7 percent of the boys met the criteria for a major depressive disorder or dysthymic disorder. These data parallel the findings on depressive symptoms and show that a tendency for females to show more depression than males emerges by age 14.

Depressive Disorders in Adults

The rate of depressive disorders in females is higher than the rate for males across all age groups of adults (see Tables 3 and 4). The rates of depressive disorders in the general population shown in Table 3 were obtained from a very large epidemiological study of mental disorders conducted by the National Institute of Mental Health (Myers et al., 1984). In this study, the Diagnostic Interview Schedule was administered to 9,543 adults in three United States cities. From the information obtained through the interview, DSM diagnoses were given as warranted. The rates in Table 3 represent percentages of people experiencing a major depressive disorder during a six-month period. These data are the best available estimate of the actual rates of unipolar depression in the United States, for these rates are not biased by individuals' willingness to seek professional help. Across all adult age groups under age 65, 4 percent of the women and 1.7 percent of the men in the study were diagnosed with a major depressive disorder. Similarly, more women than men are *treated* for depression among all adult age groups. The rates of people in each age group who were treated for unipolar depression at inpatient mental health facilities in 1980 are presented in Table 4 (National Institute of Mental Health, 1987). Across all adult age groups, 206 of 100,000 women in the general population and 138 of 100,000 men were treated for a unipolar depression.

Again, there are a few exceptions to the tendency for women to be diagnosed as depressed more often than men. As was evident in studies of depressive symptoms, there appear to be fewer sex differences in depressive disorders in college students than among people the same age who are not attending college. For example, in a study of students seeking counseling at a University of Washington psychology clinic, 19 of the 320 women and 14 of the 180 men were diagnosed as having a major depressive disorder (Stangler & Printz, 1980). This difference was not statistically significant, but signifi-

TABLE 4   *Rates of Persons Treated for Depressive Disorders, per 100,000 People*

Age group	Females	Males
18–24 years	151	123
25–44 years	266	178
45–64 years	251	141
65+ years	154	110

SOURCE: National Institute of Mental Health (1987), unpublished data on numbers of persons treated for affective disorders in psychiatric facilities in the United States; data gathered in 1980, made available to the author in 1987.

cantly more women than men were given the diagnosis of dysthymic disorder.

Another subgroup in which no sex differences in depression have been found is the Old Order Amish, an ultraconservative Protestant religious sect whose members maintain a closed society separated from the modern world. Egeland and Hostetter (1983) report a six-year epidemiological study of affective disorders among the Old Order Amish in Pennsylvania. Egeland and Hostetter established contacts within the Amish community who would inform them when a member of the community appeared "disturbed." This person would then be interviewed by Egeland or her colleagues with a well-validated, structured clinical interview (the Schedule for Affective Disorders and Schizophrenia defined in Robins et al., 1984). Over a five-year period, 21 women and 20 men were diagnosed with major depression, indicating no sex differences in the rates of unipolar depression in this culture.

The methods of Egeland and her colleagues may have led to the underdetection of some disorders, however. Because the criterion for being interviewed by the researchers was that an individual showed clear disruption in his social functioning, disorders such as depression, in which a person quietly suffers, may have gone unnoticed. These data indicating no sex differences in depression among the Amish are intriguing, however, especially in light of data showing no sex differences in other community-oriented, nonmodern cultures, which will be discussed later.

Note in Tables 3 and 4 that the rates of depressive disorders among people 65 and over appear to be lower than the rates in younger adults. Many clinicians argue, however, that biases against seeking treatment for or admitting depression are particularly strong among people 65 and over and that depression in that age range is often misdiagnosed (see Epstein, 1976; Hankin & Oktay, 1979). People 65 and over may be reluctant to admit to emotional distress and may often display depression through somatic complaints. Confusion, lack of concentration, and memory loss are also particularly common symptoms of depression in this age range, frequently leading to the misdiagnosis of senile dementia. Despite the importance of these claims, there has been relatively little empirical investigation of them (Shapiro, 1986). Some small-scale studies have found that some patients diagnosed with senile dementia improve with antidepressant drug therapy (Haward, 1977; Nott & Fleminger, 1975; Post, 1975). Because dementia is supposedly irreversible, this improvement of patients with drug therapy suggests that they had actually been suffering from depression, not dementia. In addition, one experimental study found that experienced clinicians who heard a patient talking about his symptoms on an audio recording were more likely to diagnose him as depressed if they thought he was under 55, and more likely to diagnose him as demented if they thought he was over 75 (Perlick & Atkins, 1984). These data indicate that advanced age in a patient may bias clinicians to downplay affective and motivational symptoms of depression and to interpret cognitive deficits as symptoms of dementia rather than as symptoms of depression. Such a bias might lead to the underdetection of depression in people 65 and over (although there should be no sex differences in this bias). It may be, however, that cognitive deficits *are* more likely to be symptoms of dementia than of depression as a person's age increases. That is, clinicians' bias to diagnose older adults as demented rather than depressed may be based on the actual base rates of the two disorders rather than on a misunderstanding of depression in people that age.

Another possible method of ascertaining the relative rates of depression among men and women 65 and over is to examine suicide rates in the two groups. Approximately 80 percent of people who commit suicide are depressed. Suicide statistics for the United States in 1982 show that the rate of suicide per 100,000 males age 25 to 64 was 25.9, the rate for those age 65 to 74 was 33.1, the rate for those age 75 to 84 was 48.5, and the rate for those age 85 and older was 53.9 (National Institute of Mental Health, 1987; these rates are for whites only). This increase in suicide rates with age suggests that there may be a small number of depressed men 65 and older who commit suicide rather than seek psychiatric treatment, thereby deflating the measured rates of diagnosed depressive disorders in males in that age range. By contrast, the suicide rates for females decline substantially with age. In 1982 the rate of suicide per 100,000 females age 25 to 64 was 9.2, the rate for those age 65 to 74 was 7.4, the rate for those age 75 to 84 was 6.1, and the rate for those age 85 and older was 3.9. Much more data on changes in depression rates in men and women from middle to older age is needed, however, before we can make any firm conclusions about changes in sex differences in depression during the later years of life.

Summary of Data on Depressive Disorders

Among prepubescent children, boys are more likely to be diagnosed as depressed than girls. By age 14, however, girls become more prone to depression than boys. Exactly when in adolescence this switch occurs is not clear. Among adults age 19 and older, women are about twice as likely as men to show moderate or severe levels of depression. There are a few subgroups of the population—college students, the Old Order Amish, the widowed, and perhaps people 65 and older—in which no sex differences are found.

Cross-Cultural Data on Depression in Men and Women

It is important to examine rates of depression in men and women outside the United States to determine how widespread the sex differences in depression are. If there are certain cultures in which we do not find those sex differences, then we might have some clues to the social factors that lead to the sex differences we see in the United States. On the other hand, the absence of clear cultural differences in the rates of depression in men and women would suggest that some factor universal to all women, such as a biological factor, predisposes them to depression.

Rates of Men and Women Treated for Depression

Table 5 lists several studies of sex differences in the numbers of people treated for depression in countries outside the United States. Several of these studies report data from psychiatric registers, which are comprehensive records of all people treated in psychiatric institutions and private practice in a large geographical area. All but one study (Gershon & Liebowitz, 1975) used the criteria for diagnosis of depression given by the International Classification of Diseases, or ICD (World Health Organization, 1980), which are very similar to the DSM criteria. Almost none of the studies reported in Table 5 provided data on diagnoses by age and sex, so we do not know whether there are differences between age groups in the sex differences in depression in these countries. In all the studies in this table, over twice as many women as men were diagnosed as depressed.

Table 6 presents data from studies in which the criteria used to

TABLE 5 *Studies of Treated Cases of Depression Outside the United States*

Nation	Study	Diagnosis	F:M	Comments
Denmark	Weeke et al., 1975	Depressive reaction	3.8*	Psychiatric register, 1960–64
		Neurotic depression	3.0*	
Scotland	Baldwin, 1971	Neurotic depression	2.4*	Scottish mental hospital admissions, 1967
England and Wales	Martin, Brotherson & Chave, 1957	Neurotic depression	1.7[a]	Psychiatric register, 1949–54
England	Dean et al., 1981	Psychotic depression	1.8*	Psychiatric register, 1976
Australia	Berah, 1983	Neurotic depression	1.8*	State and general hospital patients, 1978–81
	Krupinski & Stoller, 1962	Psychotic depression	3.0*	Admissions to a Victoria hospital, 1951–52
Canada	Canadian Bureau of Statistics, 1970	Neurotic depression	2.2*	First admissions to psychiatric services, 1967
Iceland	Helgason, 1977	Psychotic depression	2.9*	Psychiatric register, 1966–67
Israel	Halevi, Naor & Cochavy, 1969	Reactive depression	1.3	Census of 41 psychiatric institutions, 1964
		Psychotic depression	1.8*	
		Involutional melancholia	3.5*	
		All affective disorders	2.3*	
	Gershon & Liebowitz, 1975	Unipolar depression (Feighner criteria)	2.0*	Inpatients at psychiatric hospitals

NOTE: F:M is the ratio of females to males, corrected for the number of females and males in the sample, if possible. Chi-squares were calculated to test for sex differences in the rates of disorder.

[a] The chi-square could not be calculated, because of insufficient data.

* p < .01.

TABLE 6 *Secondary Studies of Treated Cases of Depression Outside the United States*

Nation	Study	Diagnosis	F:M	Comments
Canada	Weissman & Klerman, 1977	All affective disorders	1.7[a]	Data from the World Health Organization Collaborative Study: rates of females and males with subtypes of affective disorder were unavailable
Czechoslovakia		All affective disorders	2.1[a]	
Denmark		All affective disorders	1.8[a]	
Finland		All affective disorders	1.3[a]	
France		All affective disorders	1.6[a]	
Norway		All affective disorders	1.5[a]	
Poland		All affective disorders	1.4[a]	
Sweden		All affective disorders	1.8[a]	
Switzerland		All affective disorders	1.4[a]	
England and Wales		All affective disorders	1.8[a]	
New Zealand		All affective disorders	1.8[a]	
England	Cooper et al., 1969	All affective disorders	1.4	Admissions to a London hospital, n = 145
New Zealand	Christie, 1968	All affective disorders	2.1*	Patients given diagnosis of "affective disorder," n = 50; diagnostic criteria were unclear
The Netherlands	Saenger, 1968	Psychiatric ratings of severe depression	1.3	Persons admitted to a psychiatric hospital and rated by psychiatrist, n = 289
Hong Kong	Yap, 1965	Affective disorder (initial episode)	1.1	Diagnoses given to patients admitted to a hospital, n = 130
		Affective disorder (recurrent episodes)	1.7**	One-year follow-up of same patients, n = 62

India	Rao, 1970	Endogenous depression	0.6*	Patients treated by the author for depression, n = 62
	Mohan, 1972	Affective psychosis	1.4	Patients institutionalized in a hospital that primarily accommodates males, n = 140
Egypt	El-Islam, 1969	Nonpsychotic depression	1.0	Patients seen by the author, n = 157; diagnostic criteria were unclear
Iraq	Bazzoui, 1970	Depression	1.2	Hospitalized patients (n = 42) and private practice patients (n = 16); diagnostic criteria were unclear
Rhodesia	Buchan, 1969	Depression	1.1	Patients seen by the author, n = 77; diagnostic criteria and method of patient selection were unclear
Nigeria	Ezeilo & Onyeama, 1980	Psychotic depression Neurotic depression	0.8 1.6*	Discharge diagnosis for patients, n = 969; "no conventional diagnostic inventories available for use"
Kenya	Vadher & Ndetei, 1981	Nonpsychotic depression	2.3*	Patients being treated with chemotherapy for depression, n = 30

NOTE: F:M is the ratio of females to males, corrected for the number of females and males in the sample, if possible. Chi-squares were calculated to test for sex differences in the rates of disorder.

[a] The chi-square could not be calculated, because of insufficient data.

*p < .05.   **p < .01.

diagnose affective disorders were unstandardized or the sample of subjects was small. A number of the studies conducted in developing countries did not find significant sex differences in depression. This result suggests that something about these cultures equalizes men's and women's vulnerability to depression. Some of these studies had serious flaws, however. The two studies from India (Mohan, 1972; Rao, 1970) and the study of Nigeria (Ezeilo & Onyeama, 1980) were conducted in hospitals built to accommodate three to four times more men than women. The data from Egypt (El-Islam, 1969), Iraq (Bazzoui, 1970), and Rhodesia (Buchan, 1969) were based on the impressions of one or two psychiatrists who were not using conventional diagnostic criteria. In addition, access to psychiatric treatment is more restricted for women than for men in many developing countries (Bazzoui, 1970; Rao, 1970). So it is not clear that the rates of depression in men and women in these studies illustrate a true absence of sex differences in depression in these countries. As can be seen in these tables, the ratio of female to male depressives varies greatly from country to country. In different cultures, criteria for diagnoses are differentially weighted, and certain diagnoses are more frequently applied than others (Mazer, 1967). Even so, these studies demonstrate that women suffer more depression than men in many cultures and nations.

Community Studies of Depression Outside the United States

Table 7 summarizes studies of depression in the general populations of nations outside the United States in which interviews were used to assess depression in people not seeking any type of treatment. Again, the female-to-male ratio varies considerably from one study to the next. Across all the studies, twice as many women as men were diagnosed as being depressed. Two of the studies in Table 7 in which there are clearly no sex differences in depression —Leighton et al. (1963), a study of a tribe in Nigeria, and Bash and Bash-Liechti (1969), a study of rural Iran—were conducted in developing countries. Further, the rate of depression in these cultures was much lower than the rate in urban areas of Iran or in the African studies conducted near cities. This trend may reflect the fact that an urban population is in some ways a self-selected sample— depressives having chosen to move into the city—and thus cities may

TABLE 7 *Community Studies of Depressive Symptoms in Countries Outside the United States*

Nation	Study	Criteria for "depressed"	F:M	Comments
Sweden	Essen-Moeller, 1956	ICD: affective disorder	1.8*	Structured interview, n = 2,550
	Essen-Moeller & Hagnell, 1961	ICD: affective disorder	3.0**	Interviewed subjects from Essen-Moeller, 1956, 10 years later
Denmark	Sorenson & Stromgren, 1961	ICD: psychogenic depression and depressive neurosis	3.5**	Information taken from public records and interviews, n = 4,876
Iceland	Helgason, 1961	ICD: current affective disorder; lifetime risk of affective disorder	1.8** 1.8**	Structured interviews, n = 3,843
Australia	Henderson et al., 1979	ICD: current depression	2.6	Structured interviews (PSE), n = 157
	Byrne, 1980	Scores in the depressed range on the Zung Self-Report Depression Scale	1.4*	Same sample as Henderson et al., 1979
Uganda	Orley & Wing, 1979	ICD: affective disorder	1.6	Structured interviews (PSE), n = 206
Nigeria	Leighton et al., 1963	DSM-II: neurotic depression	0.9	Structured interviews with members of the Yoruba tribe, n = 262
Iran				
Urban	Bash & Bash-Liechti, 1974	ICD: affective disorder	3.6**	Structured interviews, n = 928
Rural	Bash & Bash-Liechti, 1969	ICD: affective disorder	1.0	Structured interviews, n = 482

NOTE: F:M is the ratio of females to males, corrected for the number of females and males in the sample, if possible. Chi-squares were calculated to test for sex differences in the rates of disorder. DSM-II = *Diagnostic and Statistical Manual of Mental Disorders*, 2d ed. (American Psychiatric Association, 1968). ICD = *The International Classification of Diseases* (World Health Organization, 1980). PSE = Present State Examination (Wing, 1976).

*p < .05.   **p < .01.

include more depressives because rural depressives move to the city to obtain treatment.

Summary of Cross-Cultural Data

Women are diagnosed as having depressive disorders significantly more frequently than men and, with a few exceptions, report more depressive symptoms than men do in most parts of the world. If the ratios for all the methodologically sound studies of depression (those in Tables 5 and 7) are averaged, the mean female-to-male ratio for depression in countries outside the United States is about 2 to 1, indicating that twice as many women as men are depressed. There is a tendency, however, for there to be no sex differences in depression in developing and rural countries.

Do Men and Women Just Show Depression in Different Ways?

Before examining the several theories of why women are more likely than men to be depressed, we should consider the possibility that there are no true sex differences in depression, but rather only sex differences in the *expression* of depression. That is, perhaps men are unwilling to show the classic symptoms of depression because these symptoms are considered unmanly, and instead exhibit depression through other symptoms. In the remainder of this chapter, I will examine the evidence supporting the idea that men deny their depressive symptoms and instead manifest depression through other maladaptive behaviors, especially alcoholism.

Reporting Biases

Some researchers have been concerned that sex differences in depression reflect men's unwillingness to admit to and seek help for depressive symptoms (Padesky & Hammen, 1977; Phillips & Segal, 1969). This hypothesis holds that men and women experience depressive symptoms with equal frequency and degree, but that men are less likely to admit to depressive symptoms because such symptoms are perceived as feminine (Chevron, Quinlan & Blatt, 1978). A number of studies have failed to support this hypothesis, however. For example, King and Buchwald (1982) predicted that if this hypothesis was true, men should be less willing than women to disclose their symptoms publicly (for example, in an interview with a researcher), and thus greater sex differences should be found when subjects are asked to disclose symptoms publicly than when they can disclose them privately (as in an anonymous questionnaire). Instead, King and Buchwald found that men were no less willing than women to disclose their symptoms to an interviewer they had never met before and that neither sex was less willing to disclose symptoms publicly than privately. Bryson and Pilon (1984) have replicated these results. Both studies, however, used college students for subjects, and we have seen that there is no tendency toward sex differences in depressive phenomena in this population.

Clancy and Gove (1974) investigated the influence of three types of biases that might affect subjects' willingness to say that they were experiencing 22 different psychological and physiological symptoms of distress.

First, Clancy and Gove had the 404 adult subjects (who were not college students) rate how socially acceptable each of the 22 symptoms were. They found that men and women gave the symptoms equal ratings of social acceptability. Second, the researchers examined sex differences in subjects' "need for social approval," as measured by a standard questionnaire. They argued that if men showed a greater need for social approval than women, this should bias the men against admitting to symptoms of distress. No sex differences in need for social approval were found, however. Finally, Clancy and Gove assessed subjects' general tendencies to say "yes" to almost any question that asked about the presence of a symptom or to agree with a particular point of view. Again, they argued that if women had a greater tendency to "yea-say" than men, this tendency might exaggerate the sex differences in depression. Instead, the women in this study showed a greater tendency than the men to "nay-say," that is, to say they did not agree with the opinions described or that they did not have the symptoms listed. Despite this tendency, women had higher scores on a measure of depression than men. These results have been replicated in similar studies (Gove & Geerken, 1976; Gove et al., 1976).

The claim that women are more willing than men to seek psychotherapy for depression has also not been consistently supported in the literature. Women do go to mental health professionals more often than men (Faden, 1977). In addition, among college students, women reported that they would seek psychotherapy based on a lower level of depressive symptoms than the level at which men said they would seek help (Padesky & Hammen, 1977). However, two studies of actual help-seeking behavior have found that men and women with similar levels of self-reported depressive symptoms were equally likely to seek psychiatric help or to consult a general practitioner (Amenson & Lewinsohn, 1981; Phillips & Segal, 1969). In addition, men and women with the same level of self-reported symptoms appear equally likely to be diagnosed as depressed in a clinical interview (Amenson & Lewinsohn, 1981). In summary, the hypothesis that the lower rates of depression observed in men reflect men's unwillingness to admit their depressive symptoms has not been consistently supported. Men appear to be just as likely to admit and seek help for a given level of depression, suggesting that the higher rates of depression in women are not merely the result of men's underreporting of depressive symptoms.

Kinds of Symptoms

Some researchers have argued that men and women are equally susceptible to depression, but that depression in men often takes the form of "acting out" behaviors instead of sadness, passivity, and crying, which are symptoms commonly included in questionnaires (Hammen & Peters, 1977). In particular, it has been suggested that the male equivalent of depression is alcoholism (Winokur & Clayton, 1967). Proponents of this argument point to statistics showing that twice as many men as women are diagnosed as alcoholics (e.g., Williams & Spitzer, 1983) and suggest that the rates of alcoholism in men make up for the absence of depression in men. This argument is bolstered by evidence that in cultures where alcohol consumption is prohibited—such as the Amish—no sex differences in depression are found (Egeland & Hostetter, 1983). In addition, many studies find high rates of depressive symptoms among alcoholic men (see Petty & Nasrallah, 1981).

Winokur and his colleagues (Cadoret & Winokur, 1974; Winokur & Clayton, 1967; Winokur, Rimmer & Reich, 1971) have argued that depression and alcoholism are genetically linked, with depressive features linked to female chromosomes and alcoholic features linked to male chromosomes. Some studies find higher rates of depression in the families of alcoholics and of alcoholism in the families of depressives than in comparison groups (Cadoret & Winokur, 1974; Cotton, 1979). These findings support the hypothesis that the two disorders are genetically linked. More recent studies, however, fail to find higher rates of alcoholism among the offspring of depressed patients than among the offspring of nondepressed patients (Merikangas, Weissman & Pauls, 1985). This result calls into question the notion that depression and alcoholism result from a similar genetic abnormality.

In addition, there is evidence that depression is as likely to be a consequence as a cause of alcoholism in men. A critical review of the literature on depression and alcoholism revealed a much greater tendency for depression to follow alcoholism, especially in men, than for alcoholism to follow the onset of depressive symptoms (Petty & Nasrallah, 1981). In patients suffering from both depression and alcoholism, most male patients reported becoming depressed at least ten years after the onset of their alcoholism (Cadoret & Winokur, 1974). The alcoholics who did not become depressed tended to have periodic binges rather than to be constant heavy drinkers. Cadoret and Winokur suggest that depression in male alcoholics often results from the toxic effects of chronic alcoholism. Other recent studies show that secondary diagnoses of depression are just as frequent among patients with psychological disorders other than alcoholism as among alcoholics (Bernadt & Murray, 1986). This finding suggests that depression frequently accompanies all types of psychiatric problems, not just alcoholism. Thus the evidence that alcoholism is the male manifestation of depression is inconsistent at best. Even if the evidence for a link between alcoholism and depression were stronger, we could not justify saying that alcoholism and depression are the same disorder or that alcoholism is a symptom of depression. Instead, these two disorders can be considered two different maladaptive responses to similar difficult circumstances. Perhaps societal restrictions against women drinking excessively may protect women vulnerable to alcoholism from developing the disorder. Likewise, perhaps societal demands on men may protect them against depression. These notions are different from saying that alcoholism is a symptom of depression. Rather, one should say that both depression and alcoholism can arise in response to environmental troubles, but that societal demands result in sex differences in the vulnerability to each disorder.

Conclusions

This review of the epidemiology of sex differences in depression suggests the following conclusions: (1) among prepubescent children, boys are somewhat more likely than girls to show depression; (2) the rates of depression in both boys and girls are quite low before puberty but increase substantially in adolescence; (3) sometime during early adolescence, girls become much more likely than boys to show depression; (4) women are much more likely than men to be depressed in all age groups between 18 and 64 years, except among college students, the Old Order Amish, and the recently widowed; (5) sex differences in depression seem to diminish or disappear among people 65 or over; and (6) women are much more likely than men to be depressed in most countries outside the United States, except in certain developing countries. In addition, there is little evidence sex differences in depression result only from men's reluctance to admit to depression or from a tendency for depressed men to become alcoholics. Any acceptable theory of sex differences in depression must be able to explain the epidemiological trends described in this chapter.

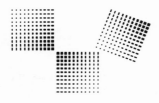

CHAPTER THREE

Biological Explanations for Sex Differences in Depression

The pervasiveness of sex differences in depression leads us to search for factors that are universal to women—such as biological factors —as possible causes of the greater vulnerability to depression in women. Researchers have proposed two general types of biological explanation for sex differences in depression. The first type of explanation arises from the belief that females are particularly prone to depression during times when their bodies experience significant hormonal changes, specifically the premenstrual period, the first few days after giving birth (known as the postpartum or puerperal period), and menopause. In addition, sex differences in depression appear to emerge sometime during or after puberty, when sex differences in the production of gonadal hormones (estrogens, progestins, and androgens) emerge. Several investigators have suggested that depression in women is brought about by changes or imbalances in levels of estrogen, progesterone, or other hormones. The second type of biological explanation attributes sex differences in depression to a greater genetic predisposition to depression in females than in males. According to these explanations, females are more likely to be depressed because the genetic abnormality leading to depression is linked to the chromosomes that determine gender. In this chapter I examine the evidence supporting both types of biological explanation of sex differences in depression.

Hormones and Moods

Claims that fluctuations in hormones have profound effects on moods in women have received a great deal of attention in the popular press and in the scientific literature. Most theories of the effects of hormones on behavior have focused on two hormones, estrogen and progesterone. Estrogen is responsible for the development of the female sex organs and secondary sex characteristics. Progesterone helps in the preparation of the uterus for the implantation of a fertilized ovum. There are four periods of a female's life during which she experiences substantial changes in the levels of these hormones. These are puberty, the menstrual cycle, pregnancy and the postpartum period, and menopause. Evidence that women commonly experience depression during these periods of hormonal change would support the hypothesis that women's greater vulnerability to depression results, at least in part, from the hormones that women produce more than men.

Depression During Puberty

As discussed earlier, before puberty boys are somewhat more likely than girls to show depression, whereas among pubescent children, girls are more likely than boys to show depression. The physical changes of puberty last for several years, beginning about age 10 and continuing to about age 18. During this period, the production of estrogen increases sharply in girls, and the production of androgens increases sharply in boys. Can the hormonal changes girls experience at puberty account for the increased vulnerability to depression that occurs for females at this time?

Brooks-Gunn and Warren (1987) have produced one of the few studies to date in which the effects of actual hormonal levels on depressive moods in girls has been assessed. In addition, these researchers compared the effect of each of the following factors on depressed mood: hormones, secondary sex characteristics (that is, breasts and pubic hair), and life events. The subjects in this study were 103 girls age 10 to 14. Depressed mood was assessed by asking the girls to complete the Youth Behavior Profile (Achenbach & Edelbrock, 1983), and life events were assessed through a questionnaire. The girls were examined by a physician or nurse to determine the extent to which they had developed secondary sex characteristics. Finally, the levels of five different hormones were assessed through blood assays. The researchers focused on estradiol because it is the principal gonadal hormone in girls and shows the largest increases in puberty of any of the hormones. The girls' estradiol levels were categorized into four sublevels according to known effects of different amounts of estradiol on sexual development.

Levels of depressive symptoms in the girls did not simply change in parallel to the changes in levels of hormones. Depressive symptoms increased as estradiol levels increased from the first to the third sublevel, but decreased as levels of estradiol continued to increase somewhat from the third to the fourth sublevel. These data suggest that girls are at increased risk of depression during the first three stages of the development of their hormonal system, when the system is first being activated. But once hormonal production becomes stabilized, girls' levels of depression decline. As we saw earlier, the greater rates of depression in girls than in boys do not emerge until age 14 or 15. By contrast, the activation of hormone production that was associated with depressive symptoms in this study occurred much earlier, around age 9 to 12. In addition, changes in hormone levels accounted for only about one percent of the changes in depressive symptoms in the girls in the study by Brooks-Gunn and Warren.

The number of negative life events the girls had experienced was a much better single predictor of depression scores than were estradiol levels: those girls with a high number of negative life events were more likely to be depressed than those with a low number. Indeed, when statistical analyses were used to assess the relative power of life events, hormonal levels, and secondary sex characteristics to predict depression, only life events emerged as a significant predictor. (Further results from this study are discussed in Chapter 8.) Although the Brooks-Gunn and Warren study provides evidence that hormonal change does have some relationship to depression levels in girls in early adolescence, this relationship is weak, and it does not appear that hormone levels affect depressed mood once hormone production has been stabilized in mid-adolescence.

A study by Eccles and colleagues (1988) showed similar results. The researchers examined the relationships between positive and negative moods and levels of five hormones in 45 girls and boys at various points in puberty. They measured the children's moods and levels of progesterone, androgen, estradiol, luteinizing hormone (LH), and follicle-stimulating hormone (FSH) three days per week for four weeks. There were few consistent patterns between hormones and moods, either within subjects across time or across subjects. In girls, high levels of estradiol were associated with high levels of positive mood and low levels of anger and impatience, and high levels of progesterone were associated with high levels of aggression. Even these relationships tended to be weak, however. In addition, the range of individual variation in the strength of the association between hormones and moods or behaviors was great. For some children the relationship between a given mood and hormone was strong and positive; for others it was strong and negative. There was little evidence that the variability in the relationships between mood and hormones had to do with the children's stage of pubertal development. Eccles and colleagues suggest that heightened levels of hormones may simply create a sensitivity in children to their environment. How they then react to their environment depends on other individual characteristics, such as coping style, and on the particular stresses they face in their environment. So far only these two studies directly address the contribution of hormones to depression in adolescent girls. In order to answer more definitively the question of whether hormones and hormonal change are responsible for the increase in depression in girls relative to boys during adolescence, we need a longitudinal study in which hormone levels and depression are assessed in both girls and boys from about age 10 to at least age 18. Then we could assess the relationship between hormone production and the increase in depression in girls relative to boys.

Premenstrual Depression

Women's menstrual cycles have long been thought to exert a powerful influence over their emotional and intellectual functioning. In particular, the premenstrual period has been thought to be characterized by a wide variety of symptoms that most or all women experience to some degree: physical symptoms such as bloating, cramps, fatigue, headaches, and breast tenderness; psychological symptoms including depression, anxiety, irritability, and inability to concentrate; and behavioral changes, primarily reflecting loss of self-control. This enormous cluster of symptoms has often been referred to as the *premenstrual syndrome* (PMS). In the nineteenth century, physicians prescribed bed rest for all women during the premenstrual week (Ehrenreich & English, 1978). For example, a physician named W. C. Taylor, in his guide to women's health published in 1871, stated: "We cannot too emphatically urge the importance of regarding these monthly returns as periods of ill health, as days when ordinary occupations are to be suspended or modified" (quoted in Ehrenreich & English, 1978, p. 111).

The modern literature in psychology and medicine also contains many assertions that for most women the premenstrual period is a time of substantial emotional and physical discomfort, as well as a time of reduced rationality and self-control. For example, an often-quoted study of premenstrual symptoms in fifteen women concludes that "there are relatively large recurring changes in symptoms and moods during the menstrual cycle which appear to have critical implications for the probability of occurrence of a large variety of impulse-laden activities" (Moos et al., 1969, p. 43). A recent review of the literature on the premenstrual syndrome for the *American Journal of Obstetrics and Gynecology* provided the following list of activities often caused by PMS: marital discord, baby battering, criminal behavior, accidents, suicides, and absenteeism at work (Reid & Yen, 1981). One piece of data frequently cited in discussions of PMS is that "a large proportion of women . . . who as pilots have serious and fatal airplane accidents do so during the menstrual or premenstrual phases of the cycle" (Moos et al., 1969, p. 37). This assertion is based on an article by Whitehead (1934), who reported *three* airplane crashes over an eight-month period in which the female pilots were reportedly menstruating (Parlee, 1974). No data were provided on how many menstruating female pilots did not crash during that same eight months. Indeed, many of the statistics showing women to be uncontrolled during the premenstrual period are based on extremely faulty or limited data (Parlee, 1974).

Even so, these data and case studies of individual women who appear to become incapacitated during the premenstrual period have led to the introduction of a new diagnosis, *late luteal phase dysphoric disorder*, to the newest edition of the DSM, published in 1986 (American Psychiatric Association, 1986). The criteria for this diagnosis are that a woman show at least five of the common symptoms of depression (for example, sadness, anhedonia, fatigue) during the week before onset of menses to a degree sufficient to interfere with her social and occupational functioning, and that these symptoms remit shortly after the onset of menses. The proposal to include late luteal phase dysphoric disorder in the 1987 edition of the DSM was controversial. Proponents of the diagnosis argued that specification of diagnostic criteria would facilitate research on the causes of and effective treatments for menstrual-related depression. Opponents argued that the evidence for the existence of premenstrual depression is so weak, and the potential for the diagnosis to bolster negative stereotypes of women's psychological competence is so great, that the diagnosis should not have been included (see Alagna & Hamilton, in press). Some people believe that the notion that women are prone to severe psychological disturbance during the premenstrual period has been and will continue to be an excuse to exclude women from positions of responsibility. In addition, there is substantial evidence against the hypothesis that women are prone to symptoms of depression and anxiety during the premenstrual period.

Evidence for premenstrual depression. One of the problems with research on PMS is that the syndrome was not conceptualized or defined clearly or consistently until recently (Rubinow & Roy-Byrne, 1984). As many as 150 symptoms, ranging from water retention to psychosis, have been said to be part of the premenstrual syndrome. One of the most popular assessment tools in studies of premenstrual symptoms has been the Moos Menstrual Distress Questionnaire (Moos, 1968). This questionnaire lists 47 symptoms divided into eight categories: pain, trouble concentrating, lowered daily activity, autonomic reactions (dizziness, vomiting), water retention, negative affect (depression, anxiety), arousal (affectionate feelings of well-being), and control (heart pounding, feeling of suffocation). Women are asked to rate, on a six-point scale, the extent to which they experienced each symptom during the premenstrual, menstrual, and intermenstrual phases of their last cycle. Unfortunately, Moos has not provided reliability or validity data for this questionnaire or cut-off levels for determining a significant degree of premenstrual symptoms (Parlee, 1973). Similar problems abound with other questionnaires on premenstrual symptoms. Even so, reviews of the modern literature on premenstrual symptoms tend to concur with Reid and Yen that "the general consensus based on questionnaire data is that 70% to 90% of the female population will admit to recurrent premenstrual symptoms and that 20% to 40% report some degree of temporary mental or physical incapacitation" (Reid & Yen, 1981, p. 86). But Reid and Yen provide no citations to studies corroborating these conclusions.

In a major methodological advance, research diagnostic criteria for premenstrual depression were developed (Halbreich, Endicott & Nee, 1983; Steiner, Haskett & Carroll, 1980). Halbreich, Endicott, and Nee introduced the Premenstrual Assessment Form (PAF), a 95-item inventory of psychological and physiological symptoms. Respondents are asked to indicate the severity with which they experience each symptom during the premenstrual period. Answers to the PAF can be compared to criteria for diagnosing a premenstrual major depressive syndrome—criteria very similar to the DSM-III criteria for major depressive disorders. Halbreich, Endicott, and Nee administered the Premenstrual Assessment Form to 335 women and found that 43 percent met the criteria for a premenstrual major depressive syndrome.

The method that Halbreich and colleagues used to assess premenstrual depression still suffered from a major flaw, however: it required women to *retrospectively* rate the severity of symptoms experienced during different periods of the menstrual cycle. This flaw introduced the possibility that respondents' biases about what they *expected* they should have experienced at different periods of the cycle might affect their reports. To overcome such potential response biases, Hamilton, Gallant, and Lloyd (in press) asked a sample of 64 women to complete a self-report inventory of depression and *then* report where they were in their menstrual cycle. In other words, the subjects did not know they were participating in a study of the effects of menstrual cycle on mood when they were completing the depression questionnaire. The correlation between the women's levels of depression and where they were in their menstrual cycles indicated that women who were closer to the premenstrual phase of the cycle had higher depression scores. Of the 44 women who were in the premenstrual phase, 36 percent scored in the depressed range of the questionnaire. By contrast, of the 20 women who were not premenstrual, only 10 percent scored in the depressed range. Even with these prospective assessment techniques, then, a substantial minority of women show at least moderate levels of depressive symptoms during the premenstrual phase of their cycle. We must be cautious about accepting the data from the study by Hamilton and colleagues, however. The proportion of women in their sample who were not premenstrual was unusually low (20 of 64). In addition, the sample was not randomly selected; women participated in the study by responding to announcements, at community group meetings and educational settings, of a new study of "moods." The women who decided to participate in the study may have been experiencing significant problems with "moods," and thus the sample may have overrepresented women with depressive disorders.

A much lower estimate of the incidence of premenstrual depression was obtained in a prospective study of 195 female undergraduates who agreed to participate in a study of "the occurrence of emotional and physical changes in relation to environmental events in young women" (Rivera-Tovar & Frank, 1988, p. 2). Every day for 90 days, these women rated the severity with which they experienced 33 symptoms, including the DSM symptoms for late luteal phase dysphoric disorder. Six of the 195 women met the criteria for this disorder: during at least two menstrual cycles they experienced at least five symptoms of the disorder for at least four of the seven days just before the onset of menses but for no more than two days once menses had begun. In other words, only 3.1 percent of the women in this sample qualified for the diagnosis of late luteal phase dysphoric disorder. This rate of the disorder is much lower than the percentage of women scoring as depressed on questionnaires in the studies described earlier. Although it is always the case that more people score in the depressed range of questionnaires than qualify for a diagnosis of depression, the discrepancy between the questionnaire studies and the study by Rivera-Tovar and Frank is unusually large. Still, it appears that at least some portion of women experience moderate to severe episodes of depression during the premenstrual period.

Biochemical hypotheses about premenstrual depression. In a review of the literature on PMS, Rubinow and Roy-Byrne (1984) list sixteen *classes* of hypotheses about the effects of biochemical changes during the premenstrual period on mood. These include hypotheses about the ovarian hormones, estrogen and progesterone; fluid and electrolyte hormones, such as prolactin, aldosterone, angiotensin, and vasopressin; other hormones, such as glucocorticoids, androgen, insulin, and melatonin; neurotransmitters, especially the monoamines and acetylcholine; and vitamin B_6 and prostaglandins. Most of the research on premenstrual mood has focused on estrogen and progesterone.

During the menstrual cycle, levels of estrogen and progesterone rise and fall sharply. Day 1 is arbitrarily defined as the first day of blood flow. During the first two weeks of the cycle, levels of progesterone and estrogen remain quite low. Around the end of the first two weeks, the level of estrogen rises and peaks, then declines again. Near the 21st day of the cycle, the level of estrogen peaks again, and the level of progesterone peaks for the first time. During the last few days before the onset of the next menstrual flow, the levels of both hormones drop precipitously and remain low until after the menstrual flow.

In many of the experiments on the effect of these biochemicals on mood changes during the menstrual cycle, one biochemical is measured over the course of the menstrual cycle in a group of female subjects, who are also asked to monitor their mood on a daily basis. In most of these studies, the subjects know they are participating in a study of mood during the menstrual cycle. Another method has been to isolate women who suffer particularly severe mood and physiological symptoms during the premenstrual period—again using self-reports—and then to measure levels of the biochemicals of interest in these women and compare these levels to the levels in women who do not report severe premenstrual symptoms. Yet another experimental method is to monitor the effects on mood of drugs altering the levels of estrogen, progesterone, or some other biochemical. For example, several studies have investigated the effects of oral contraceptives containing various amounts of estrogen and progesterone on PMS symptoms. We must be careful about making causal inferences from each of these types of study, however. Even when we find some difference between PMS sufferers and nonsufferers, this difference is not necessarily a *cause* of PMS. Similarly, when women who take a drug such as estrogen show relief from PMS, we cannot conclude that deficiencies in estrogen cause premenstrual depression. (To do so would be analogous to reasoning that because aspirin relieves a headache, headaches are caused by a deficiency of aspirin.) There is a great possibility of drawing faulty conclusions when reasoning backward from the effects of drugs to the causes of symptoms. With these methodological problems in mind, let us briefly review some of the most popular hypotheses about the effects of biochemical fluctuations on mood in women. (For other criticisms of the methodology in this literature, see Rubinow & Roy-Byrne, 1984.)

One of the earliest hypotheses about the relationship between estrogen and progesterone and mood changes was that estrogen withdrawal triggers depression and other premenstrual symptoms (Backstrom & Mattsson, 1975; Frank, 1931; Klaiber et al., 1979). The evidence for this hypothesis is indirect. Klaiber and colleagues (1979) report reductions of depressive symptoms in women given estrogen therapy. And some women ingesting estrogen in oral contraceptives also show decreases in depression (Bardwick, 1971; Moos, 1968). Another estrogen-related hypothesis holds that high levels of estrogen in conjunction with low levels of progesterone lead to tension and dysphoria. One study found that women suffering from PMS had higher estrogen-to-progesterone ratios than women who do not suffer from PMS (Backstrom & Cartensen, 1974), and two other studies found elevated levels of estrogen in sufferers of PMS (Abraham, Elsner & Lucas, 1978; Munday, Brush & Taylor, 1981).

Others have argued that declines in levels of progesterone, not estrogen, trigger depressive symptoms. Increases and decreases in levels of progesterone are correlated with increases and decreases in depressive symptoms (Janowsky, Fann & Davis, 1971). Some studies have found correlations between degree of depression in some women and the amount of progesterone in the oral contraceptives they were using (Culberg, 1972; Grant & Pryse-Davies, 1968; Kutner & Brown, 1972). And several studies have found lower levels of progesterone just prior to menstruation in PMS sufferers compared to controls (Abraham, Elsner & Lucas, 1978; Backstrom & Cartensen, 1974; Munday, Brush & Taylor, 1981; Smith, 1976).

It thus appears that there is considerable evidence for a relationship between hormonal abnormalities and some depressions during the premenstrual period. Yet there are just as many studies that do not support the hormonal theories of female depression (see Janowsky & Rausch, 1985; Rubinow & Roy-Byrne, 1984). For example, the premenstrual decline in estrogen is not the only decrease in estrogen that occurs during the menstrual cycle. Just after a midcycle peak, estrogen levels fall quite precipitously, and this decline is *not* associated with depressive symptoms (Dalton, 1964). Premenstrual symptoms are also uncommon during that part of the menstrual cycle when estrogen-to-progesterone ratios are at their highest. A number of studies have found levels of estrogen and progesterone in women who suffered severe premenstrual tension to be no different from levels in women who do not (Andersch et al., 1978; Andersen et al., 1977; Taylor, 1979; Backstrom, Sanders & Leask, 1983). And another study found that premenstrual symptoms emerged in PMS sufferers before declines in progesterone occurred in the menstrual cycle (Munday, Brush & Taylor, 1981).

Perhaps it is not estrogen or progesterone that causes depression in the premenstrual phase. Fluctuations in the mineralocorticoids during the premenstrual phase may shift the salt and water balance in the central nervous system, causing emotional symptoms (Dalton, 1964; Janowsky, Gorney & Mandell, 1967). There is evidence that aldosterone, a mineralocorticoid, may fluctuate in parallel with depressive symptoms during the menstrual cycle (Demarchi & Tong, 1972; Janowsky, Berens & Davis, 1973). Other studies, however, have found no differences in aldosterone levels between subjects exhibiting PMS and control subjects (Munday, Brush & Taylor, 1981; O'Brien et al., 1979). Other researchers have suggested that depressive symptoms in the premenstrual phase may result from excess prolactin levels (Halbreich et al., 1976) or from fluctuations in the adrenocortical hormones, such as androgens and glucocorticoids (Vermeulen & Verdonck, 1976; Walker & McGilp, 1978). But again, there is equal evidence against these hypotheses (see Janowsky & Rausch, 1985; Rubinow & Roy-Byrne, 1984).

Evidence against a premenstrual syndrome. One reason researchers may be having such a difficult time finding consistent evidence for various explanations of premenstrual depressions is that these depressions may not represent a distinct form of depression. Rather, they may simply be exacerbations of an underlying or chronic depressive disorder. Very few women who show depressive symptoms during the premenstrual period show symptoms *only* during this period (Alagna & Hamilton, in press; Rubinow & Roy-Byrne, 1984). Often these women show either symptoms across the cycle that are exacerbated during the premenstrual period, symptoms both at the time of ovulation and during the premenstrual period, or symptoms beginning soon after ovulation and increasing in severity over the entire luteal phase. In addition, many women who have severe premenstrual depression have a personal history or family history of depressions unrelated to the menstrual cycle (Rubinow

& Roy-Byrne, 1984). Again, this suggests that premenstrual depressions may often be simply an exacerbation or flare-up of an underlying depressive disorder. Finally, no treatments have been shown to be specifically effective on premenstrual depression.

Another, very different type of problem with the definition and identification of premenstrual depressions is that women's reports of premenstrual symptoms seem to be heavily influenced by their expectations of what they are supposed to experience during the premenstrual period. For example, consider a study by Abplanap, Haskett, and Rose (1979). They asked 33 women to complete daily mood ratings but did not tell the women that the study was investigating the relationship between mood and the menstrual cycle. At the end of the study they asked the same women to report, retrospectively, on their moods during the different phases of their most recent menstrual cycle, using the Moos Menstrual Distress Questionnaire. On the retrospective questionnaire, subjects reported having experienced significantly more negative symptoms during their premenstrual period than during any other period in their last cycle. When they examined the daily mood ratings of these same women, however, Abplanap and colleagues found no relationship between cycle phase and daily mood ratings (for similar results, see Parlee, 1982; Slade, 1984).

Several researchers have suggested that women have been taught to expect negative moods during the premenstrual period and that these expectations influence their retrospective reports of menstrual-related mood changes (Clarke & Ruble, 1978; Paige, 1973; Parlee, 1974; Sommer, 1973). The effect of expectancies on women's ratings of their moods was demonstrated in a study by Olasov and Jackson (1987). Their subjects were 112 female undergraduates, none of whom were taking oral contraceptives or had ever been pregnant, and all of whom had regular menstrual cycles. These subjects were divided into four groups. One group (a blind control group) was told that the study would assess how moods change from day to day but not that menstrual cycle was a factor. They were asked to rate the degree to which they had experienced, during the last 24 hours, each of 19 symptoms representing positive psychological mood (for example, happy), positive somatic mood (for example, energetic), negative psychological mood (for example, depressed), and negative somatic mood (for example, crampy). They completed this daily monitoring form each day for 40 days. At the beginning of the study, subjects were also asked to complete an expectancy questionnaire that listed the same 19 symptoms and asked subjects to rate the degree to which they *expected* to experience each symptom during their next premenstrual phase. Thus the subjects in the blind control group were not told that the focus of the study was the effects of the menstrual cycle on moods, but they were asked straightforwardly what they expected their moods to be during the next premenstrual phase. These are the same conditions as obtained in many previous studies of subjects' reports of their moods during the menstrual cycle. The researchers wished to compare the subjects' expectancies for the effects of the menstrual cycle on mood with the expectancies subjects would have when the experimenters manipulated subjects' beliefs about the premenstrual syndrome.

The subjects in the other three groups were told that the study focused on the effects of the menstrual cycle on moods. They were asked to complete the same expectancy questionnaire. Then the subjects saw a movie. The subjects in Group I saw a film in which a lecturer presented evidence "proving" that the premenstrual phase is characterized by increases in negative mood. The experimenters predicted that viewing this movie would *increase* subjects' expectations for negative mood during their next premenstrual phase. Group D subjects saw a movie in which a lecturer presented evidence "proving" that there is no relationship between mood fluctuations and menstrual cycle. It was predicted that viewing the movie would *decrease* subjects' expectations for negative mood during their next premenstrual phase. Group MC (manipulation control) subjects saw a movie about circadian rhythms and insomnia. This movie was expected to have no effects on subjects' expectations about premenstrual mood. Immediately after viewing the movies, the subjects in all three groups completed the expectancy questionnaire again. (The blind control group—Group BC—saw no film and completed the initial expectancy questionnaire only once.) Subjects in all four groups then completed daily mood monitoring forms for the next 40 days, in addition to a daily life stress questionnaire that included the item "began menstruating." At the end of the 40 days, all subjects completed the expectancy questionnaire again.

As the experimenters predicted, the film presenting evidence for premenstrual depression appeared to increase subjects' expectancies for depression in future premenstrual periods. In addition, subjects who saw this film (Group I) reported significantly more negative daily moods over all cycle phases than the subjects in any other group. Group I subjects also had more negative expectancies for future premenstrual moods than subjects in Groups D and BC. Subjects who saw the film about circadian rhythms (Group MC) but were told that the study focused on the effects of the menstrual cycle and mood showed expectancies for future premenstrual symptoms that were as negative as the expectancies of Group I and considerably more negative than those of Groups BC and D. Olasov and Jackson (1987) suggest that this result came about because women's expectancies for premenstrual symptoms are typically negative: if they are told that an experimenter's hypothesis is that the menstrual cycle affects moods, subjects will provide data confirming this hypothesis. In general, the data from the Olasov and Jackson study and the study by Abplanap and colleagues (1979) indicate that the increase in negative mood during the premenstrual period seen in many studies can be attributed to women reporting what they think they should be experiencing, rather than what they would normally experience.

The effects of the menstrual cycle on women's moods have been the focus of conjectures by clinicians and laypersons for centuries. In the last 20 years, premenstrual depression has received enormous attention in the popular media and in professional journals. Despite this attention, our understanding of the phenomenon known as premenstrual depression remains meager. Dozens of biological explanations of premenstrual depression have been proposed but no one has been well supported. This may be, in part, because the syndrome has not been defined or measured well. In addition, women's expectations about what they are supposed to experience during the premenstrual period appear to influence their reports of their experiences. Finally, depressions occurring during the premenstrual phase may be no more than exacerbations of an underlying depressive disorder, rather than a distinct type of depression.

We cannot ignore that very small group of women who do experience severe depressive symptoms during the premenstrual period, however (see the discussion of the study by Rivera-Tovar and Frank, 1988). Alagna and Hamilton (in press) argue that it may not be appropriate to give even these women a diagnosis such as late luteal phase dysphoric disorder, as has been suggested in the most recent DSM (American Psychiatric Association, 1987). The phrase *late luteal phase dysphoric disorder* presumes a biological cause for the disorder, when in reality situational factors are as clearly implicated as biological factors in the onset of the disorder. The labeling of a disorder is important because it can affect the types of research that are undertaken and funded. Alagna and Hamilton also note that "[g]iven the clear risks for stigmatization, gender- or race-specific diagnoses in particular should always provoke alarm, and require careful scrutiny" (in press). It is dangerous to imply through the choice of the label that an aspect of women's reproductive biology is central to a psychiatric illness—particularly in view of the un-substantiated folklore about the effects of menstruation on women's mental health and competence. When an official label fosters nega-tive stereotypes of women, it clearly seems premature to apply that label to a set of symptoms that are poorly understood and may not constitute a distinct disorder in themselves.

Postpartum Depression

The period just after childbirth (the postpartum period) has long been considered a period during which women's risk of most psy-chiatric disorders, including depression and schizophrenia, is rela-tively high (Cutrona, 1982). Three types of postpartum mental illness have been discussed in the clinical literature (Cutrona, 1982). The most severe is postpartum psychosis, a diagnosis given to women who completely lose touch with reality and develop delusions and hallucinations during the postpartum period (see Herzog & Detre, 1976). The estimated prevalence of such psychosis is 1 or 2 per 1,000 women. In other words, postpartum psychosis is quite rare. Some researchers have suggested, however, that even these estimates of the rate of postpartum psychosis may be inflated because new mothers who become psychotic are more likely to be hospitalized than women who are not new mothers (Pugh et al., 1963).

Are the psychoses that occur during the postpartum period differ-ent in any way from psychoses that occur during other periods, or are they simply episodes of psychoses that happen to occur during the postpartum period? Most studies have found no differences in the symptoms of postpartum psychoses and psychoses unrelated to childbirth (see Cutrona, 1982). In addition, the family histories of women with postpartum psychoses show the same high prevalence of schizophrenia and affective psychoses among family members as do the family histories of people with psychoses unrelated to childbirth. About 80 to 85 percent of women who become psychotic during the postpartum have never had a previous psychotic episode, suggesting that childbirth is a significant precipitator of psychotic episodes. About 30 to 40 percent of women who become psychotic postpartum go on to experience at least one psychotic episode not associated with childbirth (Protheroe, 1969). These trends have led most researchers to conclude that childbirth is a significant enough psychological and physical stressor to precipitate a psychotic episode in some women, but probably only in women with a substantial underlying vulnerability to psychosis.

The second type of psychological disturbance that sometimes occurs during the postpartum period is nonpsychotic postpartum depression (Cutrona, 1982). Women with this disturbance do not experience hallucinations or delusions but do experience the key symptoms of depression—sadness, apathy, tiredness, and so on. Estimates of the prevalence of nonpsychotic depression in women during the postpartum period range from 3 to 33 percent, depending on the stringency of the criteria used to diagnose depression (Cutrona, 1982). In a study of 85 first-time mothers, DSM-III criteria were used to identify women with a major depressive disorder (Cutrona, 1983). These women were interviewed on three occasions: in their third trimester of pregnancy, two weeks after delivery, and eight weeks after delivery. At these three times, 3.5 percent, 4.7 percent, and 3.5 percent of the women, respectively, were diagnosed as having a major depressive disorder. Only one woman received this diagnosis at more than one interview, suggesting that the duration of these episodes for all the other women was on the order of weeks. A total of 8.2 percent of the women in the study received this diagnosis at some time during the study.* This figure is higher than the rate of major depressive disorders in women who are not pregnant or in the postpartum period (Weissman & Myers, 1978), suggesting that women's risk for such disorders is higher during pregnancy and the

---

*The percentages of women diagnosed as depressed at these test sessions (3.5 percent, 4.7 percent, and 3.5 percent) do not add to the total percentage of women diagnosed as depressed in the study (8.2 percent), because the percentages for an individual test were based on the number of women participating in that test, which was sometimes lower than the number participating in at least one test, and that number is the sample on which the percentage is based.

postpartum period than at other times of life. (For similar results see O'Hara, Neunaber & Zekoski, 1984.)

There is some evidence that experiencing a pregnancy-related major depression puts women at an increased risk for future episodes of depression, both related to and unrelated to pregnancy. For example, Davidson and Robertson (1985) followed up on 43 women who had been treated by Robertson at some time between 1946 and 1971 for a postpartum unipolar depressive episode (diagnostic criteria were unspecified). Of these, 43 percent had had further episodes of depression not related to pregnancy, and 14 percent had had episodes related to pregnancy. Little else is known, however, about the psychiatric or family histories of women who develop pregnancy-related major depressive episodes (Cutrona, 1982). It may be that women who experience pregnancy-related episodes of major depression—like women who experience pregnancy-related psychoses—have a family history of mental disorder and a general predisposition to affective disorder.

The third type of psychological disturbance that occurs during the postpartum period is postpartum "blues." The most common symptom of postpartum blues is frequent tearfulness and crying (Yalom et al., 1968). Other symptoms include unhappiness, anxiety, irritability, and emotional lability (see Cutrona, 1982). Confusion or "fogginess" is often listed as a symptom of postpartum blues, but tests of cognitive performance have not provided evidence of such confusion in women suffering postpartum blues (e.g., Jarrahi-Zadeh et al., 1969). In addition, Cutrona notes that "such factors as fatigue and the residual effects of anesthetics used during delivery are not discussed as possible explanations for the mild 'fogginess' described by some women in the early puerperium" (1982, p. 491).

The incidence of postpartum blues has been estimated to be very high, with as many as 60 percent of women reporting at least mild, transitory symptoms of depression in the week following childbirth (see Cutrona, 1983). When standardized depression questionnaires, such as the Beck Depression Inventory, are used to assess depressive symptoms, about 30 percent of women score above the cut-off point for mild depression about two weeks after delivery (Cutrona, 1983; O'Hara, Neunaber & Zekoski, 1984). This rate of depressive symptoms is clearly higher than that among women who have not recently given birth. The rates of mild depressive symptoms drop quickly after about the second week following delivery. At eight or nine weeks following delivery, only about 11 percent of new mothers report mild to severe depressive symptoms (Cutrona, 1983; O'Hara, Neunaber & Zekoski, 1984)—a lower figure than the percentage of women in the general population who fall into the mildly depressed ranges of depression questionnaires (e.g., Eaton & Kessler, 1981).

It seems likely, however, that most studies of postpartum blues have overestimated the incidence of this problem. Most studies have used self-report depression inventories in which many normal physiological changes of pregnancy and the postpartum period (for example, fatigue, appetite change, loss of sexual interest, aches and pains) are counted as symptoms of depression. Thus women who acknowledge these typical physiological changes may appear to be depressed. To test this hypothesis, O'Hara and colleagues (O'Hara, Neunaber & Zekoski, 1984) looked more closely at the types of symptoms new mothers were reporting when they completed the Beck Depression Inventory (BDI). They divided the symptoms in this inventory into somatic symptoms (for example, appetite loss, fatigue) and cognitive/affective symptoms (for example, sadness, guilt, pessimism). Then they asked 99 women to complete the BDI once during their second trimester, once during their third trimester, and once each at three weeks, six weeks, nine weeks, and six months after delivery. At these times the percentages of women scoring in at least the mildly depressed range of the BDI (measuring both somatic and cognitive/affective symptoms) were, respectively, 46, 28, 27, 24, 11, and 11 percent. These data indicate that depression is extremely common in pregnancy but becomes much less so after childbirth and as time passes.

When the researchers looked carefully at the types of symptoms the new mothers were experiencing, they found that most were common physical complaints that might be expected during pregnancy and the postpartum, instead of the cognitive and affective symptoms of depression. In fact, when the symptoms the new mothers were reporting were compared with symptoms reported by a group of women the same age who were not new mothers, the new mothers tended to report more physical symptoms than the other women, but the new mothers reported fewer of the cognitive/affective symptoms of depression than the other women. Thus the seemingly high rates of depression in the new mothers in this study resulted from their acknowledgment of the aches and pains and problems in sleeping that come with pregnancy and having a new baby, rather than the presence of the full range of depressive symptoms.

The O'Hara, Neunaber, and Zekoski (1984) study is the first to clarify the distinctions between cognitive/affective and somatic symptoms of depression in new mothers. Before we can dismiss postpartum blues as simply somatic symptoms caused by the normal physiological changes of pregnancy, however, we need to see a replication of these results. We certainly cannot dismiss the evidence that a majority of women describe unexpected tearfulness during the first week after delivery. And even if fatigue and loss of sexual interest are caused by normal physiological changes accompanying childbirth, such symptoms can clearly cause distress for women. More important, it is clear that the risk of major depressive episodes is increased during pregnancy and the postpartum period. Thus it is important to explore potential causes of this greater risk. Three types of explanation have been proposed for women's increased risk of depression (and psychosis) during pregnancy and childbirth: biological explanations, stress explanations, and personality explanations.

Biological explanations of postpartum depression. Many biochemical changes occur during pregnancy and after delivery. Most research on pregnancy-related depressions has focused on the ovarian hormones, estrogen and progesterone. The levels of both hormones are very high during pregnancy, then drop precipitously in the first week after delivery. Depression and other psychological disturbances during pregnancy and the postpartum period have been attributed by various researchers to abnormalities in the estrogen/progesterone ratio, unusually high levels of progesterone, or abnormally rapid declines in the levels of progesterone (see Cutrona, 1982; Yalom et al., 1968). That is, women who suffer from postpartum depression may differ from women who do not in their bodies' regulation of estrogen and progesterone during pregnancy and the postpartum period. Studies testing this hypothesis, however, have found few consistent differences in hormone levels, estrogen/progesterone ratios, or rate of change of progesterone between sufferers of pregnancy-related depression and nonsufferers (Gelder, 1978; Nott et al., 1976).

Indirect evidence for a link between hormonal problems and postpartum blues comes from studies showing that some women who get postpartum blues have a history of irregular menstrual cycles (Yalom et al., 1968). In addition, there is some evidence that women who get postpartum blues have a history of symptoms of depression and anxiety during the premenstrual period (Gelder, 1978; Nott et al., 1976; Yalom et al., 1968). Because the premenstrual period and the early postpartum period are both characterized by precipitous drops in levels of estrogen and progesterone, the fact that women who tend to get postpartum blues also tend to experience premenstrual tension provides indirect evidence that abnormalities in the regulation of hormones may be associated with depression and anxiety symptoms in these women (Cutrona, 1982). There has been no consistent evidence for a link between serious postpartum depression and premenstrual tension or menstrual irregularities, however (Cutrona, 1982). Thus we have some indirect evidence that postpartum blues are linked to abnormalities in the regulation of estrogen or progesterone, but no evidence that serious postpartum depressions are hormonally based.

Other researchers have suggested that abnormalities in important chemicals in the brain, called *neurotransmitters*, cause postpartum depression. Neurotransmitters facilitate the transmission of impulses between neurons in the central nervous system. The particular group of neurotransmitters that has been implicated in depression is called the *amine group*. This group of neurotransmitters appears to play an important role in the functioning of the limbic system, which seems to regulate drives (such as the sex drive) and feelings. The amine hypothesis of depression states that abnormalities in levels of amines cause dysfunctioning in the limbic system and thereby cause the loss of sexual interest, changes in appetite, lowered motivation, and mood changes often associated with depression. This hypothesis has generated an enormous amount of research in the last fifteen years (for a review, see Baldessarini, 1986). Most of this research has focused on two particular amines, norepinephrine and serotonin. Researchers have hypothesized that abnormally low levels of these amines in the synapses between neurons cause depressive symptoms. Unfortunately, neurotransmitters cannot be measured directly in a subject's blood or urine. Thus most research on the amine hypothesis has involved measuring urine or blood levels of either the by-products of norepinephrine and serotonin or the amino acids from which these neurotransmitters are synthesized. Researchers can then compare levels of these chemicals in depressed persons to the levels in nondepressed persons.

Another research strategy for proponents of the amine hypothesis has been to treat depressed people with drugs that alter levels of norepinephrine or serotonin in the brain. Two types of drugs, called tricyclic antidepressants and monoamine oxidase inhibitors (MAOIs) have been found to relieve depression in the majority of depressed patients. Tricyclic antidepressants do so by inhibiting the reabsorption of norepinephrine and serotonin back into the originating neuron. As the name implies, MAOIs do so by inhibiting monoamine oxidase, an enzyme that causes the breakdown of norepinephrine and serotonin. Both tricyclic antidepressants and MAOIs have been found to relieve depression in the majority of depressed patients—a finding that supports the amine hypothesis of depression.

Some researchers have found evidence of differences in serotonin levels between women who suffer postpartum depression and those who do not. The focus of this research has been on tryptophan, an amino acid that is the precursor of serotonin. Two studies have found that women with relatively low levels of tryptophan in the blood show higher levels of postpartum depressive symptoms (Handley et al., 1977; Stein et al., 1976). Another study found differences between sufferers of postpartum depression and nonsufferers in the rate of change of tryptophan levels during the first four days after delivery (Handley et al., 1980). These studies suggest that tryptophan levels are related to postpartum depression levels, but they do not show that low levels of tryptophan *cause* postpartum depression. One study tested the hypothesis that low tryptophan levels cause postpartum depression by having women ingest tryptophan during the postpartum period (Harris, 1980). (A control group was given a placebo.) The women who took tryptophan showed no differences in postpartum depressive symptoms from the women who took the placebo. This finding suggests that low tryptophan levels are a correlate but not a cause of postpartum depression.

To summarize, the hypotheses that postpartum depression is caused by abnormalities in neurotransmitters and that severe postpartum depression is caused by abnormal hormonal regulation have received little support. There is some association between women's tendencies to have postpartum blues and their histories of premenstrual tension and menstrual irregularities, but there is no direct evidence that postpartum blues are caused by abnormalities in hormone levels. As the technology for assaying neurotransmitters and hormone levels improves, more consistent support for these hypotheses may be found.

Stress explanations of postpartum depression. Events that threaten a person's well-being, burden a person's ability to function from day to day, or require substantial readjustment of a person's point of view or daily activities are often called "stressful" events (see Kessler, Price & Wortman, 1985). Many women experience the last weeks of pregnancy and the first few weeks with a newborn baby as a stressful period (Holmes & Rahe, 1967). Because stressful life events appear to enhance a person's risk of depression (see Lloyd, 1980), some investigators have suggested that pregnancy-related blues and depression result from the sometimes overwhelming new challenges women face during these periods.

As Cutrona (1982) notes, the majority of women do not become seriously depressed during late pregnancy or the postpartum period. But women who experience short-term or chronic stressful events *in addition to* childbirth are at high risk for depression. Indeed, women undergoing chronic stressors (such as financial strain) or isolated stressors (such as bereavement) at the time of childbirth are three times more likely to develop postpartum depression than women not undergoing such stressors (Paykel et al., 1980). Other types of stressors associated with an increased risk of postpartum depression are illness in oneself or in a family member or ill health in the baby (Blumberg, 1980; Martin, 1977), inadequate child care resources (Cutrona, 1983), and a poor marital relationship (Ballinger et al., 1979; Braverman & Roux, 1978; Cutrona, 1983; Martin, 1977). In addition, conflictual relationships with parents, lack of close confidants, and lack of close relatives living nearby appear to contribute to postpartum depression (Ballinger et al., 1979; Gordon, Kapostins & Gordon, 1965; Paykel et al., 1980).

Thus there appears to be substantial evidence that the lack of social support and the experience of additional stressors at the time of childbirth predispose women to postpartum depressions. The argument that environmental rather than biological factors cause postpartum depression is further buttressed by evidence that adoptive mothers and biological fathers also are at increased risk for depression following the arrival of a new baby (Rees & Lutkins, 1971). These people obviously do not experience the biological changes of women who actually deliver children; thus there must be psychosocial causes of depressions in fathers and adoptive mothers. Social support and life events are not perfect predictors of postpartum depression, however. Many women who experience a great deal of stress at the time of childbirth do not become depressed (e.g., Paykel et al., 1980). Personality or biological factors may also influence differences in women's emotional reactions to childbirth. Because women with a personal or family history of affective disorders are at higher risk for postpartum depression than women without such a history (Cutrona, 1983), it may be that a woman must be biologically predisposed to depression for the stress of childbirth to lead to a full-blown depressive episode. Alternatively, certain personality factors may influence how a woman reacts to the stress of childbirth.

Personality explanations of postpartum depression. One personality theory of depression that has been applied to postpartum depression is the reformulated learned helplessness theory (Abramson, Seligman & Teasdale, 1978). According to this theory, the people most vulnerable to depression are those with a maladaptive explanatory style characterized by a tendency to attribute bad events to causes internal to oneself ("it's my fault"), stable in time ("it's going to last forever"), and global in effect ("it will undermine everything I do"). Two studies have found that women who show this maladaptive explanatory style during pregnancy are more likely to experience postpartum depressive symptoms than women who have a more adaptive style (Cutrona, 1983; O'Hara, Rehm & Campbell, 1982). O'Hara and colleagues (1982) also found that subjects' self-control was related to postpartum depression levels. Their self-control questionnaire measured subjects' tendencies to selectively pay attention to negative outcomes, to set stringent standards for personal performance, and to be excessively self-deprecatory (see Rehm, 1977). In a second study of postpartum depression, however, O'Hara, Neunaber, and Zekoski (1984) found no relationship between explanatory style and depressive symptoms (see also Manly et al., 1982). Thus tests of the hypothesis that explanatory style influences postpartum depression have had mixed results. O'Hara, Neunaber, and Zekoski (1984) did find that self-control deficits predicted postpartum depression levels, corroborating the earlier O'Hara study. These results suggest that thinking styles may influence postpartum depression, but much more research is needed to test the hypothesis.

Summary. The best-supported explanation of serious postpartum depressions is the stress explanation: women suffering postpartum depression are often experiencing stressors in addition to those associated with a new baby. It is likely that an *interaction* between such additional stress and underlying biological or psychological vulnerability to depression is necessary to cause serious postpartum depression, but we do not yet know how to characterize those biological or psychological vulnerabilities. It is difficult to generalize from this research about postpartum depression to the effects of hormonal imbalances on women's overall vulnerability to depression. There is a link between mild postpartum blues and menstrual irregularities, but this link is at best only indirect evidence for the hormonal explanation of women's depression. There is no evidence that serious postpartum depression is caused by hormonal irregularities.

Menopausal Depression

Menopausal depression was once thought to be extremely common in women. Early editions of the American Psychiatric Association's *Diagnostic and Statistical Manual* included a special diagnostic category for menopausal depression, labeled *involutional melancholia*. This type of depression was assumed to be caused, typically, by the hormonal changes occurring in a woman's body at menopause. The key symptoms of involutional melancholia were excessive guilt, anxiety, insomnia, and apathy. The term *involutional melancholia* was used more generally for depressions characterized by an abundance of physical symptoms (for example, weight loss, insomnia) and excessive guilt. A man could be diagnosed with involutional melancholia if his depression came on in his fifties or early sixties and was characterized by physical symptoms and excessive guilt.

The diagnosis of involutional melancholia was dropped, however, in the third edition of the DSM (American Psychiatric Association, 1980) in light of evidence that no unique type of depression typically arises in menopausal women. For example, Weissman (1979) obtained ratings of anxiety, physical complaints, sleep disturbance, apathy, and other symptoms of depression in 422 females who sought treatment for unipolar depression. She found no significant differences between premenopausal, menopausal, and postmenopausal women in symptom patterns or overall levels of depression. Winokur (1973) studied 71 women hospitalized for an affective disorder and found that the risk of developing depression was not higher during the menopause than during any other period of adult life. As discussed in Chapter 2, rates of depression among women actually diminish slightly with age. If there were such a thing as involutional melancholia, the rates of depression in women over about 45 years should be higher than those of younger women. It thus appears that the hormonal changes occurring in menopause are not associated with a distinct type of depression or with increases in rates of depression among women. If anything, rates of depression among women decline during menopause.

Summary

Given the paucity of evidence for the hypothesis that hormonal fluctuations or abnormalities cause depression in females, some may wonder why this notion is still firmly believed by many scientists. One reason is that experimenters investigating the effects of drugs, including psychoactive drugs in animals, have long observed that the effectiveness of these drugs in female animals depends on their current phase of the estrus cycle. Similarly, the metabolism of psychoactive drugs in human females is influenced by the menstrual cycle, although exactly in what ways is not understood (see Hamilton & Conrad, 1987). These data suggest that hormonal levels do affect the neurochemical subsystems associated with psychological disorders (including, but not exclusively, depression).

Another reason for the belief that hormonal variations affect psychological functioning is that psychotherapists often observe that women prone to depression (and to other psychological problems) frequently experience recurrences of these disorders during pregnancy, the postpartum period, or a premenstrual phase (for a review, see Rubinow & Roy-Byrne, 1984). Whether it is the psychological or the biological stress of these periods that increases the probability of an episode in vulnerable women is not known. Hamilton and Conrad (1987) suggest that, for some women prone to depressive disorders, some episodes occurring during periods of hormonal change may result from interactions between the hormonal changes and the drugs these women are taking to control their psychological disorder. The question of why women prone to psychological disorder often experience recurrences of their disorder during the premenstrual period, pregnancy, or the postpartum period is only beginning to be addressed in controlled studies. New research may show that hormonal changes exacerbate depression and other disorders in women who have a history of these disorders. For now, however, we have no clear evidence that the hormonal changes almost all females experience have substantial effects on their vulnerability to depression.

Genetic Factors

Affective disorders seem to run in families (Gershon, 1983). The rates of affective disorders in the families of persons with a unipolar or bipolar disorder are two to five times higher than the rates in families of normal controls (Weissman, Kidd & Prusoff, 1982). This aggregation of affective disorders within families may result either from genetic factors or from environmental factors shared by family members. But evidence supporting some sort of genetic transmission of affective disorder comes from studies of twins with affective disorders (see Allen, 1976). Monozygotic (identical) twins share identical genes, whereas the genes of dizygotic (fraternal) twins are no more alike than the genes of any pair of siblings. If a disorder is transmitted genetically and one twin of a set of monozygotic twins shows the disorder, the other twin will be very likely to show the disorder. When one twin of a dizygotic pair shows the disorder, the other twin will be no more likely to show the disorder than will other siblings who are not her twin. When both twins show a disorder, they are said to be *concordant* for the disorder. In a review of twin studies of affective illness, Allen (1976) found that the average concordance rate for unipolar depression was 11 percent in dizygotic twins and 40 percent in monozygotic twins. More strikingly, the average concordance rate for bipolar disorder was 14 percent in dizygotic twins and 72 percent in monozygotic twins. The substantially higher concordance rate for monozygotic twins indicates some sort of genetic transmission of the disorder. Allen argues, however, that the substantial *discordance* rate between monozygotic twins for these disorders indicates that nongenetic factors also play a strong role in vulnerability to affective disorders.

Could sex differences in depression result from a greater genetic predisposition to depression in females than in males? A number of investigators have argued that depression is the result of a mutant gene on the X chromosome (Winokur & Tanna, 1969). Because females have two X chromosomes, it is argued, they have a higher risk of depression than males. One way investigators have tested the X-linkage hypothesis of affective disorders is to examine the correlation between affective disorders and two abnormalities known to result from mutations on the X chromosome: red-green color blindness and the Xg blood group. For example, Mendlewicz, Fleiss, and Fieve (1972) examined the pedigrees of seven families in which one or more members manifested an affective disorder and one or more members had the Xg blood group. These researchers found that affective disorders and the Xg blood group were significantly correlated within the families. Those relatives who showed affective disorders also tended to have the Xg blood group. They concluded that affective disorders result from an abnormal allele on the X chromosome near the location of the Xg blood group allele. A number of other studies have also found a relationship between affective disorders and the Xg blood group or color blindness (e.g., Reich, Clayton & Winokur, 1969; Winokur & Tanna, 1969).

However, Gershon and Bunney (1976) have raised a number of concerns about the marginal statistical significance of these relationships observed in studies of the X-linkage hypothesis. In addition, Gershon and Bunney note that the family pedigrees used in these studies were often incomplete. Finally, these linkage studies assume that the alleles for affective disorders, color blindness, and the Xg blood group occur in close proximity on the X chromosome. But a large number of studies (reviewed by Gershon & Bunney, 1976) have indicated that the alleles for color blindness and Xg are far from each other.

Another way to test the X-linkage hypothesis is to examine the transmission of affective disorders from parents to children. Specifically, if a father carries the mutant gene on his X chromosome (and therefore manifests an affective disorder), all his daughters will carry the mutant gene, for the father always gives his daughters an

X chromosome. But the father will never transmit the gene to his son, for sons always receive a Y chromosome from their fathers. If a mother carries the mutant gene on one of her two X chromosomes, then her daughters and sons have an equal chance of carrying the mutant gene. In short, if affective disorders are linked to the X chromosome, we should observe father-daughter pairs of affected people but not father-son pairs, and we should observe equal numbers of mother-daughter and mother-son pairs. However, most family history studies of the X-linkage hypothesis have discovered father-son pairs manifesting an affective disorder, which is incompatible with an X-chromosome mode of transmission (e.g., Fieve et al., 1984; Gershon & Bunney, 1976; Green et al., 1973). Gershon and Bunney (1976) compiled data from these and several other studies and found that, of 106 father-son pairs in which the father had an affective disorder, 10 sons (roughly 10 percent) showed an affective disorder. This is a much higher rate than is acceptable by the X-linkage hypothesis. In addition, Gershon and Bunney found that, of 129 brother-brother pairs in which one brother showed an affective disorder, only 18 other brothers (roughly 14 percent) showed an affective disorder. According to the X-linkage hypothesis, brothers of an affected person should be much more at risk than sons of an affected father. Yet these data indicate that brothers are not significantly more at risk than sons.

One response to these data by proponents of the X-linkage hypothesis is to say that affective disorders are probably heterogeneous, with one type of affective disorder being transmitted on the X chromosome and other types being transmitted by different modes (e.g., Cadoret & Winokur, 1974; Winokur & Clayton, 1967). This is a plausible hypothesis, but researchers have not yet been able to specify what modes of genetic transmission would be associated with what subtypes of affective disorder. More recently, Cloninger and colleagues (1978) argued that most common psychiatric disorders are not likely to result from major chromosomal abnormalities on individual genes. Instead, such disorders are more likely the result of an aggregation of minor genetic abnormalities that interact with environmental variables to make a person vulnerable to the disorder. Cloninger and colleagues group all the genetic and other familial factors that influence risk for a particular disorder under the label *liability* and argue that only individuals whose liability is above a certain threshold will manifest the disorder. If one sex manifests a disorder less frequently than the other—males manifesting depression, for example—it may be because that sex has a higher threshold for the disorder. In the case of depression, however, the relative invulnerability of males may also result from nonfamilial environmental factors that protect males. Cloninger and colleagues argue that we can determine whether observed sex differences in a disorder probably result from genetic and familial factors or from environmental factors by examining the rates of the disorder in the parents and siblings of affected people. Specifically, if the sex differences in depression result from a lesser genetic loading (that is, a higher liability threshold) for depression in males, then we would expect to see *more* depression in the relatives of depressed males than in the relatives of depressed females: if depressed males are more genetically deviant than depressed females, they will be more likely to transmit their depression to offspring (and to have received their depression from their parents). If the sex differences in depression result primarily from nonfamilial environmental factors, however, we should expect no differences in the rates of depression among the relatives of depressed males and females.

Merikangas, Weissman, and Pauls (1985) applied these analyses to family history data from 133 diagnosed unipolar depressives. Complete pedigrees were obtained from all patients, and diagnostic assessments were made of all living relatives of the patients on the basis of interviews, medical records, and family history information. The researchers found that the relatives of male depressives and female depressives were equally likely to be diagnosed as depressed. These data suggest that sex differences in depression result not from genetic factors but from environmental factors.

Conclusions

The biological explanations of sex differences in depression have not been well supported. There is no evidence that women have a greater genetic predisposition to depression than men, and the hormonal explanations have received mixed and indirect support at best. To begin with, there does not seem to be as great an increase in risk for depression during periods of hormonal change as is commonly believed. Menopausal depression and long-term postpartum depression are rare. Studies seem to find evidence of significant pre-menstrual depression only when women are made aware of the focus of the study. And the increase in rates of depression in girls in early adolescence is not associated with menarche. Even among women who clearly do experience serious depression during periods of hormonal change, there has been no consistent evidence of a particular hormonal or biochemical abnormality that distinguishes them from women who do not experience such depression.

Finally, the biological explanations of sex differences in depression, as a class of explanations, cannot explain the absence of sex differences in certain subgroups, such as university students and the recently widowed. Certainly the women in these subgroups have the same biological make-up as women in groups that do show sex differences in depression. Social and environmental factors cannot be ignored as we try to explain the variations across groups in sex differences in depression.

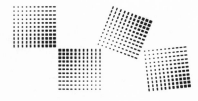

CHAPTER FOUR

Women's Social Power and Status

In Chapter 3, I examined the evidence that women's greater vulnerability to depression is attributable to biological factors. The biological explanations for women's depressions are probably the first type of explanation that many people think about, given the pervasiveness of sex differences in depression around the world. Yet the evidence for biological factors in women's depressions was weak. In this chapter, I examine a very different set of explanations for women's depressions. This set of explanations attributes women's greater vulnerability to depression to the lower status they have been afforded in societies and their lack of power, compared to men, in attaining the goals they set for themselves. Proponents of these social-role theories of women's depressions argue that the victimization of women is nearly as constant across cultures as women's biology, and thus just as powerful a possible explanation for the pervasive sex differences in depression.

The Social-Role Theories

In most cultures and for most of history, different social roles have been prescribed for men and women. A group's social role includes those activities and occupations that society deems appropriate for members of the group. The activities prescribed for women have included caring for children, cooking meals for the family, and up-keep of the family home. The kinds of paid occupations traditionally deemed "women's work" in the United States over the last several decades have included clerical work, nursing, service positions such as waitressing, and teaching in elementary or secondary school. Only in the last few decades have women entered the paid labor force in great numbers. Previously, almost all women were full-time home-makers. Many theorists have argued that women and the work they do have been less highly valued than men and the work they do. As a consequence, women have less power to influence society and less freedom to choose what role to play. Women's lack of power also leads to frequent victimization in the workplace and at home by men who have been given authority over them. According to the social-role theories explored in this chapter, women's inferior social status and lack of power in society contribute to their vulnerability to depression.

The first set of social-role theories I discuss focuses on the blatant and subtle ways women are discriminated against and victimized in society. According to these theories, women receive constant mes-sages that no matter what they do, they will never be considered as competent as men and will never have complete control over im-portant areas of their lives. As a result, women acquire a sense of helplessness and defeat and are at increased risk of becoming de-pressed. In addition, some women face direct physical and psycho-logical abuse in the form of rape, wife battering, and other forms of violence. These women are no doubt at high risk for depression just after an assault, and the sense of vulnerability and the lack of trust for others that arise from the assault may extend the risk of depression for months or years.

According to the second set of social-role theories, even when women freely choose a traditional career as a full-time homemaker they often find that this role is not highly valued and can be un-stimulating and isolating. These conditions can lead women to lose self-esteem and motivation and to become depressed. This has been called the *noxious nature of the housewife role* theory of women's depression (Repetti & Crosby, 1984). According to another theory —the *paucity of roles* theory (Repetti & Crosby, 1984)—women who are not employed outside the home often have only one source of gratification in their lives—their families. As long as all is well in the family, these women may be happy. But when there is discord in the marriage, or other trouble within the family, these women have nowhere else to turn for support and gratification. Men, on the other hand, can turn to their job and their coworkers when the home situation becomes difficult. In short, this theory holds that women often become depressed because they do not have multiple roles that can compensate for each other in times of difficulty.

We might infer, on the basis of those two theories, that women might avoid depression by having both a family life and a job outside the home. But according to the *role overload* theory (Gove & Tudor, 1973), women who work and have a husband, children, or both, face a different but equally stressful set of pressures. Most women who work outside the home still do most of the cooking, cleaning, and caring for children in the home. In essence, they carry two full-time jobs. They also face incompatible expectations in the home and on the job. They are expected to be unselfish, patient, and supportive at home, and selfish, aggressive, and self-sufficient at work. These pressures can lead to "role overload" and to the despair of depression.

Before describing the evidence that women suffer powerlessness in many areas of their lives, I want to review the psychological theory that best explains why powerlessness leads to depression: the learned helplessness theory (Seligman, 1975). According to this theory, a person who frequently experiences a lack of control over important outcomes can develop an expectation that situations in the future will be uncontrollable. This expectation of no control leads to sadness, reduced motivation, and an inability to see opportunities for controlling situations when they do arise. This condition has been termed *learned helplessness*. Seligman (1975) pointed out the similarities between the motivational, emotional, and cognitive deficits of learned helplessness and the symptoms of depression. He suggested that at least some depressions result from the belief that one has no control over important areas of one's life.

Victimization and Depression

The type of experience that would most obviously lead to a sense of helplessness in women is chronic, blatant, serious victimization, such as that experienced by battered wives. The battered wife is beaten and threatened with murder, sometimes on a daily basis, and usually feels she has no means of escaping this situation because her husband has said he will kill her or their children if she attempts to escape. Women experience such situations with extraordinary frequency. There are many much more subtle ways women can be made to feel helpless, however. For example, women who raise objections to actions or statements that they experience as sexist often are told that they are too sensitive, that they can't take a joke. Although a single such experience probably would not lead to learned helplessness, the repeated thwarting or ridicule of one's attempts to change negative aspects of one's environment might lead to helplessness, at least for some women. The following section investigates the blatant and subtle forms of discrimination and victimization women face and the evidence that these experiences contribute to helplessness and depression.

Discrimination in the Workplace

Until a couple of decades ago women were prevented from reaching men's status in education, professions, and compensation through overt, often legal sex discrimination. Women who wished to be educated and have a career often could not be admitted to the college of their choice because these institutions explicitly prohibited their entrance. Even if a woman did attain a degree in medicine or law, she found it difficult to be accepted by a professional community and to make a living. And often she was barred from key professional organizations (e.g., Ehrenreich & English, 1978).

Institutionalized discrimination. In the last two decades, the opportunities for women to enter institutions of higher learning and to find high-status, high-paying jobs have increased dramatically. While only 3.5 percent of the graduates of medical and other professional schools in 1965 were women, 32 percent of the graduates in 1986 were women (Basow, 1986). In 1965, only 11 percent of PhD's were awarded to women; by 1986 the number had risen to 37 percent. The percentage of women in the overall labor force has increased from only 31 percent in 1947 to 51 percent in 1980. A related trend is the dramatic drop in the birthrate over that period, from an average of 25 children per 1,000 population in 1955 to an average of 15 in the late 1970's (Gerson, 1985). Women are having fewer children, which gives them more freedom to enter the marketplace and

pursue careers. It might appear, then, that sex discrimination preventing women from choosing the education, career, and life course
they want is a thing of the past. Yet women today still make only
about 60 cents for every dollar a man makes for the same job (see
Fuchs, 1986). Some might attribute this discrepancy to women's recent entry into the marketplace, which would give them a relatively
low position in the seniority system. But women have been making
about 60 cents for every dollar a man makes for more than 30 years
(Basow, 1986).

There is a large—and growing—group of women who do not even
earn enough to feed and clothe themselves and their children. This
group includes newly divorced or separated mothers, many of whom
have little job experience and few marketable skills. The following
story is all too common:

"The Nouveau Poor" hit me at a precipitous moment. I read it the day before my mother went to court to involuntarily end a thirty-year marriage.
My mother spent twenty years of that marriage at home raising three children; then, just when the college tuition and the other debts were finally
paid off, my father decided to share his income (and himself) not with her,
but with a woman fifteen years his junior. Because my parents reside in a
"no-fault divorce" state, my mother was entitled to virtually nothing. Every
attorney she consulted told her that she had no right to my father's considerable assets. He has these assets because for thirty years he had a wife
to raise his children, make his meals, clean his house, and provide support
so that he could go out and earn a living. In the eyes of the law, however,
this "women's work" is worth nothing. My mother, along with many other
women, has become one of the nouveau poor. [Anonymous letter quoted by
Thom, 1987, p. 111]

The standard of living of divorced women and their children drops
approximately 70 percent in the first year following divorce, whereas
the standard of living of recently divorced men rises 42 percent
(Basow, 1986). Only 60 percent of single mothers are awarded child
support in divorce settlements, and fewer than half of fathers pay
the full amount of child support on a regular basis. Financial hard-
ship is clearly related to depression (Eaton & Kessler, 1981; Ross
& Mirowsky, 1988), so we can expect that a substantial portion
of these women are depressed. Still, women's relative poverty does
not account fully for the greater tendency of women than men to
be depressed, for women are more likely than men to be depressed
at many different levels of socioeconomic status (Eaton & Kessler,

1981). One goal of future research should be to assess whether women in poverty, such as divorced mothers who do not receive adequate child support from their former husbands, make up a substantial portion of women who become depressed.

Insidious discrimination. Even among women who are able to get a good education and find a good job, there appear to be many forms of more subtle, insidious sex discrimination that may prove even harder to fight than institutionalized sex discrimination. These forms of discrimination can be grouped into three categories: negative biases in evaluations of women's work, negative attributions for women's success, and sex segregation in jobs (the channeling of women into lower-paying "women's work").

1. *Negative biases in evaluations of women's work.* Several studies have shown that the qualifications and performances of women are evaluated more negatively than those of men, even when these qualifications and performances are identical (for a review see Wallston & O'Leary, 1981). In a classic study of such evaluative biases, college women were asked to rate journal articles for value, persuasiveness, profundity, writing style, and competence (Goldberg, 1968). The gender of the names of the authors of these papers was the only characteristic that varied from one article to another. A paper received more favorable ratings when the subjects thought the author was male than when they thought the author was female. Similarly, Fidell (1976) had psychology department chairpersons rate job applicants on the basis of profiles and found that the same profile was rated higher when a male name was attached than when a female name was attached. And Firth (1982) found that when a job application with a male name on it was sent to an accounting firm, the applicant was more likely to pass an initial screening than when the same application was submitted with a female name on it. It thus appears that women are evaluated more negatively than men even when they appear to have identical qualifications or performances. However, not all studies find differences in the ways men and women are evaluated (see Basow, 1986). Evaluative biases appear to be more likely when the criteria for evaluation are relatively subjective and ambiguous. Unfortunately, criteria for evaluations tend to become more subjective and ambiguous the higher the status and salary level of a job. Thus these evaluative biases may be operating most strongly in the higher-paying, higher-status jobs.

In their everyday work life, women have more trouble than men being taken seriously (Unger, 1975). Studies have found that when a knowledgeable man and a knowledgeable woman say the same thing, more attention is paid to the man (Gruber & Gaebelein, 1979). Women also tend to have less influence in problem-solving groups (Wahrman & Pugh, 1974) and tend to be disliked when they are assertive (Johnson, 1976). Consider this account by one woman:

I work part time at a gas station in Oakland. I pump gas, wash windows, put air in tires, check and charge batteries, check transmissions, change oil, hub jobs, and other basic things. I don't claim to be a mechanic; I'm not. But I'm getting a little tired of women asking me to get "one of the men" to check their tires, water, and oil. I've been trained on the job to do these things. . . . One woman asked me to check her transmission. I did and found that she was completely empty and suggested she add a quart of transmission fluid. She didn't believe me and asked that I get "one of the men" to check it out. So I did, and he told her the same thing. This happens every day. [Anonymous letter quoted by Thom, 1987, pp. 100–101]

This woman's account clearly illustrates that even when women gain access to the jobs they want, and perform well in those jobs, they are often still evaluated as less competent than men.

2. *Negative attributions for women's success.* In general, when a man does well at a task, evaluators tend to attribute his success to ability, but when a woman succeeds, they tend to attribute her success to luck. Conversely, when a man fails, his failure is often attributed to bad luck, and when a woman fails, her failure is attributed to lack of ability (see Basow, 1986; Feather & Simon, 1975; Taynor & Deaux, 1973). These attributional biases are particularly strong when masculine-typed, high-status tasks are involved. For example, men's high performance as surgeons or as mathematicians is attributed to ability, but women's identical performance in those fields is attributed to effort or to the easiness of the particular task (Feldman-Summers & Kiesler, 1974). However, when a task is feminine-typed —for example, cooking or infant care—there are often no differences in attributions for men's and women's performance. Other studies have found that success at masculine-typed jobs is more highly valued than success at feminine-typed jobs (Deaux & Taynor, 1973). Thus evaluators' attributional biases appear to operate most strongly in tasks that are highly valued.

One reason the attributions evaluators make for performance are important is that such attributions may affect the rewards a person receives for his performance. Heilman and Guzzo (1978) found that business school students judged both men and women more deserving of reward if their success was attributable to ability than if their success was attributable to luck or effort. In many cases a manager may tell her employees what she attributes their performances to, and these attributions may in turn affect the employees' self-esteem levels and motivation. Many studies have shown that people who attribute their failures to bad luck or lack of effort and their successes to ability tend to show more motivation, positive self-regard, and expectation of future success than do people who attribute their failures to low ability and their successes to luck or effort (Weiner, 1974). Thus the effects of the attributions made by evaluators of women's performances may be to decrease women's motivation and therefore to diminish their performances relative to men's.

3. *Sex segregation in jobs.* Men and women are largely segregated into two separate job markets (see Basow, 1986). Data from 1985 show that the great majority of employed women work in just a few types of jobs, mostly in the service sector, such as clerical work, waitressing, and retail sales. On the other hand, over 80 percent of skilled laborers, 65 percent of managers and administrators, and 60 percent of professionals (other than teachers) are male. One reason sometimes given for this sex segregation is that men and women have different talents and personality characteristics that make them suited to different jobs. Women are nurturant and patient and like detail work, which better suits them to service positions (but for some reason, not to skilled craftwork). Men are assertive, analytical, and decisive, which better suits them to business, law, and medicine. In reality, few differences are found in the talents and characteristics of men and women, particularly if they are matched in education and work experience. And the belief that women are not suited to many jobs formerly seen as men's jobs seems to be diminishing in the general public (Basow, 1986).

But the occupational choices made by young people, particularly males, are still largely sex-typed. In a recent study of more than 13,000 adolescents, 75 percent of the males chose traditionally male jobs and 47 percent of the females chose traditionally female jobs (Parachini, 1985). Several studies have found that increasing numbers of women in an occupation tend to lower its prestige and pay level

(Basow, 1986). In the Soviet Union, for example, 70 percent of the physicians are women, and medicine is considered a relatively low-status occupation. Thus even when women break into a formerly male-dominated occupation, their victory often means a decrease in the monetary and social value of the position.

The effects of discrimination on the well-being of women. The studies reviewed in this section have indicated that even when women escape overt sex discrimination, they face covert discrimination in the form of negative evaluations and attributions for their performance and segregation into low-paying jobs. Radloff (1975) argued that the constant frustration women face in society can lead to learned helplessness (see Seligman, 1975). Do discrimination and lack of power lead many women to develop learned helplessness and depression? Zappert and Weinstein (1985) surveyed 73 men and 50 women who had received an MBA from Stanford three years before. Despite the fact that the men and women received their degree from the same school, had the same number of years' experience, and were equally likely to be married and have children, the women were making an average of $25,668 per year, whereas the men were making an average of $29,676. Similarly, the men had significantly higher-status positions than the women (many men were executives). The researchers measured the respondents' perceptions of job stress, their difficulties in coping with stress in an adaptive way, their sense of conflict between their roles at home and at work, and their physical and emotional health. The women reported significantly more physical and emotional health problems than the men. Over 60 percent of the women reported feeling depressed sometimes, often, or always, compared to 44 percent of the men. Women also reported significantly more job stress than men. For example, 83 percent of the women and 59 percent of the men reported that they often or always felt they had to be the best at everything they did. The women were not more likely than the men to report dissatisfaction with their jobs, their current incomes, or their progress compared to others in similar positions, however.

In a larger and more detailed examination of the effects of sex discrimination on women's emotional well-being, Crosby (1982) found little evidence that salary discrimination often leads to depression in women. She conducted extensive interviews with over 400 employed women, employed men, and homemakers in Newton,

Massachusetts. The jobs of employed subjects ranged from factory work to professions such as law. The employed men and women were matched for job level, marital status, and presence of children, but the employed women in the sample were receiving substantially lower salaries than the men for the same jobs. The subjects were asked about their satisfaction with their jobs and home lives and their grievances about their jobs. We might predict that women as a group would have more grievances about their jobs, given their lower pay and their probable experience of some of the more subtle types of discrimination described earlier. But Crosby found no sex differences in grievances or in satisfaction with the job, even though women tended to say that they were being paid less than the "average" person in their job or less than they deserved. (For similar results, see Burke & Weir, 1976; Deaux, 1979; Ebeling, King & Rogers, 1977; Notman & Nadelson, 1973.) Women also did not seem to feel that they had less control over their jobs or other aspects of their lives than men and were not more likely than men to report feeling depressed. When asked what emotions they tended to feel in response to injustices on the job, women most often cited anger, and men most often cited depression or resignation. Thus Crosby found no evidence that sex discrimination in wages was a source of depression or unhappiness for women. Other studies have found that women and men are equally satisfied with their jobs, even when the women are clearly earning less than the men for the same job (e.g., Deaux, 1979).

One possible explanation for this phenomenon is that women, although they may acknowledge that they are discriminated against as a group, seem to be blind to their own experiences of discrimination (see also Notman & Nadelson, 1973; Walsh, 1977). Employed women in high-status positions are particularly distressed about what they view as widespread societal discrimination against women, but these same women seldom report personal experiences with sex discrimination (although they are paid less than their male counterparts). Crosby suggests that the working women in her sample were probably denying personal discrimination in part as a defense against the stress of having negative feelings about a job they had to work in daily. Another explanation that Crosby's data support is that many working women may consider themselves lucky to have as good a job as they do and thus may be willing to ignore many unpleasant aspects of it. Indeed, 70 percent of the employed women in Crosby's sample said they thought they were personally better off than most working women. Jean Baker Miller (1976) has argued that any group that has been subordinated by another group learns to ignore or accept injustices as a way of surviving. According to this argument, women have learned to be unconscious of the discrimination they face as a way of appeasing the group in the superior position in society (men) and as a way of coping psychologically with their seeming helplessness.

It may be that the blatant discrimination Crosby and others have examined does not affect women's emotional health but that more personal, subtle forms of discrimination do. That is, the pay a woman receives relative to a man may not affect her emotional well-being, whereas her sense of being respected and appreciated in her work may do so. Hamilton and colleagues (1987) argue that one of the most emotionally damaging types of discrimination against women in the workplace is sexual harassment. They define sexual harassment as "unwelcome sexual advances, requests for sexual favors, and other verbal or physical contact of a sexual nature, as these occur under . . . conditions affecting employment" (p. 156). Harassment can include pressure for dates, sexually suggestive words or gestures, deliberate touching, pressure for sexual favors, and attempted or actual rape. Many women are forced to tolerate sexual harassment because they cannot afford to quit their jobs. Here is an example:

Eight years ago I had just graduated from high school and was working as a maid in a motel for the summer. . . . I spent the summer trying to do my job as I fought off the sexual advances of the manager, who wanted me to engage in oral sex and intercourse. I was seventeen, naive, and scared. I wondered if I had done anything to entice him. I felt totally alone. I had no idea that other women had similar experiences. I felt powerless. If I quit my job, I might not have found another, and then I would not have the money I needed for college. I worked all summer, hoping that he would not overpower me, and I kept my secret to myself. I was relieved beyond words when the summer ended. [Anonymous letter quoted by Thom, 1987, p. 107]

In a survey of 10,648 federal employees, researcher Patricia Mathis found that 42 percent of all female employees and 15 percent of all male employees reported being sexually harassed at work in some way during the previous two years (U.S. Merit Systems Protection Board, 1981). Thirty percent of the women reported incidents of harassment that Hamilton and colleagues (1987) label as severe, such as pressure for sexual favors or deliberate cornering or touching. One percent of the women reported an attempted or completed rape by a coworker or boss. Between 21 and 82 percent of those who were harassed reported that their emotional or physical health worsened in response to the harassment, depending on the severity of the harassment. Women who have experienced sexual harassment often report emotional numbing and feeling confused or guilty.

Many women never tell anyone about their experience of harassment, either because they cannot themselves believe it happened or because they fear that coworkers will not believe them (Hamilton et al., 1987). Common reactions by coworkers and institutions to a woman who blows the whistle are to say the event did not happen, it was unintentional ("just a joke"), the woman brought it on herself by being seductive, or the discriminator is "basically a good guy" who should be forgiven this isolated transgression. Perhaps anticipating such responses, many women try to forget the incident, hoping it will not happen again. But harassment that is ignored usually escalates (Crull, 1984). Nine percent of the women in the study of federal employees reported leaving a job because of continued sexual harassment. Although changing jobs may let a woman escape a threatening environment, it often requires loss of income and seniority, disruption of one's work history, and problems in obtaining references for a future job. No matter what a victim of sexual discrimination does, she may face serious costs—a perfect situation for the development of a sense of helplessness. We do not know the full extent of the impact of sexual harassment on women's emotional health, in particular on women's rates of depression (Hamilton et al., 1987). Given the apparent prevalence of sexual harassment and the many ways that such experiences may cause the victim to feel helpless, the relationship between harassment and depression in women deserves further investigation.

The Balance of Power in Heterosexual Relationships

The stereotype of intimate heterosexual relationships, including marriages, is that men are the "head of the household," making most of the important decisions for the family and holding much or all of the economic power. Until recently, many countries have actually had laws specifying that men have the right to enforce their will on their wives in many areas, including how money is used, how the children will be educated, where the family will live, and even when the couple will engage in sex (Bernard, 1972).

Do men take advantage of the traditional and sometimes legal power they are given over the women with whom they have relationships? Studies that have attempted to assess objectively the balance of power in heterosexual relationships have provided mixed results. In many studies, researchers have asked subjects to indicate which partner typically makes each of several types of decisions, ranging from home decorating to moving the family (e.g., Blood & Wolfe, 1960; Centers, Raven & Rodrigues, 1971). These studies have found that the vast majority of marriages are egalitarian—the husband and wife have equal influence on the decisions made. Peplau and Gordon (1985) have criticized these studies, however, for tending to equate major decisions, over which we might expect husbands to have more influence, with minor decisions, over which wives might have more influence: "Whether the husband's decision to move the family to a new city in order to advance his career is equivalent to the wife's decision to serve the family pot roast is open to debate" (p. 272).

As an alternative approach to the study of power in relationships, Peplau (1983) asked members of dating couples in college, "Who do you think has more of a say about what you and your partner do together—your partner or you?" She found that 45 percent of the subjects thought their relationship was equal, 40 percent thought the man had more power, and 15 percent thought the woman had more power. And yet 95 percent of the women and 87 percent of the men said that in the ideal relationship partners should have equal amounts of power. Even among college students who say they believe in egalitarian relationships, then, a sizable percentage say that man has more power in their own relationship.

Recent studies in which negotiations between husbands, wives, and children have actually been observed indicate that husbands influence the outcome of discussions more than wives or children do. For example, Cooper (1988) asked husbands, wives, and children to discuss plans for a family vacation while they were being videotaped. The husband's opinions about where the family should go and what they should do influenced the final plans for the vacation more than the opinions of the wives or children did. Another observational study of discussions between husbands and wives found that, when arguments broke out, wives appeared to spend considerable time trying to prevent the escalation of conflict by affirming the husband's opinions and making positive comments (Gottman, 1979). Other studies have found that wives often disagree with and confront their husbands about decisions, however, and husbands are more likely to try to end the conflict quickly (Raush et al., 1974). Kelley and colleagues (1978) resolve this seeming contradiction by suggesting that women often see their role in an argument as the socioemotional specialists, in charge of maintaining a generally positive relationship between themselves and their husbands, but that when men refuse to continue talking about a conflict, women become frustrated and confrontational. By contrast, Peplau and Gordon (1985) argue that women are aware of their power disadvantage in relationships and that their strategies during disagreements reflect this awareness. Women are confrontational because they see no other way to influence a decision; men avoid conflict because it is a threat to their existing power advantage.

Historically, when women have voiced concerns to counselors about the balance of power in their relationships, they have not tended to receive much support (see Gottman, 1979). The woman is often identified as the troubled partner in a marriage. Psychoanalytic concepts such as penis envy give theoretical justification for denying a woman the right to disagree with and complain about her husband (see Chapter 5). Women have fared somewhat better since the behavioral, cognitive, and systems approaches to therapy have become popular. The theories behind these therapies do not assume that there are appropriate imbalances of power between husbands and wives, as psychoanalytic theory suggests.

The little data available suggest that inequalities in marriage are a source of women's greater propensity toward depression. Vanfossen (1981) interviewed 1,494 men and women about the equity of decision-making and household chores in their marriages and about their symptoms of depression. She found that low equity in a marriage was associated with high levels of depression in the employed women in this sample. But because these data were all obtained at one point in time, they cannot tell us whether low equity precedes depression or vice versa.

Violence Against Women

Sometimes, too much of the time, a husband's assertion of power in the marital relationship comes in the form of physical assault. The rates of spouse abuse are difficult to establish. Most available data come from the records of hospital emergency rooms, police arrests, hot lines, and shelters. Rates based on these records are probably underestimates, for only the most severe cases of abuse are brought to official attention. Even so, the rates of abuse—usually wife abuse—are high. In 1983, 30 domestic violence centers in southern California responded to a total of 46,528 crisis calls and provided shelter to 6,738 women and children. In a sample of 500 Brooklyn couples who were divorcing, there had been complaints of physical violence by a spouse, usually the husband, in 57.4 percent of the cases (Walker, 1983).

In an attempt to estimate the true rates of violence between couples, Gentemann (1984) interviewed a large number of women in North Carolina. Over 20 percent of these women said they had been punched, hit, or slapped hard by a relative, friend, or acquaintance. In a study of high school students, 13 percent of the girls and 9 percent of the boys said they had been the victim of physical violence by a dating partner (Henton et al., 1983). The most frequent types of violence experienced included pushing, grabbing, and shoving, followed by slapping, kicking, biting, and hitting with the fist. Perhaps even more disturbing in this study was that 27 percent of the victims of violence perceived the meaning of the violence to be love, and 41 percent of the victims were still dating the person who had abused them.

The effects of battering on women's emotional health appear to be great. Rounsaville (1978) found that 80 percent of a sample of battered women had significant depression and 53 percent qualified for a diagnosis of depressive disorder. Estimates of the rate of suicide attempts in battered women range from 25 percent (Stark, Flitcraft & Frazier, 1979) to 42 percent (Gayford, 1975).

Another particularly important type of violence against women is rape. Statistics from the Federal Bureau of Investigation suggest that approximately 90,000 women per year in the United States report being a victim of rape or attempted rape (Federal Bureau of Investigation, 1986). Police reports probably underestimate the incidence of rape to an even greater degree than they do other types of violence against women, however. Many women who are forced to have sex with a date or a husband do not define the incident as rape and therefore would not report that they have been raped. An adolescent girl wrote the following:

I am fifteen years old, and last summer I was raped by the closest friend of my boyfriend. I did not consider it rape at the time, because I knew the guy relatively well, and I didn't think you were raped by your "friends." I felt like a whore and a piece of trash; but worse than that I felt used. I felt that I had no one to turn to for help, or even someone that I could tell. It was all because I felt I had done something to make him want to have sex with me. [Anonymous letter quoted by Thom, 1987, p. 222]

It is estimated that only 10 percent of women who experience non-marital rape report the rape to police (Russell, 1984).

There have been a few large interview studies in which women in the general population are asked about their experience of rape, using a variety of questions designed to increase a woman's willingness to report a rape (Kilpatrick et al., 1985; Koss, Gidyez & Wisniewski, 1987; Russell & Howell, 1983). Kilpatrick and colleagues (1985) conducted telephone interviews with 2,004 randomly selected women in South Carolina and found that 14.5 percent of the women reported one or more experiences of attempted or completed sexual assault, 5 percent reported that they had been raped, and 4 percent reported that they had been the victims of attempted rape (see Sorenson et al., 1987). Russell and Howell (1983) found a higher rate of rape in a study using face-to-face interviews to gather information from a random sample of 930 adult women in San Francisco. The interviewers asked these women if they had ever had an experience of forced intercourse (i.e., penile-vaginal penetration), intercourse obtained by threat of force, intercourse completed when they were drugged, unconscious, asleep, or otherwise totally helpless and thus unable to consent (this is the legal definition of rape in California). These researchers found that 24 percent of these women reported being the victim of at least one completed rape and 31 percent reported experiencing at least one attempted rape. A total of 44 percent of the women had experienced either an attempted or a completed rape, and 22 percent had experienced more than one attack. The types of rape experienced by these women were evenly distributed among stranger, acquaintance, and date rapes. There were few social class differences between the women who had been raped and those who had not. The ages of the women who had been raped ranged from 18 to 64, but highest risk for rape appeared to be among women age 18 to 30. Fewer than 10 percent of the women reported the attack to the police. Russell and Howell used the data from their survey to calculate that any woman has a 26 percent probability of being a victim of a completed rape in her lifetime and a 46 percent probability of being the victim of a rape or attempted rape in her lifetime.

The initial impact of rape and other types of violence on the victim's emotional health appears to be great. Several studies have found that in the first six months after a rape or other assault, women show high levels of depression, anxiety, dismay, and many other indicators of emotional distress compared to women who are not assault victims (Burgess & Holmstrom, 1974; Kilpatrick, Veronen & Resick, 1979; Wirtz & Harrell, 1987). Some studies find that levels of distress decline substantially with time, so that by about the sixth month following the assault, levels of distress in victims are not significantly different from those in women who are not victims (Kilpatrick, Veronen & Resick, 1979; Wirtz & Harrell, 1987). Other studies, however, have found that even one year after the assault, victims are substantially more depressed and anxious than nonvictims (Ellis, Atkeson & Calhoun, 1981; Kilpatrick, Resick & Veronen, 1981). Kilpatrick and colleagues (1981) found that only 20 to 25 percent of victims were free of depressive symptoms one year following the attack. Many women tell of reliving the experience over and over in their minds for months or years following the assault.

No one except someone who has experienced rape can know the late night, quiet playback and the thousands of stirring memories ready to rear up their ugly heads at the slightest incitement. Even almost a year later, as the "anniversary" draws near, I can feel all of my original reactions once again full force, and they are something which will not recede in time. Only women who have spent lonely nights such as this one trying to exorcise the ghosts can truly comprehend the insolence and hideousness of rape. And our number is growing, faster all the time. [J. Pilgrim, letter quoted by Thom, 1987, p. 222]

Most studies of assault victims have been conducted with small numbers of victim subjects (usually 30 or fewer) who have sought help from a rape crisis center or who answered advertisements to participate in a study of rape outcome. We do not know how representative these women are of the entire population of women victims. A recent study of adults living in Los Angeles provides a less biased picture of the rates of depression and other psychological problems among victims of sexual assault (Burnam et al., 1988). Over 3,000 adults were interviewed to assess their experiences of sexual assault and psychological disorders in the recent past and the distant past. Seventeen percent of the women in the sample and 9 percent of the men reported having been assaulted at some time in their lives. Over 80 percent of the assaults occurred before the victims were 25 years old. The assault victims were much more likely than the subjects who had not been assaulted to have had an affective disorder, an anxiety disorder, or a substance abuse disorder at some time in their lives: 18 percent of the assault victims had experienced a major depressive episode, compared to 5 percent of the other subjects; 22 percent of the assault victims had a phobic disorder, compared to 10 percent of the other subjects; 20 percent of the assault victims had a substance abuse disorder, compared to 5 percent of the other subjects. The assault victims most often developed these disorders during the first year following the assault. They were particularly likely to develop a disorder if they had been assaulted as a child. In fact, subjects who had been assaulted as children remained at higher risk than control subjects for developing a psychological disorder throughout their lives.

Another approach to understanding the impact of violence on women's mental health is to examine the frequency with which women who seek help for depression or other emotional problems report being the victims of assault. Carmen, Rieker, and Mills (1984) assessed the frequency of experience of abuse in 188 persons admitted to an inpatient psychiatric ward by reviewing the hospital charts of the patients. Half the patients were diagnosed with an affective disorder. The researchers found that 53 percent of the female patients and 23 percent of the male patients had experienced some sort of serious physical or sexual abuse at some time in their life. Most of the abused males were adolescents who had been abused by their parents. Most of the abused females were adults, and the sources of their abuse included parents, husbands, and strangers.

The researchers also examined the types of symptoms that male and female abuse patients showed. The predominant symptoms of abused females were depressive symptoms; almost 70 percent of the abused females were depressed. Carmen and colleagues also gathered information on the patients' behaviors during hospitalization. They describe the abused females as follows:

In our sample, the abused females directed their hatred and aggression against themselves in both overt and covert ways. These behaviors formed a continuum from quiet resignation and depression to repeated episodes of self-mutilation and suicide attempts. Self-destructive behaviors were related to feelings of worthlessness, hopelessness, shame, and guilt. These affects escalated when anger threatened to surface, and at such times, often culminated in impulsive self-destructive episodes. Markedly impaired self-esteem was prominent among these patients as they conveyed a sense that they were undeserving of any empathic understanding or help by clinicians. [Carmen, Rieker & Mills, 1984, p. 382]

By contrast, only 27 percent of the abused males showed symptoms of depression. It was more common for the abused males to show a pattern of aggressive behaviors during hospitalization.

A much higher rate of abuse among psychiatric patients was found by Jacobson and Richardson (1987). They interviewed 100 inpatients and found that 81 percent reported at least one type of victimization experience. The rate of victimization in this study was probably so much higher than that of the study by Carmen and colleagues because Jacobson and Richardson asked pointed and detailed questions about victimization, whereas Carmen and colleagues relied on patient records for data. Brown (1988) points out that the disparity between these two studies indicates that clinicians need to ask specifically about patients' experiences of abuse in intake interviews because this information is often not volunteered by patients.

It appears that a substantial percentage of women are the victims of rape or other abuse and that many—perhaps most—of these women suffer from significant levels of depression for several months following their victimization. Of course, not all women who are depressed are the victims of abuse, so abuse is not the only source of depression in women. But the studies I have just summarized suggest that abuse is one important source of the greater level of depression in women.

Occupational Roles and Depression

Many women never face sexual harassment or victimization, or direct or indirect discrimination against them on the job. These women may still be vulnerable to depression, however. If they are full-time homemakers, they may become demoralized by the low status of their position, and the sometimes repetitive, thankless daily work. They may also find themselves without alternative sources of emotional and financial support if their marriage should be troubled or dissolve. If women have a paid job outside the home, plus a family, they often become overloaded with the work of two full-time jobs, and with the conflicting demands of the two roles.

Homemaking and Depression

Authors such as Charlotte Perkins Gilman, Adrienne Rich, and Betty Friedan have passionately described the frustration, boredom, hard work, isolation, and sense of valuelessness of many full-time homemakers, or "housewives." When these authors were first writing about women's frustrations and demoralization, popular belief held that women's most important role was raising children and that children needed the singular attention of a full-time mother in order to develop properly. Sometimes taking on this singular role cost a woman her emotional health. Consider the following passage by Adrienne Rich:

My children cause me the most exquisite suffering of which I have any experience. It is the suffering of ambivalence: the murderous alternation between bitter resentment and raw-edged nerves, and blissful gratification and tenderness. Sometimes I seem to myself, in my feelings toward these tiny guiltless beings, a monster of selfishness and intolerance. Their voices wear away at my nerves, their constant needs, above all their need for simplicity and patience, fill me with despair at my own failures, despair too at my fate, which is to serve a function for which I was not fitted. I am weak sometimes from held-in rage. There are times when I feel only death will free us from one another, when I envy the barren woman who has the luxury of her regrets but lives a life of privacy and freedom. And yet at other times I am melted with the sense of their helpless, charming and quite irresistible beauty—their ability to go on loving and trusting—their staunchness and decency and unselfconsciousness. *I love them.* But it's in the enormity and inevitability of this love that the sufferings lie. [Rich, 1976, p. 363]

In the last decade, several social scientists have argued that the higher rates of depression in women can be attributed, in part, to the lack of multiple roles and sources of gratification in women's lives and to the noxious nature of the housewife role (see Gove, 1972; Gove & Tudor, 1973).

Do housewives find their roles noxious, as some theorists claim? In a large study of satisfaction with home and work, Crosby (1982) found that housewives worked an average of 88 hours per week on housework and child care, whereas their husbands worked an average of 56 hours per week on housework, child care, *and* paid work combined. Housewives were significantly more likely than any other occupational or family-status group in Crosby's study to report dissatisfaction with their home life and their daily activities. In a reanalysis of these data, Repetti and Crosby (1984) found that this high level of dissatisfaction with home life was related to high levels of depression for housewives more than for the other groups.

Other studies of depression in different marital and occupational groups also find that housewives are more depressed than their employed husbands (e.g., Aneshensel, Frerichs & Clark, 1981; Ensel, 1982; Radloff, 1975; Rosenfield, 1980). A survey of 1,000 adults in Los Angeles found that the mean depression score of housewives was significantly higher than the mean depression score of their employed husbands (Aneshensel et al., 1981). The extent to which being a housewife is associated with high levels of depression appears to depend on the social status of the couple and on the quality of the couple's marriage, however. Repetti and Crosby (1984) found that housewives whose husbands have low-status jobs showed elevated levels of depression and that those whose husbands have high-status jobs did not. One possible explanation is that the high-status wives could afford to hire others to perform some of the more noxious tasks of homemaking, allowing them to have outside activities that provided multiple roles in their lives. Low-status housewives probably had to perform the noxious domestic duties themselves and did not have as many outside activities to provide different sources of pleasure.

Levels of depression in housewives appear to be related to the quality of their relationship with their husband (Vanfossen, 1981). About 1,500 homemakers and employed married men and women were asked about the intimacy in their marriage, the affirmation of worth they received from their spouse, and their symptoms of depression. Among the housewives, the affirmation received from the spouse and the level of intimacy in the marriages were significantly related to the women's levels of depression. Affirmation from the husband was particularly important for positive emotional health among the wives who said they disliked housework. That is, housewives who said they found housework boring and unfulfilling were particularly likely to be depressed if they perceived that their husbands did not provide adequate affirmation of their worth. Affirmation and intimacy in the marriage were not as closely linked to levels of depression in husbands or employed wives as in housewives. For example, low levels of intimacy in the marriage were associated with higher levels of depression in both the housewives and the employed husbands, but not in the employed wives. For the employed wives, a low level of equity in household chores and decision-making was a significant predictor of depression. Because these data are cross-sectional, they cannot tell us whether low affirmation, low intimacy, or depression comes first. But they suggest that the emotional well-being of housewives may be somewhat more dependent on the women's self-definition and on the affirmation of worth they receive from their husbands than is the emotional well-being of women who engage in paid work.

According to the paucity of roles theory (see Repetti & Crosby, 1984), anyone who has only one source of gratification in her life should be at increased risk of depression because she does not have other activities to fall back on if that one source should disappear. In fact, there is evidence that not having separate work and family roles can be a risk factor for depression in anyone: men who have never married or who are widowed report more depression than married men (Aneshensel, Frerichs & Clark, 1981; Radloff, 1975). Crosby (1982) found that single men reported even more loneliness and social isolation than housewives.

Role Overload and Depression

The noxious aspects of the housewife role do not necessarily mean that housewives report more depression than other groups of women. Gove and Tudor (1973) suggested that women who have both a work role and a family role in essence have two full-time jobs and that this role overload contributes to the high levels of depression in employed wives and mothers. This theory may explain why many studies comparing rates of depression in housewives and working wives find that housewives are not more depressed than married, employed women (Aneshensel, Frerichs & Clark, 1981; Radloff, 1975; Roberts & O'Keefe, 1981): both groups show high levels of depression, always higher than employed, married men. Crosby (1982) found that among both high-status and low-status employed subjects, women spent over twice as much time as men in child care. Employed mothers also did two to three times more housework than employed fathers. This ratio was true even among couples with high-paying jobs that might allow them to hire help. Crosby counted the average number of hours per week spent in paid employment, work around the house, and child care. The women in her sample worked an average of 69 hours per week, whereas the men worked an average of 56 hours per week. The group with the highest average number of weekly hours was high-status housewives at 96 hours, followed by high-status working mothers at 90 hours, low-status working mothers at 84 hours, and low-status housewives at 81 hours. Yet employed women expressed no more dissatisfaction with the way things were going at home than men, even though they were doing considerably more work.

In a more direct study of the role overload hypothesis, Zappert and Stansbury (1984) found that nearly two-thirds of female students in the medical, engineering, and graduate schools at Stanford University anticipated problems in combining a career and family when they left school, compared to only one-third of male students in those schools. The married women in this sample were doing significantly more housework than the married men. Nearly 50 percent of the married women but only 1 percent of the married men reported that they stayed home when their child was ill. The women in this sample were significantly more depressed than the men and had poorer health overall.

Other studies have found, however, that women who have both families and paid work are at lower risk for depression than full-time homemakers (Gore & Mangione, 1983; Kandel, Davies & Raveis, 1985; Repetti & Crosby, 1984). For example, Kandel, Davies, and

Raveis (1985) assessed depression in 197 women and found the lowest levels of depression in married employed mothers. Women who had only two of these roles showed somewhat higher levels of depression. Women who had only one of these roles showed levels well above the cut-off point for severe depression and nearly twice as high as women with all three roles. The detailed pattern of depression scores in this study suggested that having a job was most strongly associated with good emotional health in these women. In particular, work seemed to have a buffering effect on women who were undergoing strains in their marriage.

In a longitudinal study of depression in women, Aneshensel (1986) obtained depression scores from 490 women at two times one year apart. She too found that women who were having marital problems showed less depression if they were employed than if they were not (see also Cleary & Mechanic, 1983). Women who were undergoing occupational strain (for example, inadequate monetary rewards or excessive job demands) also showed elevated levels of depression. Being married buffered these women from that strain, but only if the marriage was supportive. In contrast, simply having a job did seem to help women deal with stress in their marriage (for similar results, see Verbrugge, 1983).

Along the same lines, other studies have found that the amount of support a woman receives from her partner in both emotional and practical arenas will determine whether she experiences role overload. Vanfossen (1981) found that working wives whose husbands willingly shared housework were significantly less depressed than those whose husbands did not share housework. Working wives were particularly likely to be depressed if there were frequent disagreements between the couple over housework. Similarly, Repetti (in press) found that working women who saw the division of labor at home as inequitable and who reported little cohesion in their family were significantly more depressed than women whose husbands shared housework and who had cohesive families. Ross and Mirowsky (1988) also found that difficulty in arranging child care was a contributor to depression in employed wives. Having children was not in itself related to levels of depression in these women, but those who could not find adequate child care or whose child care arrangements were cumbersome had high levels of depression.

Increasingly, women are also becoming the primary care-givers of elderly parents and parents-in-law. Of the current eight million care-givers of the elderly, most are daughters, with an average age of only 46 (Bernardy, 1987). These women often work part time or full time and still have their own children at home. Having responsibility for parents, children, a job, and a household leads to significant emotional and physical deterioration in at least some women (Brody, 1985; Cantor, 1983). Much research needs to be done before we know the full impact of this set of burdens on women. This research should be given a high priority because the percentage of the population that is elderly will increase substantially over the next twenty years.

A number of other situational and personality factors may affect the relationship between multiple roles and women's emotional health (McBride, 1988). For example, women who work for pay as care-givers (in nursing homes or elsewhere) may be stressed by having to be nurturant and patient both on the job and at home. In short, they may not gain as much benefit from having a job outside the home because their job is so much like their duties at home. And women whose duties on the job do not match their sex-role attitudes—for example, a feminist woman working as a secretary to a chauvinist man—may not find the job beneficial to their health. These and other hypotheses about the effects of situational and personality factors remain to be tested. It is probably true, however, that any role can be either stressful or beneficial depending on the characteristics of the role and the person (see Repetti, in press).

Explaining the Epidemiology of Sex Differences in Depression

Social-role theories can explain some of the special trends in the epidemiology of sex differences in depression. First, consider the emergence of women's greater vulnerability to depression in early adolescence. It is during early adolescence that children begin to think about and even choose their adult occupations. By a large margin, girls still choose (and are encouraged to choose) to study feminine-typed disciplines such as home economics and teaching, and boys still choose to study masculine-typed disciplines such as science and math (Randour, Strasburg & Lipman-Blumen, 1982). Even in high school, then, girls begin to associate themselves with low-status occupations and boys with high-status occupations. In addition, girls may be told that their range of options for occupations and lifestyles is naturally lower than that of boys. Thus adolescent girls may already be facing biases in others' evaluations of their capabilities, restrictions in the choices given to them, and undervaluation of the work they choose to do. These conditions could contribute to the increase in depression in girls relative to boys that we observe during adolescence.

Dating also begins during adolescence. Although society's expectations that males and females will act according to certain roles in a heterosexual romantic relationship have lessened somewhat over the last twenty years, the traditional roles are still enacted much of the time (Buss, 1988). The male is expected to initiate the date, choose the activities, make the first sexual advances, and so on. The female waits for his cues, all the time ready to protect herself from him. It is probably anxiety-provoking for an adolescent boy to make the first phone call to a girl he likes. But it may be depression-provoking for an adolescent girl to sit waiting for the phone call (especially if it does not come) and to try to send out cues that she is interested in a boy without inviting trouble. The girl's situation seems ripe for the development of learned helplessness. Further reasons why adolescence may induce helplessness in females but not in males are discussed in Chapter 8.

The second epidemiological trend that might be explained by social-role theories is the evidence that there are no sex differences in depression among college students. In Chapter 2 I suggested that this trend might result from a self-selection of healthy women in the college population. But perhaps the lack of sex differences in depression among college students may indicate that the roles, opportunities, and experiences of men and women in college are closer to equal than in other settings. Especially in the last ten years, women have been encouraged to enroll in the same math and science courses as men. At the least, women have nearly the same opportunities for study as men. There are usually many campus activities and organizations that provide both women and men with multiple sources of pleasure and self-expression. These activities also provide the chance for women and men to get to know each other outside traditional heterosexual romantic relationships. This opportunity may lead to somewhat less gender stereotyping and thus to more equitable relationships within couples who do develop a romantic interest. Thus college may be a setting in which the roles and status of men and women are as close to equal as they ever are. If social-role theories of depression are correct, this equality should help to equalize the rates of depression in the sexes.

A third finding in the epidemiology of sex differences in depression was the lack of differences among the Old Order Amish, although there were some questions about whether all the depressed women in this population were detected. But if Amish women and men really experience equally low levels of depression, it may be because the work of women in this society is valued as highly as that of men. The work and family roles of men and women in Amish society are rigidly fixed. But because the members of this society live as though in the nineteenth century, women's making of clothing and food is as important as men's farming and building. In addition, family life and children's well-being are extraordinarily important in this society, so a woman's service as wife and mother is highly valued. Thus the unique structure and values of Amish culture may protect Amish women from depression.

Finally, social-role theories may help us understand why rates of depression seem to increase in old age in men but not in women. Throughout adulthood, men have their work to provide clear feedback about their worth, an outlet for self-expression, and a way of structuring their daily activities. Work also provides a haven from any problems in marriage or children's lives. When a man retires, he encounters for the first time in his adult life a lack of clear guidelines for what he must do to gain praise or a sense of his own competence and worth. He must decide each day what to do with himself. This change is a welcome relief for some men but may be overwhelmingly threatening to others. When a man spends all his time at home, he may have no place to turn if there are marital problems or if his children are in distress. These enormous changes in men's lives, compounded by the physical deterioration they may experience, may be enough to make many men depressed. For a woman who has not been working in the paid labor force, older life brings few changes in her daily routine except for the now-constant presence of her retired husband at home. But her sources of meaning and worth—namely her family and home—remain the same. Once her children have left home, she may find the time to pursue outside interests and activities, thereby actually increasing her number of sources of pleasure and self-worth. This rationale may explain why some studies show a decrease in depression among women as they pass from middle to older age.

Conclusions

Several aspects of women's social roles may predispose them to depression. If a woman works full time, she may face overt and subtle discrimination that will make her feel unable to accomplish her goals. Whether she works or not, she has a substantial chance of becoming the victim of sexual or physical abuse. If she turns to a role as full-time homemaker and mother, she faces a high work load, isolation, and dependency on her family for affirmation, all factors that may lead to depression. If she attempts to combine work and a family, she must often cope with two full-time jobs. There is evidence that each of these conditions is associated with elevated levels of depression in women, but the evidence is mixed at best, except regarding the effects of victimization on women's emotional health. Moreover, social-role theories cannot explain why only a minority of women who experience the pressures described by the social-role theories develop depression.

A number of theories have been proposed to explain why some people develop depression in response to stress and others do not. Most of these theories posit some personality characteristic that influences people's reactions to stress. Some suspected personality characteristics include excessive dependency on others for one's self-esteem, lack of assertiveness, and the tendency to blame oneself for bad events. Many theorists have argued that females are more likely than males to develop personality characteristics that increase vulnerability to depression. In the next chapter I review theories of male and female personality development, focusing on those personality traits said to predispose people to depression; in Chapter 6 I review the evidence that women have depression-prone personalities.

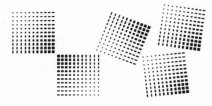

CHAPTER FIVE

Female and Male Personality Development

Personality is usually conceptualized as a set of attitudinal and be-havioral characteristics that a person shows consistently in many situations across time. If a woman seems to be cheerful and caring for others most of the time and in most situations, for example, we might say she has a friendly personality. These consistent attitudinal and behavioral characteristics are sometimes referred to as *traits*. Some examples of frequently cited traits include honesty, cheerfulness, trustworthiness, independence, and assertiveness. Most people be-lieve that males and females have different personality traits. Males are thought to be more task-oriented, analytical, assertive, emotion-ally stable, and competitive than females (Broverman et al., 1972). Females are thought to be more people-oriented, gentle, nurturant, emotional, nonassertive, and self-sacrificing than males. There are three types of theories about the development of personality charac-teristics: psychoanalytic theories, behavioral theories, and cognitive theories.

Sigmund Freud's psychoanalytic theory of personality is consid-ered the classic personality theory. Freud argued that the biological drives we are born with interact with early childhood experiences to create traits: that males and females develop different personality traits because they are born with different reproductive organs. Ac-cording to this theory, females develop a set of personality traits, such as passivity, dependency, and a tendency to be self-sacrificing, that predispose them to depression.

Several decades after Freud began writing on the development of personality traits, a group of psychologists known as behaviorists called into question the claim that traits exist. One notable critic of the concept of personality traits is Walter Mischel (1968, 1973), who argued that people are too inconsistent in their behavior in different situations for there to be any underlying trait driving their behavior. For example, Mischel (1968) showed that he could get people to display honest behavior or dishonest behavior by changing the situations in which he placed them. People act, said Mischel and many others (e.g., Bandura, 1973), according to the rewards and punishments that will result from their actions, not according to underlying traits. As for sex differences in tendencies to act one way or another, Mischel argued that male and female children are not born with different personalities, but rather are exposed to different reinforcement contingencies; that is, girls and boys are rewarded and punished for different types of behavior and thus show different patterns of behavior.

Behaviorists interested in depression and other emotional disturbances have noted that some patterns of behavior are clearly more adaptive than others. For example, a person who is frequently passive will not gain many rewards and, according to a behaviorist theory of depression, is likely to become depressed (Lewinsohn, 1974). The behaviorist explanation of sex differences in depression is that females are more likely than males to adopt behavior patterns that reduce their control over the environment, such as non-assertiveness and dependency, and thus are more likely to develop depression.

In the late 1970's a number of theorists broke from strict behaviorist explanations of people's behavior and argued that an equally important determinant of behavior is the way people think about a situation (in other words, their cognitions). People form expectancies of the consequences of their actions, and of what other people want them to do, which guide their behaviors (Bandura, 1977). People also think about the causes and implications of events, and these cognitions can affect their optimism and how they feel about themselves (Abramson, Seligman & Teasdale, 1978; Beck, 1976; Rehm, 1977). According to these cognitive/behavioral theories, people can develop habitual styles of thinking about events, called *cognitive styles*. Cognitive styles can in turn lead to consistencies in how people act and react in a variety of situations. There are adaptive and maladaptive cognitive styles, and certain maladaptive styles can lead to depression (Abramson, Seligman & Teasdale, 1978; Bandura & Cervone, 1983; Beck et al., 1979; Rehm, 1977). Some theorists have suggested that women are more likely than men to adopt maladaptive cognitive styles that lead to depression (see Nolen-Hoeksema, 1987). These styles include the tendencies to blame oneself when bad events occur, to have pessimistic expectations, and to believe that one has little control over one's life. These cognitive styles develop in response to controllable and uncontrollable events as well as to the expectancies that important people in one's life, such as parents, voice about one's prospects and abilities.

Psychoanalysts, behaviorists, and cognitivists all attribute women's greater vulnerability to depression to roughly the same set of characteristics, whether these characteristics are considered personality traits, behavior patterns, or cognitive styles. These characteristics include the tendencies to be nonassertive and to internalize hostility, to be dependent on others for one's self-esteem, and to blame oneself and be self-effacing. In this chapter I describe how each type of theory explains the development of these characteristics in females; in Chapter 6 I examine the evidence that females possess these characteristics more than males and that these characteristics contribute to depression in women.

Psychoanalytic Theories

The term *psychoanalysis* refers to a complex theory of human development and to a method of psychotherapy. According to psychoanalytic theory, human behavior is motivated by drives and needs of which a person is usually unconscious. When unconscious drives conflict with each other or with the constraints of reality, a person may exhibit maladaptive behaviors that she does not understand. The goal in psychoanalytic therapy is to help the patient recognize the conflicts that motivate her maladaptive behavior and learn to resolve these conflicts in more adaptive ways. Freud is probably the best known of the psychoanalytic theorists. One of the most controversial of Freud's theories is his description of female personality development (see Mead, 1974; Millet, 1970; Mitchell, 1974; Williams, 1979). Several of Freud's contemporaries and many current feminists have accused Freud of "phallocentrism," or a masculine bias in his ideas about female personality. Freud himself considered his theory of female personality to be speculative and underdeveloped. Nonetheless, psychoanalytic theory has strongly influenced how clinicians treat female patients and how females think about themselves (Lee & Hertzberg, 1978). Many concepts from the psychoanalytic explanation for female depression have been popularized through the mass media.

Freud's theories are extremely difficult to present clearly, in part because Freud made liberal use of metaphors for complex psychical processes and in part because he varied the meaning of some crucial theoretical terms slightly from one essay to another. Unless a reader has considerable background in Freud's writings, isolated passages from his essays can appear ridiculous. Mitchell (1974) has accused Freud's feminist critics of presenting such passages out of context in an effort to discount all Freudian theory. In order to present fairly a classical psychoanalytic perspective on depression in women, I review at some length the basic Freudian concepts, Freud's theories of depression, and his theories of female and male personality development. (For a comprehensive review of Freud's theories on female and male development, see Mitchell, 1974.)

Some Basic Psychoanalytic Concepts

Freud (1905) argued that all people are born with a store of psychic energy or "libido." Although Freud meant the term *libido* to refer to all biological drives, including hunger and thirst, the term is most often used today to refer to the drive for sexual gratification. The primary task of development, according to Freud, was to learn how to satisfy one's libidinal impulses while conforming to societal norms for self-control. Freud postulated three systems involved in the processing of psychic energy: the id, the ego, and the superego. The id is the system of unconscious, instinctual, uncontrolled libidinal drives. The superego is the system of parental standards, restrictions, attitudes, and ideals internalized by the child. The harsh restrictions and demands of the superego battle against the impulses of the id. The function of the ego system is to moderate the demands of the id and the superego in the face of the constraints of reality.

Freud argued that a child is oriented at different stages of development toward gratification of libidinal impulses through the stimulation of different areas of the body. If a child does not receive adequate stimulation of, or receives too much stimulation of, the target body areas, the child will be "stuck" or fixated at that stage. Fixation at a stage of psychosexual development results in characteristic personality traits. Essentially, Freud argued that too little gratification of a child's libidinal desires at a given stage impedes the child from "working through" the stage and developing adaptive means of channeling his energies. The symptoms of mental disorders, according to Freud, often represent maladaptive attempts to gratify these needs or to hold back or "repress" impulses and desires from consciousness.

Freud's Theory of Depression

In developing his theory of depression, or *melancholia*, Freud (1917) pointed to the similarities between melancholia and mourning. Both the mourner and the melancholic experience reduced energy, diminished joy in life, and hopelessness. Like the mourner, the melancholic perceives that she has lost something. She is different from the mourner, however, in that her loss may be real or imagined. Freud argued that when we love another person, we invest much of our libidinal energy in that person. If we lose the object of our love, we must withdraw the libido we have invested in the love object and redirect it at another object. In healthy mourning, the withdrawn libido is transferred to a new object. But, Freud asserted, if the libidinal energy cannot be reinvested in an object, it will be turned inward onto the person's own ego. All of the anger the individual feels against the lost love object will also be turned inward. This "anger turned inward" results in the self-punishment, self-denigration, and guilt seen in melancholia.

Freud argued that vulnerability to depression will be greater in people with "oral-dependent" and narcissistic personality traits. People with such traits are excessively dependent on others. Upon the loss of a love object, people with "oral" traits are prone to turn their anger inward, a trait that Freud describes as part of the depressive process. And because their dependency on the lost love object is great, the hostility directed at the love object—which now has been directed inward—will also be great.

Male and Female Personality Development

Freud's explanations of the psychological differences between males and females centered on the anatomical differences between the sexes and on the different roles during intercourse and parenting that he believed are dictated by these anatomical differences. Freud (1925) acknowledged that patriarchal societies severely restrict the range of behaviors males and females can exhibit and impose an inferior social role on females. But, he argued, patriarchies arise because of the different reproductive roles of males and females. Females' inferior social status derives from their "necessarily" passive role in mating. According to Freud, then, the primary source of differences in male and female personalities is the fact that males have penises and females have vaginas and give birth.

Because of the sustenance and sexual stimulation (in baths and playing) children receive from their mother, the mother becomes the first target of a child's sexual love. Both boys and girls fantasize about sexual intimacy with their mother and are jealous of any affection she shows toward other children or toward adults. At some time in the phallic stage (age 3 to 6), male and female children make a very important discovery: girls do not have a penis. Freud contended that the female child is devastated by this discovery and blames her mother for withholding this most desired possession. When she realizes that her mother also lacks a penis, the girl turns to her father, whom she hopes will give her his penis. The realization that their mother has no penis leads both male and female children to devalue the mother and all other women. The male child's sexual attraction to his mother continues despite any disrespect he may have for her. This sexual attraction to the parent of the opposite sex is what Freud termed the *Oedipus complex*. Attraction to the opposite-sex parent is accompanied by hatred of the same-sex parent, who is seen as the child's rival for the loved parent. Eventually, a male child will come to fear that his rival (his father) will punish him for his desire for the mother by castrating him. This "castration complex" leads the boy to suppress, or bring under rational control, his attraction to his mother. Learning to keep one's instinctual drives and impulses under rational control facilitates the development of the superego. In Freud's terms, the castration complex in boys destroys the Oedipus complex and leads to the formation of the superego.

The psychic development of girls, once they realize that females do not have a penis, takes a different path from that of boys. The girl feels she has been castrated. She turns to her father, hoping he will provide her with the penis her mother has denied her. The girl's hostility toward her mother is increased by her envy of the mother's intimate relationship with the father. Thus the castration complex destroys the Oedipus complex for boys but leads to the Oedipus complex for girls. Furthermore, Freud felt that there is no alternative mechanism for girls to destroy their Oedipus complex, so that females are never really forced to develop a superego, to put their instinctual emotional lives under rational control.

In "Female Sexuality" (1931), Freud described three lines of development a girl may follow when she realizes that neither her father nor anyone else can provide her with a penis:

1. If the girl can replace her desire for a penis with a natural substitute—a baby—then the girl will develop "normal femininity." She will renounce active roles in favor of the passive sexual role that can provide her with a "penis baby."

2. Freud labeled the second line of possible development the *masculinity complex* (1931, p. 242). The girl may rebel against the "anatomical reality of her castration" and against the passive sexual role resulting from that reality. She may cling to her masculine libido, retaining the desire to be active and aggressive sexually and socially. Freud felt that this line of development often leads to lesbianism.

3. The girl may so greatly devalue herself when she realizes she has no penis that she rejects her sexuality totally. She will cease any masturbation and will not transfer her sexual sensitivity and desire for stimulation from her clitoris to her vagina (as she must if she is to enjoy her role in intercourse). As a woman, she will be frigid, inhibited, and neurotic.

Freud felt that even if a female follows the first line of development, her self-control and her character will still suffer from never having resolved her Oedipus complex. Helene Deutsch (1944), who developed Freud's ideas about the female psyche in great detail, argued that the female personality is characterized by passivity, masochism, and narcissism. Passivity, as a general characteristic, derives necessarily from the passive female role in intercourse. The masochism inherent in a woman's personality allows her to derive pleasure from defloration, intercourse, and childbirth—all supposedly abhorrent and painful experiences. Finally, female love is essentially narcissistic love because the goal of a love relationship is to replace the penis, which the female feels she has lost. Deutsch felt that passivity, masochism, and narcissism are balanced in a healthy woman such that the woman can thoroughly enjoy the sexual and social roles to which she is destined by her sex. A number of experiences can lead to an imbalance in this triad, however, and the result will be behavior that is excessively passive, masochistic, or narcissistic.

According to classical psychoanalytic theory, the tendency toward narcissistic love relationships makes women particularly vulnerable to the depressive process (Mitchell, 1974). The female looks to males to make up for her inadequacies, but she is inevitably and frequently disappointed. When love objects are lost, she has lost a crucial part of herself. Her ego, already injured by the realization of her castration, is confronted by the hostility she feels toward the introjected love object, and melancholia is likely to occur as a result.

Criticisms of the Classical Psychoanalytic Theory of Female Development

Even among Freud's contemporaries, there were many psychoanalysts who did not agree with his and Deutsch's conception of female development. One of the earliest critics of Freud's conceptualization of female development was Karen Horney, who was trained in Berlin by Freud's colleagues, Abraham and Sachs, in the early 1900's. Marshaling anthropological, sociological, and clinical evidence, Horney (1935) challenged several assumptions and methods in classical psychoanalysis, including (1) the emphasis on sexual drives and anatomy in personality, to the exclusion of environmental and cultural influences on personality development; (2) the view that the male is the prototypical human being; and (3) the claim that one could describe a universally applicable psychology of the human on the basis of a small sample. Horney suggested methods for improving psychoanalytic research and offered new perspectives on human development, particularly the development of females. Her descriptions of female conflicts have been the basis of many modern popular "theories" of female behavior (Mitchell, 1974).

As early as 1917, Karen Horney began to raise a number of questions about Freud's most basic assertions concerning human development. In general, Horney wished to deemphasize the role of instinctual drives in personality development. Disagreeing with Freud's assumptions that mental health and personality were fixed soon after birth, she placed much more emphasis on the physiological and psychological changes that occur in adolescence. She also emphasized the plasticity of personality development, in terms of both its openness to environmental influences and the control a person has over his or her own development.

Horney had two particular disagreements with Freud's views of female development that are especially important to explanations of depression in females: she questioned the role of penis envy in the development of female personality and argued that social-role demands exerted a strong influence on female personality. First, Horney denied that penis envy was at the core of female personality development. She did not deny that females envy the penis, but she could not accept Freud's assertion that penis envy results from a girl's realization that she has been castrated. Rather, Horney suggested that the female's envy of the penis represents her deep envy of the greater physical and social power of males. Moreover, Horney asserted that envy is not confined to females. She felt that each sex envied the other. Indeed, she was impressed with the strength with which men envy women's reproductive role, the ability to bear a living human being (see also Mead, 1974). This envy, combined with the social unacceptability of any desire in a male to be female in any way, leads men to undervalue women in order to maintain their own self-esteem. In "The Problem of Feminine Masochism" (1935), Horney seemed incredulous that women have internalized this undervaluation so wholeheartedly.

Horney felt that Freud and other psychoanalysts had committed a grave error in the collection of observations leading to Freudian theories of female personality: Freud and the other theorists were using the societal ideal of womanhood to describe what they thought was the inherent female character. Horney felt that this fallacy was committed by Freud and sustained by other psychoanalysts primarily because psychoanalysts typically were male in those days. Indeed, if the ideals of female psychoanalysts did not conform to the Freudian assessment of their sex's development, they were accused of denial and repression.*

Horney insisted that a woman was just as capable as a man of developing an "independent character"—that is, a sense of self-worth independent of her relations to a man. Moreover, seeking such independence and pursuing activities contrary to those mandated by the traditional social role of women were not signs of a woman's denial of a personality and lifestyle dictated to her by her reproductive role. About the Freudian conception of the natural role of women in society, Horney wrote:

> This attitude toward women, whatever its basis and however it may be assessed, represents the patriarchal ideal of womanhood, of woman as one whose only longing is to love a man and to be loved by him, to admire him and serve him, and even to pattern herself after him. Those who maintain this point of view mistakenly infer from external behavior the existence of an innate instinctual disposition thereto, whereas, in reality, the latter cannot be recognized as such, for the reason that biological factors never manifest themselves in pure and undisguised form, but always as modified by tradition and environment. [1934/1967, pp. 182–83]

Horney's reference to "biological factors . . . modified by tradition and environment" illustrates her view that the personality of a man or woman is shaped by the complicated interplay between biological needs and drives and external, environmental demands and experiences. Her explanation for the prevalence of depression in women thus must involve instincts and environmental influences and must show how particular interactions between these two forces result in a depression-prone personality. In "The Overvaluation of Love," Horney (1934/1967) traces the development of what she termed "a common present-day feminine type" (p. 182). Horney discussed the growing depreciation of the role of women in the economic lives of their families and communities resulting from the industrialization of what had formerly been women's work (see also Ehrenreich &

---

*In *An Outline of Psychoanalysis*, Freud states, "We shall not be so very surprised if a woman analyst who has not been sufficiently convinced of her own desire for a penis also fails to assign adequate importance to that factor in her patients" (*Collected Papers*, 1964, Vol. 23).

English, 1978). Whereas before the Industrial Revolution a woman's skills and labor had been indispensable to the survival of her family and the collective in which she lived, those skills and labors were being replaced by more efficient modern tools and services. Furthermore, the resources of women were not being rechanneled into more modern uses. Rather, the woman's role was compressed "into the narrower sphere of eroticism and motherhood" (1934/1967, p. 183) because of the traditional definition of the capabilities and place of females.

As mentioned earlier, Horney was impressed with the extent to which women accepted the definition of themselves as instinctually drawn to love relationships. Women expected men to provide complete fulfillment of their needs, desires, and strivings. The overvaluation of love relationships and the unrealistic expectations put on those relationships, which resulted from the woman's investment of her whole self-worth in her love relationships, led to rivalry between women for men. In "The Problem of Feminine Masochism" (1935), Horney predicted that masochistic tendencies can result in part from a "surplus of marriageable women, particularly when marriage offers the principal opportunity for sexual gratification, children, security, and social recognition. This condition is relevant inasmuch as it favors emotional dependence on men, and generally speaking, a development that is not autonomous but fashioned and molded by existing male ideologies. It is pertinent also insofar as it creates among women a particularly strong competition from which recoil is an important factor in precipitating masochistic phenomena" (p. 255).

Horney's explanations for psychological phenomena were not exclusively sociological ones. Although she raised serious disagreements with classical psychoanalytic theories of psychological disorders, her own theories drew heavily from Freud's theory of the stages of psychosexual development. Horney took Freud's work very seriously and carefully analyzed his observations, assumptions, and conclusions with a reverent eye. She questioned many of his assumptions and reinterpreted many of his observations. But a careful reading of her work pertaining to women and depression reveals that she was not a social-role theorist. She was a psychoanalyst who believed in a great deal of environmental influence on the psychosexual development of a person.

Three of Horney's papers are especially illuminating about her views on the prevalence of depression in women: "The Distrust Between the Sexes" (1930/1967), "The Overvaluation of Love" (1934/1967), and "Personality Changes in Female Adolescents" (1935/1967). Horney's "common present-day feminine type" was a woman fraught with conflicts within herself that were manifested through several psychological "disorders": hypochondriasis, homosexuality, anxiety, and depression. But the manifestation of the conflicts were not as important to Horney as were the *themes* of the conflicts. In the women to which Horney was referring, these conflicts involved the women's relationships to men and to work. Horney's psychoanalytic background becomes apparent when she explains the development of these conflicts.

The origin of the conflicts besieging the "common present-day feminine type" seems to be the competition with one's mother or sisters for the love of a man—usually one's father—during the development of the Oedipal complex. Particularly if a little girl's attraction to her father is confounded by his favoritism toward an older sister, the girl suffers a great loss of self-esteem in the rejection by her love object. Subsequently, gaining the love of a man becomes important in reestablishing her self-worth and in proving that she is really "normal." However, the wounds to her self-concept resulting from the rejection by her love objects cripple the girl's expression of her "natural femininity." At the same time, the victory of a sister or other female in winning the love of a girl's early love objects leads the girl to hate the victor—and any potential victor—and to wish harm upon these rivals. Yet the girl feels guilty about wishing harm upon her sister or any other female, and she fears that the same harm will be inflicted on her because of her wishes. Thus a conflict develops between her drive to prove her self-worth by winning the love of a man and her guilt and fear about her feelings toward her rivals.

Horney discussed three phases that women often go through during their lives as they strive for reestablishment of their self-worth: the man-hating phase, the achievement-striving phase, and the despair phase. The pain of losing early love objects may create in a woman the desire never to be vulnerable to a man again. She will still be compelled to win the love of men, but she will not allow herself to become dependent on them. Rather, she must make men dependent on her so that she wins the prize but takes few risks of being hurt. In fact, a woman may seek revenge for her childhood loss by making a man dependent on her precisely so that she may reject him as she herself was once rejected. This misguided motivation for entering into a relationship inevitably leads to a poor choice of a partner, disappointment, and further loss in a relationship. Thus the woman is caught in a vicious circle that only serves to lower her self-esteem further.

According to Horney, women caught in this circle often attempt to escape it by channeling their competitive drive into achievement situations at work. The woman still seeking revenge for her denunciation by her first love object strives for recognition as "a winner": "[T]hey expect, without being aware of it, to achieve distinction from the very outset. . . . Their inevitable failure they do not ascribe to their unreal and excessive expectations, but regard it as due to their general lack of ability. They then are inclined to drop whatever work they are doing at the time; they thus fail to attain that knowledge and skill, through patient labor, which is indispensable to success; and thereby they bring about a further and permanent increase in the discrepancy between increased ambition and weakened self-confidence" (1934/1967, p. 209).

Finally, this incessant inability to achieve the unreasonable and misguided ambitions she holds in compensation for her perceived inability to reestablish her self-worth pushes the woman into despair. She believes she is incompetent to achieve any goal. She avoids competition and any exercise of her natural capabilities, for she presupposes her own failure. Of course, this conviction that she cannot do anything protects the woman from the failure and defeat that she has often imposed upon herself and that she dreads. Horney suggested that this posture of weakness, dependency, and helplessness may at times be an unconscious "scheme" to act in precisely those ways that tradition says will attract a man. Nevertheless, a woman's repression of her wishes to hurt those who have hurt her—her mother, her sisters, and other women with whom she has competed, as well as the men who have rejected her—and the unfulfillment of her malformed expectations for herself and her life lead the woman to react by succumbing to depression.

Horney felt that the "feminine type" was increasingly common in her day because of the narrowing of women's participation in economic spheres and the extra weight being put on the woman's erotic and maternal roles. Thus it is pertinent to ask to what extent Horney's model of depressive development is relevant to contemporary society, in which women are gaining freedom from their reproductive roles and freedom to pursue intellectual, nondomestic roles. Although females are not restricted to roles as wives and mothers in contemporary society to the degree that they were in Horney's time, Horney thought the incidents during psychosexual development that contribute to depression were independent of social influences. She regarded the girl's Oedipal attraction to the father, and the "wish to receive from the man," to be innate and universal in females. Because all girls go through this phase of development even in today's society, it is inevitable that many girls still feel slighted by their father and feel that he favors other females. This perceived rejection is the origin of a conflict between the desire to acquire love and the guilt for the harm the girl wishes upon her rivals and rejecting love objects. These are precisely the conflicts that Horney said propel the female onto the insidious paths described above.

Horney also assumed that every female has "maternal instincts." She discussed the conflicts that arise between these instincts and the time and energy involved in pursuing activities other than motherhood. Even if a woman escapes the conflicts resulting from rejection by the father and has every opportunity to pursue intellectual interests, very powerful conflicts can result from the difficulties of pursuing both maternal instincts and interests outside the home. Horney suggested that these conflicts between maternal instincts and intellectual pursuits, exacerbated by societal demands on the woman to follow only her maternal instincts, predispose women to masochism. If one accepts Horney's assumption that females are born with powerful maternal instincts, it is natural to assume that the trade-offs in time and energy between following those instincts and developing a career outside the home can create conflicts that predispose women to self-abasement of some kind. However, Horney predicts depression only for those women who carry the extra burden of an obsession with love relationships that resulted from their experiences of rejection by their earliest love objects.

Contemporary Psychoanalytic Theories

A number of other psychoanalytic theorists, including Abraham (1960), Rado (1928), Fenichel (1945), and Bibring (1953) have also viewed obsessions with love as an important predisposing trait for depression. Recently, the idea that women base their self-esteem more on love relationships than do men has become popular again, particularly with the publication of Chodorow's *The Reproduction of Mothering* (1978), Scarf's *Unfinished Business* (1980), and Gilligan's *In a Different Voice* (1982). Chodorow (1978) provides the most detailed account of how girls' experiences during childhood lead them to put great value on relationships. Her arguments are based on a derivative of psychoanalytic theory called *object relations theory*. According to this theory, the type of personality that women develop is most prone to depression.

Freud had described the ego as a complex regulatory system that controls and directs the impulses of the id in line with the constraints of society. Many of Freud's followers became interested in the ego as the seat of personality and the sense of self. Beginning with Heinz Hartmann, and including Ernst Kris, David Rapaport, Erik Erikson, and many others, a subgroup of psychoanalysts, often called the "ego psychologists," focused on the ego and its role in personality development. Two schools of thought developed within ego psychology. The first school, led by Erik Erikson, was concerned with the adaptation of personality to reality throughout the life cycle, through the resolution of conflicts between competing goals or forces, such as dependency and autonomy. The second school, the object relations school, originated with Melanie Klein and emphasized the importance of the relationships between the child and significant others in the child's life in the development of personality. According to object relations theory, one's concept of self is always a self-in-relationship (Chodorow, 1978). That is, we develop our concept of self from our relationships with important others early in life. As adults, we re-create aspects of earlier relationships, especially early relationships that were unresolved or ambivalent.

Two members of the object relations school, Jacobson (1971) and Bibring (1953), were primary contributors to an ego-oriented theory of depression. Early in personality development, the infant's concept of self is fused with its concepts of others in its life (Jacobson, 1971). With development, the infant learns about the differences between itself and the rest of the world. A realistic concept of self begins to grow in the ego, while concepts of powerful others grow in the superego.

The most crucial period in the development of personality is the point at which the infant realizes his relative helplessness in relation to the external world. Prior to this point, the underdevelopment of his concept of objects as separate from himself allows him to perceive himself as controlling his entire environment, each component of which is perceived as a component of himself. The realization that he is not omnipotent motivates the infant to seek the security of a stronger person, typically the mother figure, as a love object. If this love object is understanding of his need for security, accepting of his sometimes bumbling attempts at self-assertion and reality testing, and supportive of his growth as a unique personality, then he will establish a realistic self-ideal and appropriate boundaries between himself and others.

If the mother figure is hostile, aggressive, selfish, and demanding, on the other hand, the infant will submit to being victimized for the sake of survival. But in order to cope with the terrifying reality that the person he relies upon for physical and emotional sustenance is inconsistent or even hostile, he will split his image of his mother into the "good" mother and the "bad" mother. The bad mother will be repressed from consciousness along with his image of himself as rejected, unlovable, and worthless. At the same time, the image of the good mother—and of the "good" self that is loved by the good mother—are glorified unrealistically. The infant needs to support the powerful, good image of the love object in order to justify being victimized. He will make few attempts to become independent from the love object, to develop a realistic and distinctive sense of self, for fear of completely losing the love object. Thus, says Jacobson, instead of developing a distinct image of himself apart from the rejecting love object, the infant fuses his image of himself with his image of the love object.

The frustration of his attempts at gaining love and satisfaction from his mother figure will arouse rage and hostility in the infant. Lashing out at the real love object threatens his security, however, so he will turn his anger inward on the part of himself that is the image of the bad mother. At the same time, he will continue to glorify his image of the good mother. This see-saw action between bolstering the image of the good and powerful mother and self, and aggressing against the bad mother and self, can continue through a lifetime if the child never develops a concept of himself with his own values, interests, and desires. Instead, the glorified image of the rejecting love objects and the self-image derogated because of failure to receive love are fused into a representation on which hostility and rage are inflicted. This negative self-representation and self-directed hostility result in feelings of helplessness, worthlessness, emptiness, disillusion, and poor relationships with other people. Jacobson (1971) regards these feelings as the primary depressive disturbance. The depressive person may make secondary attempts at restitution of self-esteem and worth by intense efforts to be loved by a new love object. But his lack of a self-defined identity will hamper the development of healthy relationships.

In summary, Jacobson states that the depressive person lacks barriers between his own self-concept and his images of the external world. Overly valued images of good and powerful love objects are internalized and provide excessive internal standards against which the bad, weak self is measured. The depressive person's hostility is turned inward against both the excessive ideal self and that part of the self that is helpless to meet the standards of the ideal self.

Other ego-analytic conceptions of depression share Jacobson's emphasis on dependence and lack of autonomy as factors that increase vulnerability to depression (e.g., Arieti & Bemporad, 1980; Bibring, 1953; Rado, 1928). Nancy Chodorow (1978) has described how the socialization of females makes them less likely than males to gain a realistic sense of self separate from their mother. She argues that girls are not encouraged to separate from their mothers to the extent that boys are. Very early in their lives, boys are viewed by their mothers as separate people because they are of a different gender. Thus autonomy and self-reliance are encouraged in boys. By contrast, mothers often see their daughters as extensions of themselves and attempt to maintain a symbiotic relationship with their daughters (Chodorow, 1978). This symbiosis is at the same time blissful for the daughter and extremely threatening to her growing need for autonomy. Thus her love of her mother is ambivalent; she will tend to split her image of her mother into the good mother and the bad mother and to vacillate between these two images. More important, however, she will not develop a core sense of self separate from her ambivalent relationship to her mother. In the extreme, such a lack of development can lead to psychosis. But in the much less extreme version of this scenario that occurs in the lives of most females, girls learn to base their sense of self largely on their relationships with others. That is, they do not develop distinct images of themselves as autonomous beings, but instead develop images of themselves only in terms of their relationships with others. In addition, because girls' relationships with their mothers are so ambivalent, their relationship with others in adulthood—and the sense of self that is based on these relationships—will be characterized by ambivalence and conflict. According to Jacobson and other ego psychologists, this type of conflicted self-concept, tied to relationships with others, predisposes females to depression. In addition, their greater concern with relationships makes women rely more heavily on the opinions and affection of others (Chodorow, 1978). They may also be willing to tolerate abuse from people in their lives in order to gain occasional expressions of acceptance and love. This abuse can lead both to frequently unsatisfying lives and to repression and internalization of one's aggression (Chodorow, 1978).

Psychoanalytic and ego-analytic perspectives on depression and female development pervade popular psychology and much of the clinical literature. Analytic formulations are popular because they provide the richest, most comprehensive accounts of human behavior of any psychological theory. Yet it is this very richness that makes these accounts almost impossible to test adequately. This is no reason to reject psychoanalytic ideas out of hand, but neither should psychoanalytic theories be accepted in blind faith.

Summary of Psychoanalytic Theories

Freud argued that penis envy shapes the personalities of women, making them prone to narcissistic love relationships, which in turn make them prone to introject hostility and become depressed. In addition, Freud and Deutsch held that masochism is a necessary feature of women's personalities, enabling them to take pleasure in intercourse and child-bearing. This general trait of masochism also increases women's chances of becoming depressed. Horney, among others of Freud's contemporaries, disagreed that necessary character traits for women include masochism and narcissism. Instead, Horney argued, women tend to appear masochistic and narcissistic because they have been forced by the patriarchal society to base their self-worth on love relationships. This forced self-definition leads females to compete hostilely with other females for lovers, but also to feel guilty about this competition. Even women who escape basing their self-esteem on love relationships and instead find meaningful careers will feel guilt and conflict about renouncing maternal instincts in favor of work. Horney argued that women tend to internalize this guilt and thus become depressed.

Finally, proponents of the object relations school, such as Chodorow and Jacobson, argue that females do not develop an autonomous sense of self separate from their mothers because mothers see their daughters as extensions of themselves and attempt to maintain a symbiotic relationship with them. Sons, on the other hand, are encouraged by mothers to become separate beings early in life. As a result, females' self-concepts are defined much more in terms of their relationships with others (especially their ambivalent relationship with their mother) than are males' self-concepts. Females also tend not to express dissatisfaction and anger at their lovers and friends because they fear losing those relationships. According to object relations theory, such a nonautonomous self-concept makes one more prone to helplessness, self-derision, and depression.

Behavioral Theories

Even Freud acknowledged that the environment plays a role in the development of personality characteristics. But he and other proponents of psychoanalytic theory saw the role of the environment as secondary to the role of biological drives. The behaviorists, who came into power in American psychology in the early twentieth century, argued that the role of the environment was primary in the development of psychological characteristics. Theorists such as B. F. Skinner and John Watson embraced the position of John Locke (1632–1704), who stated that a child is born as a *tabula rasa*, a "blank slate" onto which experience writes all the psychological characteristics the child will come to exhibit. The behaviorists identified two basic learning processes that they said lead to particular types of behavior patterns, including sex-typed behaviors, that a child will acquire: direct reinforcement and observational learning.

Direct Reinforcement of Sex-Typed Behavior

If a child is consistently rewarded for a behavior, the likelihood of her showing that behavior again in the future is increased (Thorndike, 1911). If a child is consistently punished for a behavior, on the other hand, the likelihood of her showing that behavior again is decreased. Thus if a boy is consistently rewarded for showing certain behaviors, such as assertiveness, emotional control, and independence, then he is likely to continue showing those behaviors. If the boy is consistently punished for showing certain behaviors, such as passivity, crying, and clinging, he is likely to cut back on those behaviors. Mischel (1968) emphasized the situation-specificity of behaviors, including sex-typed behaviors. That is, children learn behaviors in the context of specific situations and will not necessarily transfer learned behaviors to new situations. Thus a boy might show aggressive behaviors at home if he is rewarded for such behaviors there, but not show aggressive behaviors at school if he knows he will be punished for such behaviors in that situation. The main point in the theory is that there are no underlying traits that are innately more prevalent in boys than in girls or vice versa. Rather, boys and girls are rewarded and punished for different groups of behaviors. This differential reinforcement of boys and girls has been referred to as *sex-role socialization*. Because the theorists have focused on the effects of society's reinforcements of patterns of behavior, their theory is referred to as *social learning theory* (see Bandura, 1986).

Parents certainly say that they treat male and female children differently (Block, 1979a; Fagot, 1978). They say they encourage boys more than girls to compete, to hide their feelings, and to be physically active and independent. Parents say that they give girls more warmth and affection than boys, and that they treat girls more gently, trust them more, and watch over them more. Some studies find that parents have higher aspirations for their sons' eventual careers and accomplishments than their daughters', and parents say they push their sons more than their daughters to achieve high goals (Barnett, 1979; Hoffman, 1977). These self-report studies must be interpreted cautiously, however, because the parents may just be telling researchers what they think they should be doing, not what they are really doing in interactions with their children. Indeed, Fagot (1974) found little relationship between parents' attitudes toward proper child-rearing and their actual behaviors toward their children.

Most observational studies of parents' reinforcements of sex-typed behaviors have focused on parents' reactions to the types of toys their children play with or the types of games the children play (see

Huston, 1983). Parents tend to react more positively when their children are engaging in sex-typed play than when the children are not (e.g., Fagot, 1978; Langlois & Downs, 1980). For example, parents will show more signs of approval when a girl is playing with a dollhouse than when she is playing with army toys; they will show more approval when a boy is playing with trucks than when he is playing with a tea set. When parents play with their children, they play more roughly with boys than girls, and encourage boys more than girls to play active, physical games (Parke & Suomi, 1980). Fathers seem more concerned than mothers that their children not violate norms for sex-appropriate behavior. Fathers are particularly likely to react negatively to feminine-typed behaviors by their sons; the very idea of their son wanting to play with dolls or to wear frilly clothes creates fear and disgust in many fathers (Goodenough, 1957). Girls, on the other hand, are given more freedom than boys to cross the lines and to engage in the types of play and activities deemed masculine.

A few other observational studies have found that parents communicate higher expectations and demands for independent work in boys than in girls; in turn, parents respond more quickly to girls' requests for help and focus more on the interpersonal aspects of the situation with girls (Block, 1979a; Golden & Birns, 1975; Rothbart, 1971). Huston (1983, p. 430) argues, "When parents respond quickly to a girl's request for help, they may communicate their low evaluations of the child's competence; when they demand independent effort from a boy, this may signify confidence in the child's ability."

Parents are not the only potential source of reinforcements for sex-typed behavior in children. Perhaps teachers have that potential as well. Observational studies do show that teachers often treat boys and girls differently, but not necessarily in ways that would reinforce sex roles. Teachers tend to criticize, reprimand, and show other types of disapproval to boys more than girls (Cherry, 1975; Dweck et al., 1978; Serbin et al., 1973). This may be because boys simply misbehave more often than girls. Teachers do not appear to reinforce sex-typed behaviors, such as emotionality or aggression, differentially in boys and girls (Etaugh & Hughes, 1975; Smith & Green, 1975). Instead, they reinforce task-oriented, mastery behaviors and punish negative behaviors such as aggression in both boys and girls.

Children may also receive pressure to conform to sex roles, at least in regard to play activities, from their peers. Children show preferences for playing with same-sex peers as young as 2 years (Jacklin & Maccoby, 1978), and by age 3 they show disapproval of other children who play in cross-sex activities (Fagot, 1978; Lamb & Roopnarine, 1979). Again, boys are more likely than girls to be punished by their peers for crossing the line to play with the toys of the other sex (Fagot, 1977).

So there is evidence that children are reinforced by parents and peers for engaging in sex-typed activities and playing with sex-typed toys. Parents may also encourage more physical activity, and perhaps more independence, in boys than in girls, although the evidence for this is weaker. Studies that have attempted to show that children are directly reinforced for showing many of the other personal or social characteristics associated with the stereotype of their sex (such as dependency, social orientation) have found little evidence that these characteristics are differentially reinforced by adults (see Huston, 1983; Maccoby & Jacklin, 1974). In addition, recent studies indicate that children often choose to engage in sex-typed play, even when they are pressured by adults to engage in cross-sex play (Maccoby & Jacklin, 1987). Thus the extent to which children's propensity to play in ways deemed appropriate for their sex is the result of reinforcements from adults or the children's free choices is unclear.

Observational Learning of Sex-Typed Behavior

The other basic learning process behind sex-typing is observational learning. Bandura (1973) pointed out that children and adults often acquire behaviors by seeing others rewarded for these behaviors. In his famous series of "Bobo doll" experiments, Bandura had children watch other children or adults physically attack a plastic doll. Some of the children then saw the attackers punished or rewarded for their aggression. Other children saw the attackers get away with their aggression without any consequences. When given an opportunity to attack the doll themselves, the children who saw the attacker rewarded for aggression, or get away with aggression, were much more likely to attack than the children who saw the attacker being punished for aggression. Bandura argued that the children learned the consequences of attacking the doll simply by observing the consequences experienced by the previous attackers.

As for sex-typing, social learning theorists have argued that children learn many behaviors deemed appropriate for their sex simply by watching their parents and others exhibit such behaviors. In his Bobo doll experiments, Bandura found that the greater the similarity between an attacker and an observing child, the more likely the child was to learn the attacker's behavior through observation. Thus it has been argued that children are more likely to learn the behaviors of their same-sex parent because similarity facilitates observational learning.

An important point to add about observational learning is that children can come to show patterns of behavior not only because they are directly reinforced for these behaviors, but also because they come to *expect* to be reinforced through observational learnings. Indeed, some social learning theorists argue that people's expectations of the consequences of their behavior are more important determinants of behavior than the actual reinforcements society provides (Bandura, 1977; Mischel, 1973; Seligman, 1975). If a girl comes to expect that a boy she likes will not like her if she acts assertively on a date, for example, she will act passively on the date. It may be, however, that the boy prefers assertive girls and thus will not be pleased with his date's passivity and so will not "reward" her for it. The girl may continue to act passively, however, because her expectancy of being punished for assertiveness outweighs the actual punishment for nonassertiveness. Thus behavior patterns, including sex-typed behaviors, can result even from inaccurate expectations about the consequences of behaviors.

Girls and boys have many opportunities to observe some kinds of sex-typed behaviors. Even when mothers are employed outside the home, they tend to do much more of the housekeeping, cooking, and child care than fathers (see Chapter 4). Mothers are most likely to be in low-status, traditionally feminine jobs (for example, teaching, clerical work, nursing), whereas fathers are more likely to be in high-status, traditionally masculine jobs (such as business management or law). The portrayal of men and women in television and movies is extraordinarily stereotyped, say many critics (see the review by Huston, 1983). Males are portrayed as aggressive and often clever, in high-status positions, and in control. Females are often portrayed as passive, seductive, and unintelligent.

Do children model their behaviors after the adults in their lives and in the media? Despite the amount of television children watch, there is little evidence that viewing sex-stereotyped characters affects children's behaviors (Greer, 1980; Perloff, 1977). Children who watch more television, even those who especially like shows that stereotype men and women, do not show greater sex-typed behavior themselves. The evidence that children learn sex-typed behavior by modeling their same-sex parents is mixed. The degree to which children show sex-typed behaviors is not related to the degree that their parents are sex-typed, as would be expected if observational learning were taking place (Maccoby & Jacklin, 1974; Smith & Daglish, 1977). On the other hand, when children are exposed to adults showing behaviors that contradict sex stereotypes (for example, women as police officers, men cooking dinner), their beliefs about what is possible or true about the behaviors of males and females can be changed (e.g., Atkin, 1975). The children's own behaviors often do not change upon exposure to counter-stereotypical models, however. Thus existing studies have not suggested a strong contribution of observational learning on children's adoption of sex-typed behaviors.

Cognitive Theories

The final set of theories about how children come to adopt sex-typed behaviors and personality traits is known as *cognitive theory*. Lawrence Kohlberg (1966), one of the first proponents of a cognitive perspective on sex-typing, argued that children actively construct cognitive representations of the world and that these representations, or *schemas*, then guide the child's behavior. One of the most important schemas a child constructs is the gender schema (Bem, 1974). One of the first realities a child notices about the world is that there are two sexes. According to Kohlberg, children begin to classify people, including themselves, according to sex as early as age 3. They go on to develop their concepts of what it means to be a female or a male in terms of appearance, abilities, psychological characteristics, and activities. Children make their own behavior conform to their concept of what a person of their sex is supposed to be like. The particular content of the child's concept of male and female is determined by cultural and social norms. Thus all children will develop a gender schema as a natural part of cognitive development, but the content of their schemas for male and female will reflect what their observations lead them to believe differentiates the sexes in their own society. Since most societies view females as unassertive, dependent, emotional, and humble, girls will adopt these characteristics, because they will be part of the girls' gender schema. Boys will adopt the characteristics associated with the masculine gender, namely assertiveness, independence, rationality, and self-confidence.

Kohlberg's theory seems to predict that children will show more and more sex-typed behavior as they age and their gender schemas develop. Kohlberg argued, however, that children will be most rigid in their adherence to sex-typed behavior when their gender schemas are fragile and under development: their lack of certainty about which characteristics are essential to being a member of their gender and which are not will lead them to be overzealous in their adherence to all characteristics even remotely associated with their gender. Thus Kohlberg predicted that children would show the greatest amount of sex-typed behavior during those years of early childhood when they were forming their concepts of gender, and then show declines in sex-typed behavior as they came to understand which behaviors and characteristics were an essential part of being a male or being a female. Children do seem to be very rigid in their judgments of what males and females can do and how they are supposed to behave early in the development of their concepts of gender (see Huston, 1983). From about age 3 to age 8, their knowledge of the activities and characteristics deemed appropriate for each sex grows steadily, and they become more flexible in judging what is and is not crucial to being a male or female.

The evidence that the extent to which children's behavior is sex-typed depends on the development of their gender schema is mixed, however. As children's understanding of gender develops during the preschool years, their tendency to want to play with children of the same sex and to play in sex-typed activities increases. There is little evidence, however, that the development of gender schemas leads to sex-typed personality characteristics such as assertiveness, emotionality, and independence (see Huston, 1983). Children know which personality characteristics are associated with each sex in early-to-middle childhood. Yet both boys and girls show increasing preference for masculine activities and valuing of masculine personality characteristics (such as independence) in middle childhood. Thus it would appear that the cognitive theory of how males and females acquire the personality characteristics thought to contribute to the sex differences in depression has not been well supported. This theory has proved difficult to test, however, so we may not want to dismiss it on the basis of current evidence (Huston, 1983). There are differences from one person to another in the strength of gender schemas, and these individual differences may mask developmental changes (see Bem, 1974).

Conclusions

Psychoanalytic theory, behavioral theory, and cognitive developmental theory describe different processes by which females and males come to adopt different personality traits or behavior patterns. All these theories assume that sex differences in personality and behavior exist—that females tend to be more nurturant, passive, modest, dependent, and people-oriented than males, and that males tend to be more assertive, self-confident, independent, and task-oriented than females. And although psychoanalytic, behavioral, and cognitive behavioral theories of depression identify different *processes* by which certain personality characteristics lead individuals to depression, there are commonalities in the personality characteristics said to be risk factors for depression. Specifically, these theories hold that nonassertiveness, dependency, and the tendency to be self-effacing put an individual at risk. Because these characteristics are supposedly more common in females than in males, females are more vulnerable to depression than males.

CHAPTER SIX

The Contribution
of Personality Differences to Sex
Differences in Depression

If it is true that females are more nonassertive, dependent, and self-effacing than males, several theories of depression suggest that these sex differences in personality lead to the sex differences in depression. Psychoanalytic theorists argue that people who cannot express their anger openly and who are excessively dependent on others for self-esteem will be most likely to internalize their hostility and develop depression (Arieti & Bemporad, 1980; Bibring, 1953; Chodoff, 1972; Freud, 1917). The behavioral theories of depression also suggest that dependency on others and lack of assertiveness contribute to a person's vulnerability to depression. For example, Lewinsohn (1974) argued that nonassertive people are not able to bring about the outcomes that they desire and thus may become depressed. Similarly, Seligman (1975) argued that a sense of helplessness to control important events in life arises from nonassertiveness and leads to depression. Being very dependent on others can also contribute to a sense of helplessness, and thus to depression, because control over important events is out of a person's hands.

Cognitive theories of depression have suggested that a tendency to overreact to the opinions of others, instead of relying upon one's own internal standards, can undermine one's sense of competence and self-efficacy and contribute to depressive symptoms such as lowered motivation, passivity, and pessimism (Bandura & Cervone, 1983; Rehm, 1977).

Finally, a reformulated version of the learned helplessness theory of depression (Abramson, Seligman & Teasdale, 1978) predicts that excessive humility is a risk factor for depression. This theory focuses on the attributions or explanations people give for the good and bad events in their lives. People who habitually explain bad events in terms of causes that are internal to them ("it's my fault"), stable in time ("it's going to last forever"), and global in effect ("it will undermine everything I do") and who also explain good events in terms of external, unstable, specific causes are more prone to depression than people with a more adaptive explanatory style (Peterson & Seligman, 1984). So people with the maladaptive style tend to blame themselves for bad events, and do not take credit for good events. They also do not expect things to go well in the future. This self-effacing, pessimistic style leads to nonassertiveness and depression (Peterson & Seligman, 1984).

Thus several theories of depression suggest that nonassertiveness, dependency, and the tendency to be self-effacing (that is, to make self-derogatory, perhaps pessimistic attributions for events) predispose people to depression. If indeed women are more likely than men to develop these characteristics, it would follow that these sex-typed personality characteristics lead to the sex differences in depression. But before we conclude that we have solved the puzzle of sex differences in depression, we must evaluate the evidence that females are more nonassertive, dependent, and humble than males.

Nonassertiveness and Internalizing Hostility

Are females less assertive than males? To answer this question, we first must define what we mean by *assertiveness*. One assertiveness-training manual for women defines assertiveness as behavior intended to "communicate honestly and directly" (Bloom, Coburn & Pearlman, 1975). Such communication may take the form of expressing disagreement or anger with others, expressing one's preferences when decisions are being made, and refusing to accept the demands of others. Other characteristics associated with assertiveness are persistence and confidence in the face of frustration and the ability to pursue one's goals despite obstacles and risks. There are three bodies

of literature providing information about sex differences in assertiveness: literature on verbal assertiveness, especially in the face of
confrontation (Do women "talk back" to those who confront them,
or do they allow themselves to be victimized?); literature on sex differences in influenceability (Are women more likely than men to give
in to social pressure and do what others want to do?); and literature
on risk-taking and persistence under challenge (Are women worse
at risk-taking than men, and do they often become helpless when
frustrated?).

Verbal Assertiveness

There have been several reviews of the literature on sex differences
in assertiveness or aggressiveness (Eagly & Steffen, 1986; Frodi,
Macaulay & Thome, 1977; Maccoby & Jacklin, 1974, 1980). Many
of these reviews have coupled studies of what we might call assertiveness (that is, talking back when confronted) with studies of
physical aggression. But one review (Frodi, Macaulay & Thome,
1977) divides the literature into studies examining direct physical or
verbal aggression by subjects who have not been provoked, direct
verbal aggression or assertiveness by subjects who have been provoked, and indirect or "displaced" aggression by subjects who have
been provoked. Males are consistently more likely than females to
show direct physical aggression toward others. For example, Buss
(1961) had subjects deliver light shocks to other subjects (who were
actually also experimenters) for supposedly making an error on an
experimental task. Men were more willing than women to deliver
shocks. But there were no consistent sex differences in any other
types of aggression in the studies reviewed by Frodi and colleagues.
Among the conclusions of this review was that females, when provoked, are just as likely as males to show verbal aggression. That is,
females were just as likely as males to "talk back." There was also
no evidence to support the notion that females tend to show indirect
hostility. (Among twelve studies of indirect hostility, four showed
that men were more likely than women to show this type of hostility,
and eight showed no sex differences.) Thus the studies reviewed by
Frodi and colleagues suggest that men are more likely than women
to show physical aggression toward others, even when they are not
provoked to do so by others' behavior. But there is little evidence
that men are more likely than women to assert themselves verbally

when provoked or that women tend to use indirect means to express aggression toward others.

Even in studies of physical aggression, there are large inconsistencies from one study to the next in sex differences in physical aggression. Recently, Eagly and Steffen (1986) have identified a number of social and attitudinal factors that help to explain this variability across studies of sex differences in aggressiveness. Eagly and Steffen predicted that females would be less likely than males to act aggressively when there was some chance that they would be physically retaliated against for their aggression, when they believed that their aggression would cause significant harm to another person, when they expected to feel guilty or anxious about being aggressive, or when they had an audience that heightened their awareness of the social undesirability of aggression in females. In other words, Eagly and Steffen argued that women probably do not have a *trait* of non-assertiveness that makes them act nonassertively in most situations but that some situations may constrain women's ability or desire to act aggressively.

To test these hypotheses, Eagly and Steffen reviewed all studies of aggressive behaviors published between 1967 and 1982 in which adults were put into situations designed to elicit aggressive or assertive behaviors. They coded each study for the following variables: (1) whether the aggressive act in question was a physical or a psychological act; (2) whether the subject was given free choice to aggress or not to aggress, or was forced to perform some aggressive act and allowed only to choose the *level* of aggression; (3) whether the subject knew he or she was under surveillance in the experiment; and (4) the amount of provocation used to elicit aggression by the subject. In addition, Eagly and Steffen asked 97 female and 103 male undergraduates to rate short descriptions of the procedures in each study for the following variables: (1) the likelihood that the aggressive behavior would cause harm to the target; (2) the likelihood that performing the aggressive behavior would cause them (the under-graduate raters) guilt or anxiety; (3) the amount of danger they would face if they performed the same act; (4) the likelihood that they would perform the same act given the same situation; (5) the likelihood that the typical male would perform the same act; and (6) the likelihood that the typical female would perform the same act.

The female raters said that the acts in these studies would cause more harm to the target, more guilt and anxiety in them, and greater danger for them than did the male raters. The female raters also rated themselves as less likely to perform the aggressive acts than did the male raters. Respondents of both sexes rated the typical female as less likely to perform the aggressive acts than the typical male. These data indicate that females expect more negative consequences of aggressive acts than males and that both sexes believe females are less likely to perform these acts than males. Eagly and Steffen's analyses of the overall behaviors of the actual subjects in these studies (not the raters) indicate that female subjects were less likely to perform aggressive acts than male subjects were. But the sex difference in likelihood of aggression was small. Only 34 percent of the studies showed that males were significantly more likely to be aggressive than females. Eagly and Steffen found support for most of their predictions about factors that would account for the presence or absence of a sex difference in aggression. The tendency for males to aggress more than females was greater in studies of physical aggression than in studies of psychological aggression, in studies where the privacy of the aggressive act was insured, and in studies where (according to the ratings of the undergraduates) females more than males expected the aggressive act to cause the target harm, to cause the aggressor guilt and anxiety, or to put the aggressor in danger.

Eagly and Steffen concluded that there does not seem to be a general tendency for males to be more aggressive than females. Rather, situational constraints and sex differences in beliefs about the *consequences* of aggression determine whether males and females show aggression. Females do not aggress as much as males when the type of aggression called for is physical instead of psychological or when they believe there is some danger that they will be retaliated against physically. The reason these considerations do not inhibit aggression in males as much as in females is probably that males are physically stronger than females and thus can often defend themselves better against retaliation. When females expect their aggression to cause the target harm, they are less likely to be aggressive, but when they expect little harm to come to the target, they will be aggressive. When an aggressive act is to be performed in private rather than in public, males are more likely to aggress than females. Eagly and Steffen suggest that this trend occurs because males are more likely to conform to social norms of nonaggression in public than in private. Finally, aggressive acts that female undergraduates but not male undergraduates said would cause them guilt and anxiety were less likely to be performed by female subjects than by male subjects in the studies. Eagly and Steffen note that these results are in line with data on sex differences in empathy, which indicate that women show more empathic distress over the troubles of other people than do men.

What can we conclude from the Eagly and Steffen (1986) review of studies about sex differences in assertiveness and aggressiveness? First, there is some tendency for males to show more aggression than females, but the difference is small. Second, the likelihood of females showing an aggressive act is mediated by their beliefs about the consequences of that act: if they believe they are in danger of retaliation, they are less likely to act. Females are also less likely to act aggressively if they expect harm to come to their target or if they expect to feel guilty or anxious about being aggressive. This finding suggests that females are less likely than males to perform more harmful, severe aggressive acts, but just as likely to perform aggressive acts that are not hurtful—the definition some theorists use for *assertive* acts.

One drawback in most studies of aggression is that they have been conducted with college students, among whom sex differences in many variables are often smaller than in the general population of adults. In addition, most of these studies examined interactions with strangers rather than among friends and spouses (see Krebs & Miller, 1985). But the existing studies of nonviolent behavior between spouses also challenge the notion that women tend to be nonassertive (Frost & Averill, 1982; see also Gottman & Levenson, in press; Peplau, 1983; Raush et al., 1974). For example, Frost and Averill (1982) found that women were just as likely as men to have been angry at their spouse or lover in the previous week. Whereas men tended to avoid and deny responsibility for these conflicts, women tended to want to talk with their spouse or lover about the conflict. Similarly, Raush and colleagues (1974) found that during high-conflict situations between married couples, women were more likely to be "coercive" and "personally attacking" than men, whereas men were more "resolving" and "reconciling" than women. Thus these studies on aggression and conflict in close relationships suggest that women may actually be more likely than men to remain engaged in conflicts. This conclusion certainly contradicts the stereotype of women as nonassertive. Even though women may remain engaged —and sometimes aggressive—in conflictual interactions with men, they may still emerge from these conflicts feeling frustrated and helpless, for men tend to withdraw from conflict or declare a conflict settled long before women are satisfied that a resolution has been found (Gottman, 1979).

The primary point, however, is that there is little evidence that women suffer from a trait of nonassertiveness. Clearly, there are some situations in which women tend to be less *aggressive* than men, but such restraint often results from rational assessments by women of the physical danger they risk by being aggressive or of the harm they would do to another person. Women who are often faced with the fact that acting assertively or aggressively will bring harm to themselves or others may come to feel helpless and depressed. For example, battered wives often know that their husbands may kill them or their children if they try to escape, and their sense of helplessness leads to depression. But this explanation is different from saying that many women are by nature nonassertive and are therefore more depressed than men.

Sex Differences in Influenceability

Most textbooks on social psychology and attitude change assert that women are much more likely than men to conform to the demands and opinions of others. Eagly (1978) notes that most writers characterize sex differences in influenceability "in such terms as 'large, strong, clear' and 'well-established' and claim that [they are] both 'general' and 'consistent'" (p. 87). In addition, most writers assert that these sex differences clearly result from socialization into sex roles: females are encouraged to assume the passive, conforming stance that is part of the feminine sex role, and males are encouraged to assume the forceful, influential stance that is part of the masculine sex role. Eagly (1978) points out, however, that these claims are based on a handful of studies, most of which were done in the 1950's and several of which report no statistical tests for sex differences in their measures of influenceability.

Eagly (1978) therefore set out to review studies of sex differences in influenceability and to assess the consistency of their findings.

She first examined studies of persuasion in which subjects heard arguments about some issue; agreement with these arguments was assessed as an index of the subjects' persuadability. Eagly found 62 such studies in which researchers performed statistical tests for sex differences in persuadability; 51 of these studies (82 percent) reported no sex difference, 10 studies (16 percent) found females to be more persuadable, and 1 (2 percent) found males to be more persuadable. Thus the vast majority of studies found no sex difference in persuadability, but among those that did find a difference, women usually appeared to be more persuadable than men.

Eagly (1978) also reviewed studies of conformity in which one member of a group voices an opinion that is known to differ from the subject's opinion. Later, the subject's change in opinion toward that of the other person is assessed as a measure of conformity. Usually, these experiments have involved some group pressure for the subject to conform, or at least some awareness of surveillance of the subject's responses by group members. Sex differences have been found more frequently in conformity studies than in persuadability studies. Of 61 conformity studies reporting the results of statistical tests for sex differences, Eagly found that 38 (62 percent) found no difference, 21 (34 percent) found females to be more conforming, and 2 (3 percent) found males to be more conforming. Thus, in these studies of conforming, a substantial minority found that women were more conforming than men. The degree of sex difference in conformity tended to be larger in studies with considerable surveillance over the subjects' responses: females tended to be more conforming than males when they knew their responses were being watched. Eagly suggests that the subjects may have felt particularly strong pressure to act in accord with the role for their sex when others were watching them.

Simply tallying the number of studies finding or not finding sex difference in influenceability is a rather crude way of assessing the evidence for sex difference. In many of the studies that did not show a statistically significant sex difference, there may have been some mean difference in men's and women's scores that was rendered statistically insignificant by characteristics of the study (such as small sample sizes). By contrast, in some studies that report a significant sex difference, the magnitude of this difference may be very small. In the last decade statistical methods have been developed to aggregate data from several studies and to assess the magnitude of an apparent sex difference in some important variable (Glass, McGraw & Smith, 1981). These techniques, called *meta-analysis techniques*, provide indices of the size of effect that sex has on the variable in question. That is, the *effect size* statistic provided by a meta-analysis tells us to what extent any variability can be attributed to sex.

Eagly and Carli (1981) performed a meta-analysis on the studies of persuasion and conformity described above and found that, when all studies were combined, there was a significant difference in men's and women's influenceability. Women were more likely than men to be persuaded and to conform. But the effect size of sex in this difference was small: only 1 percent of the variability in persuadability and conformity was accounted for by sex.

Most of the studies in the Eagly and Carli (1981) review were laboratory studies conducted with college students. The sex differences in influenceability may be greater in the general population. There have been several studies of leadership and assertiveness in organizational settings. Most of these studies have been careful to compare only men and women who have the same status on the job, for job status should have considerable effect on a person's ability to persuade and influence others. In general, when men and women with same job status are compared, few sex differences in influenceability are found (Barthol, 1978; L. K. Brown, 1979; S. M. Brown, 1979; Osborn & Vicars, 1976; Terborg, 1977). Male and female managers show essentially the same levels of influenceability. Indeed, the sex differences in assertiveness in actual organizational settings tend to be smaller than those found in laboratory settings.

Eagly (1983) suggests that the common notion that women are less assertive at work than men probably results from the fact that women usually have lower-status jobs than men, and status determines assertiveness on the job (see also Kanter, 1977). People mistakenly interpret these differences in assertiveness as sex differences rather than job status differences. Other researchers have argued, however, that women's tendency to be nonassertive leads to their low status in the job market (see Lockheed & Hall, 1976). Women who are assertive and influential on the job will attain high-status positions, but most women do not face up to challenges or take risks at work and thus do not attain high-status positions.

Risk-Taking and Persistence Under Challenge

The study of sex differences in risk-taking behavior most often cited as evidence that females are averse to risk-taking is a study of children by Slovic (1966). Slovic asked 735 boys and 312 girls age 6 to 16 to play a game in which they could pull any of nine switches on a panel and receive some candy. If they pulled a tenth "disaster" switch, they lost all the candy they had previously won. The "disaster" switch was indistinguishable from the other switches, and its location on the panel of ten switches was unknown to subjects. Because the probability of pulling the disaster switch increased with the number of switches pulled, stopping performance of the task was interpreted as an index of risk-taking tendencies. Slovic found that girls stopped pulling switches earlier than boys at all age levels except age 6 to 8. This pattern of results is often cited as evidence that females are not as good as males at risk-taking.

A number of additional results from the Slovic study are seldom mentioned in discussions of sex differences in risk-taking, however. Sex differences in the number of switches pulled were significantly large only among children age 11 or age 14 to 16. In addition, the average number of switches pulled by the girls came closer to the optimal number given the risks of the game. As a result, girls won an average of 2.20 spoonfuls of candy, whereas boys averaged only 1.84 spoonfuls. Thus the Slovic (1966) study does not provide strong support for the claim that males are better at taking risks than females.

Other studies often cited as showing that women buckle under pressure come from the literature on achievement motivation and learned helplessness. Most studies in this literature follow a particular design. Subjects are asked to work on a series of puzzles or tasks, some of which are unsolvable, and experimenters focus on the subjects' performance on solvable tasks that come after a few unsolvable tasks. Some subjects remain persistent and expect success on the new, solvable tasks. These subjects are labeled *mastery-oriented* subjects. Other subjects show lowered motivation, an inability to see that new puzzles are solvable, and lowered expectations for success on the new, solvable tasks. These subjects are labeled *helpless* subjects. Published articles and textbooks frequently state that following failure, females are much more likely than males to show a helpless pattern of behavior, including lowered motivation, passivity, and lowered expectations for succeeding in the future (e.g., Dweck & Licht, 1980). If it is true that females are more prone to helplessness than males, this vulnerability could explain in part why women have trouble achieving high-status positions: such achievements require sustained motivation and expectations of success in the face of repeated failures and frustrations. And as discussed earlier, a greater tendency toward helplessness may also contribute to women's greater vulnerability to depression.

Some studies have found that females are more likely than males to show lowered expectations of success following failures (e.g., Dweck & Bush, 1976; Eccles, Adler & Meece, 1984; Gitelson, Petersen & Tobin-Richards, 1982). For example, Eccles and colleagues (1984) had adolescent students complete a series of puzzle tasks, some of which were unsolvable. Subjects were asked for their expectancies for success before the first puzzles were attempted and again after failures at the tasks. Males and females had equally high expectancies for success before starting the puzzle tasks, but females had lower expectancies for future success than males after failures. These results are in line with the hypothesis about sex differences in helplessness. Eccles and her colleagues did not, however, find any sex differences in actual persistence at tasks that followed failures or in the percentage of future tasks completed correctly. Thus, although males and females stated different expectancies for success at future tasks, they did not show differences in performance at those tasks, as would be predicted by the helplessness hypothesis. (For similar results, see Parsons et al., 1982; Sweeney, Moreland & Gruber, 1982.) Many other studies have also found little or no evidence for consistent sex differences in helplessness following failure in either children or adults (e.g., Beck, 1977; Diener & Dweck, 1978; Dweck, 1975; Dweck & Repucci, 1973; Nicholls, 1975; Rholes et al., 1980; Roberts & Nolen-Hoeksema, 1990).

Results from laboratory studies of helplessness may not be generalizable to everyday achievement settings, however. Women may be more likely than males to show helplessness when confronted with actual frustrations and failures on the job. Eccles (1985) notes a number of sex differences in approach to careers that might indicate a greater lack of persistence in women than in men. First, women are less likely than men to pursue advanced degrees in all fields, including feminine-typed fields. Second, women are less likely than men to try to climb the corporate ladder to high-status positions, and when they do try, their rise is slower than that of men (Frieze et al., 1978; Vetter, 1981). Finally, when faced with a conflict between family or social life and advancement of their career, women are more likely than men to abandon or diminish their involvement in their career (Baruch, Barnett & Rivers, 1983; Bryson, Bryson & Johnson, 1978).

Eccles (1985) warns, however, that these differences between men's and women's approaches to their careers may result from differences in the value men and women assign to different activities in their lives rather than from any sex differences in strength under pressure. Women may not value advanced degrees, prestigious jobs, and high salaries as much as men do, and thus they may choose not to sacrifice the activities they do value highly, such as having a family, for the sake of the job. Eccles (1985) presents data from a study of adolescents' choice of courses in school that indicate that the subjective value males and females place on different courses correlated more closely with their choice of course than did their expectancies for success, or past successes at such courses. (See also Eccles, Adler & Meece, 1984.) In other words, females chose not to take math in this study because they put a relatively low value on math, not because they felt helpless to succeed at math. Eccles and colleagues argue that it is not appropriate to assume that females value and desire the same goals as males or that females' tendency not to accomplish males' goals reflects personality or ability deficits in females. Further evidence for this interpretation of sex differences in achievement patterns is needed, but Eccles clearly raises an important point about the standards against which we judge the accomplishments of the two sexes.

The Clinical Literature

In many types of empirical studies, we find little evidence that women are less assertive than men. When sex differences in assertiveness are found, they tend to be small. It can be argued, however, that the measures of assertiveness in many empirical studies are not subtle or sensitive enough to detect the kind of sex differences in assertiveness that are relevant to depression in women. Another source of information about such sex differences is the clinical literature. Frost and Averill (1982) searched this literature and found very little discussion of possible sex differences in anger and its expression. Even in an international congress on psychoanalytic views on aggression, none of the presentations dealt with possible sex differences in anger or aggression. In recent years feminist psychoanalysts have asserted that denial of anger is a source of many neuroses in women (e.g., Kaplan, 1986). But these theorists provide essentially no evidence for sex differences in anger and its expression. Even in the literature that would be most likely to present evidence for sex differences in aggression and its relation to sex differences in depression, then, there is no support for such a relation.

Summary

The literature on verbal assertiveness, influenceability, risk-taking, and helplessness does not provide substantial support for the claim that women tend to be much less assertive than men. When sex differences are found in this literature, women tend to show less assertiveness than do men, but these sex differences are always very small and were found in only a subset of studies. Nor does the literature support the hypothesis that women's greater tendency toward depression is caused by a tendency to be nonassertive. It seems unlikely that the enormous sex differences in depression can be accounted for by the small and inconsistent sex differences in assertiveness. It may be that some women become depressed because they tend to be nonassertive and internalize hostility, but the same is probably true of some men as well.

Sex Differences in Dependency

This section presents the evidence for the theory that women are more likely than men to be dependent on others, making them more vulnerable to depression. Some theorists claim that women are more concerned with relationships and are more likely to base their self-esteem on relationships than are men, and that this tendency contributes to their greater vulnerability to depression. A more specific theory is that women tend to be more reactive to and dependent on the evaluations of others in evaluating themselves, and that this tendency contributes to their greater vulnerability to depression.

Concern with Relationships

A number of studies have shown that females describe themselves as more socially oriented than males do (see Maccoby & Jacklin, 1974). Females report higher liking of others and rate relationships as a more important component of life than do males. But when researchers have attempted to observe behaviors that might index social orientation or dependency, the findings about sex differences have been inconsistent. One problem is in measuring social orientation and dependency. A number of different behaviors have been used to index dependency: seeking help, consolation, reassurance, or protection; remaining near others; touching and clinging to others; and trying to get others' attention. These behaviors do not correlate well with each other, indicating either that some of them do not index dependency or that there is no coherent construct of dependency. Behaviors that have often been used to indicate a general social orientation have included help-giving and sensitivity to social cues.

Maccoby and Jacklin (1974) reviewed 32 studies of sex differences in touching and proximity to parents and in resistance to separation from parents. These tests were conducted primarily with infants and preschoolers. In eight of these studies, girls showed more of these behaviors than boys; in seven of the studies, boys showed more of the behaviors than girls. In the remainder of the studies there were no sex differences. Thus this review gives little evidence of greater dependency in females than in males, at least early in life. But because these studies were conducted with children rather than adults, we cannot draw conclusions from these studies about dependency in adults. Because psychoanalytic theory says that sex differences in dependency arise from early childhood experiences, however, the negative evidence in the Maccoby and Jacklin review is relevant to the psychoanalytic argument.

There is also little evidence that parents encourage dependency more in girls than in boys. Maccoby and Jacklin (1974) reviewed observational studies of parents' restrictiveness and encouragement of emotional attachment with boys and girls. They found that boys actually receive more restrictions on independent behavior than girls, apparently because boys are somewhat more obstreperous than girls.

Similarly, in 39 studies of parental warmth, nurturance, and acceptance, they found no consistent evidence that mothers or fathers show more of these behaviors toward one sex or the other until puberty, when parents become less likely to display affection openly to boys than to girls.

Block (1976) criticized the Maccoby and Jacklin review for focusing too much on young children and on laboratory studies of parent-child behavior. Block argued that there are consistent and substantial differences in the ways parents treat boys and girls. As evidence, she provided self-report data from parents on their parenting behaviors and retrospective accounts from young adults of the behaviors of their parents when they were children. These data support the stereotype that parents emphasize achievement and competition, control of the expression of affect, and independence for sons and encourage warmth and physical closeness, trustworthiness, and "ladylike" behavior for daughters. Almost none of the differences were significant at the level required when a great many comparisons are being made, however.* The other problem with such data is that self-reports are open to the biases of subjects to respond in ways that fit stereotypes of differences in how boys and girls are treated.

Perhaps women are not more dependent than men, but only more socially oriented. There have been fewer studies of sex differences in behaviors indexing general social orientation than there have been for dependency. The few that have been done do not clearly indicate a greater social orientation in females than in males. Females do seem to have somewhat more intense relationships with a few friends than males do, but males tend to have more friends than females do. Thus it is not clear that friendships are more important to females than to males. In their observational studies of children in six different cultures, Whiting and Edwards (1973) found no sex differences in help-giving behavior among children age 3 to 6. Among children age 7 to 11, girls tended to offer more practical and emotional support than boys. But children who give help tend to be more assertive

---

* Block compared 91 parenting behaviors for sex differences. When so many comparisons are made, it is advisable to divide the usual level of statistical significance ($p=.05$) by the number of comparisons (91). In this case, the p-level necessary for acceptance of a result as significant is .0005. Almost none of the comparisons of parents' behaviors toward boys versus girls reached this level of significance. In fact, few even reached a $p=.05$ level of significance.

and less in need of reassurance than children who do not give help (Hartup & Keller, 1960). Thus help-giving does not appear to be a dependency-related behavior.

In an extensive review of help-giving in adults, Eagly and Crowley (1986) found that men are more likely than women to give help to others in many situations. Eagly and Crowley focused on social psychology experiments in which the experimenter sets up a situation where subjects have the option of helping someone in obvious need. They found that the amount of danger to the help-giver was an important predictor of sex differences in help-giving: women were less likely to give help than men when there was some chance that they would risk harm, especially physical harm, in doing so. When there was little risk of harm in the situation, there were essentially no sex differences in help-giving behavior.

These data do not directly address the view that women overvalue love relationships and invest their self-esteem in these relationships more than men do. Cochran and Peplau (described in Peplau & Gordon, 1985) asked men and women to rate the importance of a number of factors in relationships. The males and females in this study (UCLA students) did not differ in the importance they assigned to a secure, intimate attachment, but women were more likely to rate autonomy and independence as important factors in a relationship than men were. Cochran and Peplau acknowledge that their results may be specific to a college population. But other studies have found that women tend to have a more practical, less romantic view of intimate relationships than men do. Men fall in love more readily than women (Rubin, Peplau & Hill, 1981). Women tend to consider pragmatic issues, such as their potential partner's earning power, reliability, and trustworthiness, more than men do. Among young married couples, women tend to give greater importance than men to feeling emotionally involved with their spouse, being able to talk over issues with their spouse, and maintaining independence and self-reliance (Parelman, 1983). Men tend to give greater importance than women to feeling responsible for their spouse's well-being, putting their spouse's needs first, and spending time with their spouse. These studies indicate that men and women may have somewhat different sets of concerns in relationships, but not that women are more invested in relationships than men are.

Indeed, there is some evidence that the risk to men's emotional health is greater than the risk to women's when they lose a close relationship. When an intimate relationship ends, the male partner is at least as likely as the female partner to become depressed (Bernard, 1972). Males react with long-term depression and physical illness to the death of their spouse more often than do females (Stroebe & Stroebe, 1983). These trends have been explained in a number of ways. Some theorists argue that men tend to rely on women to provide emotional richness in their lives because men have trouble experiencing and expressing emotionality (Chodorow, 1978). Thus when a spouse or lover leaves, a man also loses his source of emotional life. Others have argued that men become reliant on women, especially wives, to resolve the daily hassles in their lives and to provide a sounding board for their daily complaints and concerns. When his wife dies, a man literally does not know how to care for himself and does not tend to have anyone who knows him well enough to care and listen (see Stroebe & Stroebe, 1983). These speculations remain untested, however.

The fact that women appear to be less likely than men to become depressed upon the loss of an intimate relationship contradicts the psychoanalytic views that women depend on relationships for their self-esteem and become depressed when such relationships are lost. There may be another type of link between relationships and depression in women, however. It may be that women do not get depressed when relationships end, but rather during relationships. As discussed in Chapter 4, being married is associated with relatively low levels of depression for men but not for women (see Radloff, 1975). Other evidence for a link between being in an intimate relationship and being depressed is found in children and adolescents. For example, Simmons and colleagues (reported in Simmons & Blyth, 1987) found that girls who were dating in junior high school were more likely to be depressed than girls the same age who were not dating, but that there were no relationships between dating and depression in boys. These data indicate that certain aspects of heterosexual relationships are associated with increased levels of depression in females. Studies reviewed in Chapter 4 suggest that these aspects might include imbalances of power, amounts of responsibility for housework and child care, and the potential for physical abuse.

A modern psychoanalytic version of the argument that women are more dependent on relationships has gained considerable attention. Chodorow (1978) and others (e.g., Deutsch, 1944) have argued that women form closer bonds with their daughters and encourage less autonomy in them than in their sons because they know that their daughters will probably be mothers. Likewise, girls identify with their mothers more than boys do because girls know they will probably be mothers. The bond between mothers and daughters, then, tends to be extremely strong and enduring. Because girls are not encouraged to develop an autonomous self as much as boys are, girls tend to think in terms of relationships more than boys do. Particularly if their mothers are unaffectionate but very controlling, girls have difficulty separating from their mothers, which can lead to depression. Another version of this argument is that girls never separate from their mothers to the extent that boys do, and thus develop conflicts about autonomy and independence that contribute to their tendency toward depression (see Chodorow, 1978; Deutsch, 1944).

A number of contemporary empirical studies have reported that depressed women recall their parents, especially their mothers, as unaffectionate, withdrawn, and overcontrolling (Blatt et al., 1979; Jacobson, Fasman & DiMascio, 1975; Lamont, Fischhoff & Gottlieb 1976; Parker, 1979). These studies suffer from a major methodological problem, however. Depressed people selectively remember and perhaps exaggerate negative experiences (Beck, 1967; Blaney, 1986). The retrospective accounts of parents provided by depressed women may also be subject to this biasing error.

Dauber (1984) used the "subliminal psychodynamic activation" method to study the effects of messages related to autonomy on depressed college women. In subliminal psychodynamic activation, subjects are given a 4-millisecond exposure to stimuli containing content related to the kinds of unconscious motives that psychoanalytic theory implicates in psychopathology. In Dauber's study, subjects were exposed either to the phrase "Leaving mommy is wrong" or to the phrase "Mommy and I are one." Dauber hypothesized that the phrase "Leaving mommy is wrong" would increase depressive affect in women who were already depressed by intensifying the conflict underlying their depression. By this reasoning, the phrase "Mommy and I are one" should reduce depression by "activating reassuring and otherwise gratifying fantasies of oneness with a good, symbiotic mother" (Dauber, 1984, p. 10). Subjects also viewed a control phrase, "People are talking." Dauber presented these stimuli to 18 women who were mildly or moderately depressed. The subjects completed a depression questionnaire immediately prior to and immediately after viewing each stimulus phrase. Dauber found that subjects' depression scores increased significantly upon viewing the phrase "Leaving mommy is wrong." Depression scores decreased slightly after the subjects saw "Mommy and I are one" and the control phrase.

Dauber (1984) concluded that these results support the ego-analytic conception of depression as the result of conflicts over autonomy and dependence. Yet as Dauber himself points out, other studies (e.g., Schmidt, 1981) have found that in general the subliminal presentation of negative self-statements, such as "I have been bad," increases depression in depressed college students. Such statements do not refer to autonomy or dependence issues. Thus the phrases used by Dauber may have increased depressed affect simply because they were negative statements, not because they tapped a specific underlying conflict.

It appears, then, that there is little current evidence to support the belief that conflicts over autonomy stemming from females' relationships with their mothers contribute to their tendency toward depression. Females are not dependent on the presence of a relationship (particularly with a man) for protection against depression. Instead, males are more likely to become depressed over the breakup of a relationship than females are. More generally, there is some evidence that being in a relationship may be a source of depression for at least some women.

Reactivity to the Evaluations of Others

Even if women do not tend to invest their self-esteem in relationships more than men do, their self-esteem may nevertheless be more dependent on the evaluations of others. According to cognitive/behavioral theories, a tendency to be overly reactive to the opinions of others, instead of relying upon one's own internal standards, undermines one's sense of competence and self-efficacy and contributes to depressive symptoms such as lowered motivation, passivity, and pessimism (Bandura & Cervone, 1983; Rehm, 1977). Lenny (1977) reviewed the literature on women's self-confidence in achievement settings and concluded that, compared to men, women express more self-confidence when they receive positive feedback and less self-confidence when they receive negative feedback (e.g., Feather, 1969; Feather & Simon, 1971). When no feedback about performance is available, women tend to expect to do less well and give lower evaluations of their performances than do men.

Roberts and I (1990) conducted a laboratory study of men's and women's self-evaluations after different types of feedback on their performance. We asked undergraduates to work on a series of difficult puzzles, some of which were unsolvable, and periodically measured the subjects' persistence, perceptions of productivity, self-efficacy, and self-satisfaction as they worked on the puzzles. Subjects were divided into four experimental groups, each of which received a different type of feedback from the experimenter. In the negative feedback group, subjects were told they were not doing as well on the task as expected. In the positive feedback group, subjects were told they were doing better than average on the task. In the irrelevant feedback group, subjects were given positive feedback unrelated to their performance—they were told, "You have a very steady hand." In the control group, subjects received no feedback on their performance.

The men and women in this study did not differ in their persistence or performance at the puzzles, but there were sex differences in subjects' reactions to the different types of feedback. The largest of these differences occurred in the changes in subjects' ratings of self-satisfaction after receiving feedback. Whereas the men's self-satisfaction tended to increase after all types of feedback, women's self-satisfaction increased after positive feedback but decreased after negative feedback. Similarly, women increased their ratings of self-efficacy after positive feedback but substantially decreased their ratings after negative feedback. There were no significant differences in men's self-efficacy scores resulting from different types of feedback. These findings support the claim that women's self-evaluations are more reactive to feedback than men's.

One other substantial sex difference was that men showed a greater self-enhancing bias than women in their estimates of their productivity in finishing puzzles. In general, men tended to overestimate their productivity and women tended to underestimate their productivity. Men were particularly likely to increase their estimates of their productivity after receiving negative feedback: "Here men showed clear evidence for a self-enhancing resistance to the negative evaluation of their competence, in a manner which would seem to be maximally protective of self-esteem. Rather than using the external evaluator's information as a diagnostic of their lack of competence to attain goals, the male subjects instead positively evaluated themselves as vastly more competent than was actually the case" (Roberts & Nolen-Hoeksema, 1990, p. 27). Other researchers have found a tendency for males to be more likely than females to engage in self-enhancing estimates of their own competence and control (e.g., Golin et al., 1979; Martin, Abramson & Alloy, 1984). Having such self-enhancing biases and an illusion of control has in turn been associated with reduced risk of depression (see Alloy & Abramson, 1982).

Thus there is some evidence that women's self-evaluations are more reactive than men's to the evaluations of others and that women are less likely to have an optimistic bias or illusion of control in their self-evaluations. No one has tested the extent to which these sex differences in reactions to feedback account for the sex differences in depression, however. In addition, it might be that the greater attention women seem to pay to the opinions of others makes them more likely than men to gather important information that can help them eventually to perform better than men. That is, both negative and positive feedback often contains useful information on more appropriate strategies for approaching a task. Having self-enhancing biases may protect one's self-esteem against negative feedback in the short run, but it may lead in the long run to persistence at inefficient strategies, even when information about more appropriate strategies is available (Roberts & Nolen-Hoeksema, 1990). Thus women may show more short-term negative reactions to negative feedback than men do, but they may learn from this feedback and change their strategies in ways that can lead to more optimal performance and accomplishment of goals. Our study did not test this hypothesis, but future studies should sort out the advantages and disadvantages of being sensitive to the evaluations of others.

Summary

Although there is some evidence that women rely more than men on external feedback in making self-evaluations, we do not know whether such a tendency accounts for the sex differences in depression. Nor is there evidence for the claim that women invest their self-esteem in close relationships with men and that this investment contributes to their greater tendency to become depressed. Depression in women may be related to the quality of *ongoing* relationships, but men are more prone to depression than women following the loss of a close relationship.

Causal Attributions

There have been many studies of sex differences in attributional tendencies. In most of these studies, subjects are asked to work on puzzles or other cognitive tasks and then to make attributions for their success or failure at these tasks. Several studies have shown that women tend to make more external attributions than men, attributing outcomes to luck or task difficulty (Bar-Tal & Frieze, 1977; Deaux & Farris, 1977; Feather, 1969; Simon & Feather, 1973; Sweeney, Moreland & Gruber, 1982). Most studies have found that women are more likely than men to attribute both success *and* failure to external factors, especially luck (see Frieze et al., 1982; Sohn, 1982). According to attribution theory, the greater tendency of women than men to attribute successes to luck should make them less likely than men to take credit for their successes—a tendency that might contribute to women's problems in gaining recognition for their work and in increasing their job status. But this tendency for women to make external attributions should also make women less likely than men to blame themselves for their failures and thus less likely to react negatively to failures. That is, if a woman attributes her failures to bad luck but a man attributes his failures to lack of ability or some other internal attribution, then the woman should react less negatively to her failures than the man to his.

Sweeney, Moreland, and Gruber (1982) studied the relationship between sex differences in attributions for performance and sex differences in reactions to poor performance. They asked college students to explain their performance on an examination. They found that women who performed poorly on the test rated luck and task difficulty as more important factors in determining their failure than did men who performed poorly. (There were no sex differences in the importance assigned to ability and effort as causes of failure, or in any type of attribution for success.) The greater tendency of women than men to attribute failure to external causes was not associated with any sex differences in how subjects felt about their failure at the test, however: men and women showed equally negative reactions to failure.

The sex difference in external attributions in this study was slight, however, which may explain why this sex difference did not lead to sex differences in feelings about failure. Two separate reviews of the literature on sex differences in attributions have concluded that the tendency for women to rate external factors as important causes of events more often than men do is very slight, and that the results of different studies are inconsistent (Frieze et al., 1982; Sohn, 1982). In addition, the kinds of attributions for which studies do find sex differences (most often attributions to luck) are not the most common kind of attributions subjects give for events. Both men and women are most likely to attribute their performances to ability or effort. There is no consistent evidence for sex differences in the use of ability and effort attributions (Sohn, 1982).

The literature on sex differences in attributions has been criticized on many grounds (e.g., McHugh, Frieze & Hanusa, 1982). Most of the studies in this literature have asked subjects to make attributions for their performance on laboratory tasks such as anagrams or other puzzles. These tasks may be too artificial and the results of these studies may not mimic people's true behavior (Sweeney, Moreland & Gruber, 1982). Other critics have argued that these tasks could be construed as masculine-typed and that women might not give maladaptive attributions for their performances if feminine-typed tasks were used (McHugh, Frieze & Hanusa, 1982). Weak support for this claim has been found in a few studies (e.g., Berndt, Berndt & Kaiser, 1982), in which women tended to give somewhat more self-enhancing attributions than men for outcomes in feminine-typed tasks such as social interaction, and men tended to give somewhat more self-enhancing attributions than women for outcomes in masculine-typed tasks such as competitive achievement situations. These sex differences in attributions were very small, were not always found when predicted, and were only marginally statistically significant, however.

Perhaps the most important problem with previous studies of sex differences in attributions in adults, however, is that almost all these studies have been conducted with college students. Because sex differences in most personality and behavioral variables (including depression) are diminished or nonexistent in college students, we cannot dismiss the possibility that this absence of a sex difference is an artifact of the population used in these studies.

Several studies on sex differences in attributions have been conducted with children (e.g., Eccles, Adler & Meece, 1984; Gitelson, Petersen & Tobin-Richards, 1982; Nicholls, 1975). It is often claimed that studies such as these have shown consistent and substantial sex differences in attributional tendencies, with girls making much more maladaptive attributions than boys. One of the studies most frequently cited to support this general conclusion was conducted by Nicholls (1975), who asked children to work on a series of difficult tasks, first in a practice session and then in a test session. Some problems were solvable, others unsolvable. After both the practice session and the test session, Nicholls asked the children whether they thought their success or failure resulted from luck, ability, effort, or task difficulty. Girls were significantly more likely than boys to attribute failures in the practice session to lack of ability, and boys were significantly more likely than girls to attribute failures in the practice session to bad luck. No significant sex differences were found in attributions to effort or task difficulty for the practice sessions, or in any type of attribution for the test sessions. Nor were there significant sex differences in the children's persistence at test tasks: despite the differences in boys' and girls' attributions about their performance on practice tasks, boys did not persist more at actual test tasks than girls did.

Many other studies of sex differences in children's attributions have found no evidence that girls make more maladaptive attributions than boys (e.g., Parsons et al., 1982). Indeed, my colleagues and I found that boys showed a much more maladaptive explanatory style than girls (Nolen-Hoeksema, Girgus & Seligman, in press; see also Chapter 7). We asked elementary school children to make attributions for a wide variety of academic, social, and athletic events and found that boys were much more likely than girls to make pessimistic, self-derogatory attributions for negative outcomes. This result is exactly what the reformulated learned helplessness theory would predict, given that boys tend to show more depression and achievement problems before puberty than girls. That is, claims made on the basis of previous studies that girls are much more likely than boys to give maladaptive attributions (and as a result to show helpless behaviors following failure) always stood in contradiction to the well-established tendency for *boys* to have more achievement problems and emotional problems than girls.

We are still left with the question of why some previous studies have found that girls make more maladaptive attributions than boys, and our study and other studies have found either no sex differences in attributions in children or that boys are more maladaptive than girls in their attributional biases. There are at least three explanations for the differences between the results my colleagues and I found and the results of other studies of sex differences in children's attributions. First, the methods of assessing explanatory tendencies in our study and the methods in previous studies were different. In previous studies, children were asked to explain their performance on cognitive tasks such as anagrams. In our study, however, children were asked to explain events in a number of domains, including schoolwork, peer relationships, family relationships, and extracurricular activities. Girls may give more maladaptive explanations than boys for academic successes and failures, but boys' explanations for bad events in most other domains are *much* more maladaptive than girls'. Eccles and colleagues (1984) found that when children are asked for their explanations for their performance both in feminine-typed subjects such as English and in masculine-typed subjects such as math, the children show no sex differences in explanatory tendencies. Thus the tendency seen in the achievement motivation studies for girls to give more maladaptive explanations than boys is apparently confined to a narrow range of cognitive tasks.

Second, in previous studies children were usually asked to voice their attributions for their performance to an experimenter. In our study, my colleagues and I used a questionnaire to assess attributions. It may be that girls are more modest and boys are more self-aggrandizing in the attributions they voice to an adult, and that boys reveal their more pessimistic explanatory tendencies on an anonymous questionnaire. That is, girls may be more self-confident and boys less self-confident than they admit in a public-disclosure setting such as a lab study.

Third, in most previous achievement motivation studies children were asked whether their success or failure at a task resulted from task difficulty/ease, effort, luck, or ability. Frieze and Snyder (1980) have shown that when children are given the opportunity to voice attributions for their performance spontaneously, they almost never cite luck and often make attributions other than the typical four, such as wanting to do well. This finding suggests that forcing children to choose from among the traditional four attributions for their performance may lead to a distorted picture of children's true attributional tendencies. In our study, children were asked to consider a wide variety of attributions for different events, with the goal of assessing children's tendencies to choose internal versus external, stable versus unstable, and global versus specific attributions. Our results indicate that, when given more opportunity to exercise their attributional biases, boys reveal a more pessimistic bias than girls do.

In summary, the hypothesis that sex differences in depression result in part from sex differences in attributional styles has received support in some studies of children. Boys are more likely than girls to be depressed, and boys show more maladaptive attributional styles than girls. The evidence for this hypothesis from studies of adults is inconclusive, however, largely because most studies have been conducted with college students. These studies show little consistent evidence for sex differences in attributional tendencies, but there is also little evidence for sex differences in depression in college students. We clearly need a study of sex differences in attributional styles and related sex differences in depression among the general adult population.

Conclusions

In this chapter I have examined various claims that sex differences in certain personality characteristics lead to sex differences in depression—specifically the claims that females are less assertive than males, more likely than males to internalize hostility, more dependent than males on others, and more likely than males to blame themselves and make maladaptive attributions for events. Each of these characteristics has been said to make women more vulnerable than men to depression. There is evidence that women tend to be less physically aggressive than men, but little evidence that females are generally more nonassertive and passive or that they have a strong tendency to avoid conflict and internalize hostility. Indeed, women appear to be more likely than men to confront conflictual situations, at least within marital relationships.

There is some evidence that women are more reactive than men to the evaluations others make of them, but no evidence that women are more dependent than men on love relationships for their emotional well-being. Indeed, males appear to have stronger negative emotional reactions to losses of relationships than do females. Several studies have revealed few if any consistent sex differences in the kinds of attributions males and females make for events. The most salient feature of the literature reviewed here, however, is the absence of evidence for some of the most commonly held beliefs about sex differences in personality: that women are less assertive, more dependent, and have worse attributional styles than men.

One reason that such beliefs persist may be that journals and other media tend to be biased toward publishing studies that find sex differences in the variable of interest. In addition, authors of such articles may be prone to emphasize these differences, even when they are very small, using language that suggests much bigger differences. For example, a study by Dweck and Repucci (1973) is often cited as showing sex differences in attributions for failure and in the tendency to become helpless. Dweck and Repucci conducted a typical helplessness experiment in which children worked on solvable and unsolvable puzzles. The children's persistence at the solvable puzzles and their expectations of success were taken as measures of helplessness in the face of frustration. The children were also asked to complete a questionnaire that assessed their tendency to attribute successes and failures to internal or external causes, and specifically to ability or effort. In reporting the results of this study, Dweck and Repucci did not mention any sex differences in persistence at the task or in expectations of success. Some of their data appear to indicate that the girls in this study solved the puzzles faster than the boys, although Dweck and Repucci did not mention this difference in the text. In describing the analyses of subjects' attributions for their performance, Dweck and Repucci reported that statistical tests revealed no significant sex differences in the choice of internal attributions for failure of success, in the tendency to attribute success to ability or to effort, or in the tendency to attribute failure to lack of ability. There was a significant sex difference in the tendency to attribute failure to effort, however: boys were more likely to attribute their failures to lack of effort than were girls.

In their discussion of the results of this study, Dweck and Repucci did not mention that there were no sex differences in any of the helplessness measures or that there were sex differences in only one of the attributional measures. Instead, they *highlighted* the one sex difference in attributional tendencies, suggesting that "the fact that . . . female subjects were less likely to internally attribute failure to lack of effort than their male counterparts suggests that females might be more prone to deterioration of performance in the face of failure" (1973, p. 116). Yet the authors reported no sex differences in performance deterioration among their results. It is therefore even more puzzling that the authors went on to state that "the data indicate a slight tendency for females to succumb to the effects of low expectancies, and for the females who slowed down to do so to a greater extent than the males" (1973, p. 116). Dweck and Repucci acknowledged that these sex differences did not approach significance in this experiment, but we are left wondering why they mentioned these data in the discussion section but did not report them in their entirety anywhere in the paper. Nevertheless, such overstated claims about sex differences in helplessness and attributions have influenced further studies and reviews of the literature.

Clinicians and social scientists sometimes argue that laboratory studies are too insensitive to detect sex differences in personality (e.g., Block, 1976; Chodorow, 1978). In their work with nonstudents —and perhaps with psychiatric patients in particular—these clinicians and social scientists may see plenty of evidence of sex differences in personality. For example, most women who seek treatment for depression may have significant problems with assertiveness or dependency, whereas depressed men may carry different concerns into therapy.

Although we should not dismiss clinical experience as an important source of information about the different types of problems men and women face, we must be cautious about basing any theories of men's and women's personalities on such information. Like other researchers, clinicians are vulnerable to the biases that may lead them to gather evidence in such a way as to bolster their initial hypothesis about a situation (Chapman & Chapman, 1969). Clinicians who begin with the assumption that there are differences in men's and women's personalities may use this assumption to guide their search for information about the causes of depression in their male and female clients. They may look for signs that a woman who is depressed tends to be nonassertive or dependent, for example, while ignoring potential sources of depression in women that do not fit common beliefs. Thus, we should insist on clear evidence from objective studies of the causes of depression in men and women that the sex differences in depression are due to sex differences in personality traits.

CHAPTER SEVEN

Sex Differences in Responses to Depression

The explanation for sex differences in depression that I discuss in this chapter is based on my own work on individuals' responses to their own symptoms of depression (Nolen-Hoeksema, 1987). There appear to be individual differences in the ways people respond to symptoms of depression. Some people tend to focus inward on their symptoms and on the possible causes and consequences of those symptoms; I have labeled this approach a *ruminative* style of responding to depression. Others try to distract themselves from their symptoms through activity or other means; I have labeled this approach a *distracting* style of responding to depression. There is increasing evidence that people who engage in ruminative responses to depression tend to have longer and perhaps more severe episodes of depression than people who engage in distracting responses to depression. In addition, women appear more likely than men to show a ruminative response style for depression, and men appear more likely to show a distracting response style for depression. Thus the sex differences in depression may be attributable, at least in part, to sex differences in responses to depression.

Response Styles for Depression

The response styles theory of depression (Nolen-Hoeksema, 1987) proposes that the way a person responds to depressive symptoms will affect the duration and severity of depressive episodes. People who engage in ruminative responses to depressed mood will experience amplification and prolonging of the mood, whereas people who engage in distracting responses to depressed mood will experience relief from that mood. Ruminative responses are cognitions and behaviors that repetitively focus the depressed person's attention on her symptoms and the possible causes and consequences of those symptoms. Examples of ruminative responses to depression are isolating oneself to think about how one is feeling, writing in a diary about how one is feeling, and repeatedly telling others how bad one feels. The focus of ruminations, as described here, is on one's symptoms of depression (sadness, apathy, fatigue) and not on an external event—although the person may consider recent events as possible causes of the symptoms. Ruminations are one type of response to depression, one way of attempting to regulate one's mood, rather than part of a generally obsessive style of thinking about events and decisions in one's life.

People who focus on their depressive symptoms may be trying to alter those symptoms. In fact, most people may ruminate for at least a short while when they experience symptoms of depression, just as most people examine a cut or bruise to determine its severity. Depression is an unpleasant state, and people may typically turn their attention inward when they become depressed in an attempt to evaluate and remove this state (see Carver & Scheier, 1981; Duval & Wicklund, 1972). According to the response style theory, however, rumination is often not helpful, and people who continue to ruminate for extended periods will experience an amplification of their depression.

Distracting responses are cognitions and behaviors designed to draw a person's attention away from his symptoms of depression. (Examples include engaging in an activity with friends and working on a hobby that takes concentration.) There are a few responses to depression that may be distracting but are also inherently maladaptive because they can lead to negative consequences for a person's health and social and occupational functioning. (An example is engaging in violence or reckless behavior such as driving quickly on mountain roads.) Although these behaviors may distract a person and help to relieve depression in the short run, they often lead to more depression in the long run because of their consequences. There are many distracting responses to depression that are not inherently dangerous, however, and these responses are the focus of the response styles theory. Distracting responses to depression must also be distinguished from what some researchers call the *repressive defense style* (see Weinberger, in press). This style is characterized by a lack of awareness of one's own experiences of distress and a denial that one ever feels distress. By contrast, the response styles theory defines distracting responses to depression as attempts to regulate or relieve depressive symptoms through certain activities. By definition, then, a person must acknowledge that he is experiencing depression before it can be said that he is using distracting responses.

There are at least three mechanisms, described in detail below, whereby rumination enhances and prolongs a depressed mood. First, depressed mood appears to create a negative bias in people's thinking such that their memories and inferences tend to be pessimistic (Bower, 1981; Teasdale, 1985). Because of this effect of mood on thinking, people who think about the causes and consequences of their depressed moods while they are depressed will be more likely to reach negative conclusions concerning these issues than people who distract themselves from their mood and wait until the depressed mood has lifted to consider these issues. A second mechanism by which rumination increases depression was stated by Zullow and colleagues (Zullow, 1984; Zullow et al., 1988). They argued that the tendency to dwell on negative circumstances—their definition of rumination—enhances the effects of maladaptive cognitive styles because maladaptive cognitions are brought to mind relatively more often by rumination. Finally, rumination interferes with attention and concentration (Kuhl, 1981; Lewinsohn et al., 1985). This interference leads to increased failures and a greater sense of helplessness in controlling one's environment, factors that contribute in turn to depression. Engaging in activity to distract oneself when depressed, on the other hand, increases one's chances for controlling the environment and for obtaining positive reinforcers, thereby dampening an existing depressed mood.

Rumination Allows Depressed Mood to Affect Thinking

Most studies on the effects of negative mood on memory, learning, and problem-solving have been inspired by the semantic-network theory (see Bower, 1981; Clark & Isen, 1982; Ingram, 1984; Teasdale, 1983), which states that memories are often connected by associations with a person's mood at the time the memories were stored. Thus all memories associated with a negative mood (for example, memories of the death of a parent) are linked in a network. When people find themselves in the mood associated with these memories, the network containing the memories is activated, enhancing the probability of retrieving the memories. Other theorists have extended the semantic-network view to argue that negative beliefs or schemas about the self and the world are also more accessible when people are in negative moods (Pietromonaco & Markus, 1985; Teasdale, 1983). Thus when people are in negative moods, they may be more likely to use pessimistic beliefs about their own competence or about the goodness of the world to interpret ongoing events than when they are in positive moods. More recently, Schwarz and Clore (in press) have also argued that negative moods often influence people's evaluations of themselves, other people, or circumstances. That is, when asked to make evaluations, people ask themselves, "How do I feel about it?" If they are in a negative mood, they may decide that a negative evaluation is appropriate.

The great majority of studies testing these hypotheses have been conducted in laboratory settings. Sad mood is induced in one group of subjects with the help of sad music, sad stories, or hypnotic suggestion. Neutral and positive moods are induced in other groups of subjects. Then the different groups are compared on their attention to, learning of, and memory for mood-relevant materials (such as negatively toned words), their interpretations of events, and other cognitive tasks. In support of the idea that moods affect thinking, studies have found that, compared to people in neutral or happy moods, people in sad moods show the following behaviors: (1) they have selective recall of sad memories from their lives (Bower, 1981; Clark & Teasdale, 1982; Teasdale & Fogarty, 1979); (2) they remember more false negative evaluations of them made by an experimenter (Natale & Hantas, 1982); (3) they interpret their own behavior in social interactions more negatively (Forgas, Bower & Krantz, 1984); (4) they rate their life satisfaction as low (Schwarz & Clore, in press); (5) they form more negative impressions of others (Forgas & Bower, 1987); (6) they make more negative interpretations of thematic apperception test (TAT) cards (Bower, 1981); and (7) they are less likely to show an optimistic illusion of control over outcomes (Blaney, 1986).

Based on results such as these, Teasdale and colleagues (Teasdale, 1983, 1988; Teasdale & Fogarty, 1979) have argued that one way depression is maintained in depressed people is through the effects of depressive mood on memory, information-seeking, and problem-solving. Greater access to unhappy memories, enhanced sensitivity to negative information about one's current situation, the probability of making negative interpretations about that situation, and interference with problem-solving resulting from depressed mood can all exacerbate the mood. Increasingly negative mood leads to increasingly negative thinking, and a vicious circle between mood and thinking develops, spiraling the depressive into deeper and deeper depression.

Evidence that rumination increases a person's chances of falling into this vicious circle comes from studies of the effects of self-focus on cognition and depressed mood. For example, Pyszczynski, Holt, and Greenberg (1987) induced self-focus in one group of depressed subjects by having them write a story about themselves and other-focus in another group of depressed subjects by having them write a story about others. The self-focused depressives were more pessimistic in their expectancies for future events than a group of nondepressed subjects, but the other-focused depressives were no more pessimistic than the nondepressed subjects (see also Carver, Blaney & Scheier, 1979). Self-focus also appears to increase the probability that a person will make an internal attribution for negative events (Buss & Scheier, 1976; Duval & Wicklund, 1972; Fenigstein & Levine, 1984; Hull & Levy, 1979). In addition, Turner (1978) found that persons high in self-consciousness described themselves more in terms of stable and global traits than those low in self-consciousness. Self-focused people should experience increased hopelessness about their ability to control bad events or moods to the extent that they blame those events or moods on their own negative traits (Abramson, Seligman & Teasdale, 1978).

Studies also indicate that self-focus enhances depressed mood. Depressed psychiatric patients report more negative mood when made self-aware by the presence of a mirror than do depressed patients who are not made self-aware (Gibbons et al., 1985). Similarly, having subjects self-focus while being put through a depression-inducing procedure such as reading lists of increasingly negative traits results in significantly greater increases in depressed mood than having subjects read the same list of traits without the encouragement to self-focus (Scheier & Carver, 1977; Scheier, Carver & Gibbons, 1979). These studies indicate that self-focus enhances existing depressed moods, perhaps by making it more likely that a person will engage in negatively biased information-processing. A primary characteristic of rumination, as defined by the response styles theory, is self-focus. Thus the results of these studies lend credence to the prediction that rumination will contribute to an existing depressed mood because the mood will negatively bias the content of the person's thoughts about her depression.

Rumination Enhances the Effects of a
Pessimistic Explanatory Style

Many studies have found that people with a pessimistic style of explaining the negative events in their lives are at increased risk for depression (see Abramson, Seligman & Teasdale, 1978; Peterson & Seligman, 1984). Zullow and colleagues (Zullow, 1984; Zullow et al., 1988) have argued that the effects of a pessimistic explanatory style are enhanced by a tendency to ruminate over negative events because rumination brings the pessimistic explanations to mind frequently. Zullow (1984) found that college students who showed both a tendency to ruminate over negative events and a pessimistic style of explaining events were more prone to depression than were students who only showed rumination or a tendency toward pessimistic explanations.

Rumination probably also enhances the effects of other maladaptive cognitive styles. Beck and colleagues (Beck et al., 1979) have argued that depressed people have negative views of themselves, the world, and the future and tend to interpret events in ways that support their negative views. In people who are prone to episodes of depression, endorsement of negative beliefs and attitudes appears to increase as level of depression increases (Miranda & Persons, 1988). This trend may occur because people who are prone to depression tend to ruminate in response to their initial symptoms of depression, thereby enhancing the activation of their negative beliefs. Although this hypothesis has not been tested directly, Teasdale and colleagues have found that depression-prone people who are taught to distract themselves from their negative thoughts show a quicker recovery

from depression than people not taught to use a distracting response
style (see Teasdale, 1985).

Rumination Interferes with Instrumental Behavior

Lewinsohn and colleagues (1985) have suggested that rumination
exacerbates depression by interfering with instrumental behavior.
Support for this argument comes from a study by Kuhl (1981),
who asked subjects what they would do in response to a number of hypothetical negative events. He labeled subjects who chose
such responses as "I would think about what just happened" as
state-oriented and subjects who chose such responses as "I would
do something to correct the situation" as *action-oriented*. Subjects
were given a series of unsolvable puzzles. State-oriented subjects
showed more helpless behaviors on subsequent tasks than did action-
oriented subjects. Kuhl found that state-oriented subjects' helplessness occurred not because they came into the experiment with a
generalized belief that they could not succeed, but rather because
their excessive ruminations about their failures at the first set of tasks
appeared to interfere with learning in subsequent tasks. With regard
to depression, Kuhl argued that state-orientation may explain certain symptoms of depression: if a person thinks obsessively about
the problems associated with his depression, even simple behaviors
such as eating may be inhibited.

A number of other studies of achievement-related behaviors have
found that poor performance on exams is associated with the tendency to ruminate on self-related, task-irrelevant cognitions (e.g.,
Brockner & Hulton, 1978; Heckhausen, 1980; Sarason, 1975). In
addition, poor performance leads to lowered expectancies for future
success, lowered self-evaluations, lowered motivation to meet new
challenges, and worse performance on subsequent tasks. Laboratory
studies also have shown that the simple act of self-focusing interferes with subjects' performance on cognitive tasks and with their
effective interpersonal behavior (Coyne, Metalsky & Lavelle, 1980;
Fenigstein, 1979; Strack et al., 1985). These studies thus indicate that
the kind of self-focus involved in ruminative responses to depression
interferes with optimal behavior and that the resulting poor performance is associated with lowered self-evaluations and expectancies
for future successes and therefore with the accumulation of addi-

tional failures. Such conditions can contribute to a person's sense of helplessness and thereby exacerbate his depression (Seligman, 1975).

Responses and the Duration of Depressed Mood: Tests of Predictions

The most straightforward prediction following from the response styles theory is that people who engage in ruminative responses to depression will suffer longer periods of depression than those who engage in distracting responses. The results of studies conducted by my colleagues and me support this prediction. In a laboratory study of the response styles theory, Morrow and I first induced depressed mood in subjects by playing sad music and having subjects imagine their mother dying (Morrow & Nolen-Hoeksema, 1989). After the mood-induction procedure, subjects engaged in one of four randomly assigned activities designed as simulations of response styles for depressed moods. These activities were either ruminative or distracting, and either passive or active. In the ruminative/passive group, subjects silently read sentences such as "I wonder why things turn out the way they do," "Some days I **feel** upset," and "I want to **understand** things." These sentences were presented separately on cards, and subjects were told to read through them and focus on the one word in each sentence that was printed in boldface. Subjects in the distracting/passive group also read sentences printed on cards, but these sentences stated facts such as "Napa Valley is in **northern** California" and "Canada's biggest industry is **lumber**." Again, subjects were told to read the sentences and concentrate on the one word in each sentence that was printed in boldface.

In the ruminative/active group, subjects were given cards printed with adjectives such as *dissatisfied, depressed, confident*, and *independent* and were asked to sort the cards into piles according to how well each adjective described them. Markers for the piles were positioned around a 10-by-12-foot room so that subjects had to walk around the room in the process of sorting, thereby being more physically active than subjects in the passive groups. In the distracting/active group, subjects also sorted cards into piles around the room, but the cards were printed with the names of countries, and the subjects were told to sort them into groups according to industrialization.

Our primary prediction was that subjects in the distracting groups would show greater decreases in depressive mood than would the subjects in the ruminative groups. Our weaker prediction was that activity would decrease depression more than would passivity, largely because activity aids in distraction. Our results strongly supported these predictions. The greatest remediation of depressive mood occurred in the subjects in the distracting/active group, followed in order by the subjects in the distracting/passive group, the ruminative/active group, and the ruminative/passive group. Indeed, subjects in the distracting/active group showed levels of depressive mood lower than the levels they had shown *before* the mood-induction procedure. By contrast, subjects in the two ruminative groups were still significantly more depressed than they had been before the mood-induction procedure.

In a field study of the response styles theory, Morrow, Fredrickson, and I asked 49 undergraduates to keep diaries in which they recorded two times per week whether they had felt depressed at any time in the previous three to four days and, if so, what they did in response to their depressive symptoms (Nolen-Hoeksema, Morrow & Fredrickson, 1989a). Subjects indicated how they had responded to their symptoms by checking off items on a list of eight distracting and eight ruminative responses. Examples of distracting responses were "I did something I enjoyed, like a sport or going to a movie" and "I talked to friends about anything but my mood." Examples of ruminative responses were "I tried to determine why I felt the way I did" and "I talked to friends about how I was feeling."

We first identified all new onsets of depression of at least moderate severity; that is, we identified subjects who said they had felt at least moderately depressed in the last few days but had not reported feeling depressed on the previous report. These subjects were then divided into two groups according to whether their responses were more ruminative or more distracting. The initial levels of depression in these two types of episodes were not different, largely because we selected episodes of at least moderate depression. But when subjects reported ruminating in response to their initial symptoms, they continued to report at least moderate levels of depression for significantly longer than they did when they had distracted themselves from their initial symptoms. In addition, when we examined all times at which subjects reported experiencing a depressed mood in the previous few days, the extent to which subjects ruminated rather than distracted was significantly correlated with the average level of severity of their depression.

Sex Differences in Responses to Depression

I have argued that one factor contributing to sex differences in depression is sex differences in responses to depression (Nolen-Hoeksema, 1987). Women appear more likely to engage in ruminative responses when depressed, thereby amplifying their symptoms and extending depressive episodes. Men appear more likely to distract themselves from depressed moods, thereby dampening their symptoms. Evidence for sex differences in responses to depression comes from a number of self-report studies. For example, Morrow, Fredrickson, and I presented college students with a list of ruminative and distracting responses for depression and asked them to recall the last time they felt depressed and to rate how frequently they engaged in each of the behaviors or thoughts on the list when depressed (Nolen-Hoeksema, Morrow & Fredrickson, 1989b). Respondents were encouraged to rate the items according to what they generally did, not what they thought they *should* do. Examples of ruminative responses included "tried to determine why I felt the way I did" and "tried to analyze my mood." Examples of distracting responses included "did something I enjoyed, such as playing a sport or a musical instrument, or going to a movie" and "decided not to concern myself with the mood." The women in this sample rated themselves significantly more likely to engage in ruminative responses than did the men; conversely, the men rated themselves significantly more likely to distract themselves when depressed than did the women.

Similar sex differences in responses to depressed mood have been found in other studies (Chino & Funabiki, 1984; Funabiki et al., 1980; Kleinke, Staneski & Mason, 1982). For example, Kleinke, Staneski, and Mason (1982) found that male college students were more likely than female college students to say they coped with depression by thinking about other things, ignoring their problems, or engaging in physical activity. Female students were more likely to say they cut down on responsibilities and activities when depressed, confronted their feelings, and blamed themselves for being depressed. Evidence that women tend to ruminate when depressed whereas men tend to distract themselves also comes from the diary study described earlier (Nolen-Hoeksema, Morrow & Fredrickson, 1989a). When we examined subjects' responses to periods of depressed mood of at least moderate severity, we found that women were more likely than men to say they had ruminated in response to their depressive symptoms and that men were more likely than women to say they had distracted themselves. These sex differences in response styles were in turn associated with sex differences in depressive experiences. The average severity of the depressive symptoms reported by women was greater than that reported by men. Women also tended to report more severe depression at subsequent reports than men did.

Carstensen, Morrow, and Roberts (1988) also found evidence of sex differences in responses to negative emotion in a study of conflicts in 17 heterosexual couples. Each member of the couple called into an answering machine every time the couple had a conflict of some kind. Subjects were strictly instructed not to discuss their responses and to call in independently. If there were no conflicts between the couple, the subjects called in at the end of the day to report that fact. When subjects called in, they reported on the nature of the conflict, the primary emotion they had experienced in relation to the conflict, the severity of that emotion, and what they had done in response to that emotion. The women in these couples were more likely than the men to experience sadness in relation to the couples' conflicts and to focus on their emotion or to engage in some emotional expression in response to their negative emotion. The men were more likely than the women to engage in distraction or to say that they had decided not to concern themselves with their mood.

Butler and I conducted another study on sex differences in response styles (Butler & Nolen-Hoeksema, 1988). This study was a laboratory analog study in which sad mood was induced in subjects and the subjects were then given a choice of doing either an emotion-focused, ruminative task or a distracting task. The emotion-focused task involved ranking a list of emotions according to how well they described the subject's current mood. The distracting task involved ranking a list of nations by level of industrialization. We predicted that the women would choose the ruminative task when depressed and that the men would choose the distracting task. Indeed, 70 percent of the women chose the emotion-focused task, and

57 percent of the men chose the distracting task. Thus data are accumulating to show that women are more likely than men to engage in emotion-focused, ruminative responses to depression. Men are somewhat more likely than women to chose to distract themselves when depressed. In addition, these sex differences in response styles are associated with sex differences in depressive experiences.

Although women's greater tendency to ruminate may lead them to suffer increased rates of depression, men's tendency to distract themselves, when taken to maladaptive extremes, may also lead to certain types of pathology. Men are much more likely than women to engage in some inherently maladaptive activities, perhaps in an effort to distract themselves from negative moods. For example, in questionnaire studies, men appear more likely than women to say that they respond to depressed moods by drinking alcohol (see Nolen-Hoeksema, 1987). People who rely on alcohol as a method of coping with emotions are at increased risk for becoming abusers (Cooper, Russell & George, 1988; Farber, Khavari & Douglass, 1980). In addition, Gjerde, Block, and Block (1988) found that dysthymic adolescent males appeared aggressive, antagonistic, and disagreeable, whereas dysthymic adolescent females appeared ruminating, unconventional, and ego-brittle. Some researchers have argued that sociopathy and alcoholism are the male manifestations of an underlying depression (Williams & Spitzer, 1983). By contrast, I would argue that women and men learn different ways of responding to negative moods and that these differences in response styles lead to sex differences in propensities toward certain types of disorders.

Why are women more ruminative and men more distracting in their responses to depressed moods? Being active and controlling one's moods are part of the masculine stereotype; being inactive and emotional are part of the feminine stereotype. From a very young age, children describe themselves and others in terms of sex-role stereotypes, even before their actual behavior conforms to the appropriate stereotype (Brown, 1956; Nadelman, 1974). Parents reinforce certain behaviors consistent with these stereotypes, showing particular concern that boys not exhibit feminine or "sissy" behaviors (Goodenough, 1957; Maccoby & Jacklin, 1974). Thus the distracting, active response style of men may result simply from acceptance of the sanctions against emotionality in males. Rumination in women may not be specifically encouraged by parents or others—

parents and teachers do not appear to reward girls for passivity and contemplation—but may result instead from the fact that girls are not rewarded for activity as much as boys are (Dweck et al., 1978; Serbin et al., 1973). In addition, because women are told that they are naturally emotional, they may come to believe that depressed moods are unavoidable and cannot be dismissed easily when present (see Chapter 9). Such an attitude would decrease the probability of women taking actions to distract themselves from their moods.

Another reason men may be more likely than women to distract themselves when depressed is that they experience greater negative physiological arousal in conjunction with a depressed mood than women do and want to decrease this arousal as quickly as possible. Gottman and Levenson (in press) review several studies indicating that men show greater autonomic nervous system and endocrine system activation in relation to conflict and negative mood than do women, and that they experience this heightened arousal as negative. Gottman and Levenson argue that the well-documented tendencies for men to use avoidance and withdrawal to end conflict quickly, in contrast to women's desire to remain engaged in a conflictual discussion until resolution, might be attributed to sex differences in levels of physiological arousal during conflict.

In summary, one source of sex differences in depression may be sex differences in response styles for depression. Women appear more likely than men to engage in the ruminative response style and in turn are more likely to show depression. But men's greater tendency to distract themselves in response to depression, when taken to the extreme, may predispose them to alcoholism and sociopathy. Neither constant rumination nor constant distraction is an optimal way of responding to distress.

Explaining the Epidemiological Trends in Sex Differences in Depression

Can the response styles theory explain variations in sex differences in depression across cultural groups, age groups, and history? Among adults of retirement age and older, we often find either no sex differences in rates of depression or a tendency for men to be depressed more than women. This decrease in the sex differences in depression appears to occur because the rates of depression in men rise relative to the rates in women, which tend to remain stable or perhaps even decline in older age (see Chapter 2). One reason that rates of depression rise in older men may be that retired men no longer have work to distract them from depression when it arises. That is, men may have a ready-made source of distraction in the daily demands of the workplace. When they retire, men lose this distractor and may thus have more opportunity to ruminate when they feel depressed. By contrast, women who are not employed outside the home have less structure and fewer built-in distractions during the day (at least once their children are in school or have left home) and thus have more opportunity to ruminate. When a couple reaches retirement age, the amount of structure and distraction in a homemaker's day does not decrease. Indeed, she may have more distraction than before because her husband is now at home all day. This shift may explain why rates of depression in women remain stable or decrease with age, whereas rates of depression in men increase with age.

A second epidemiological trend in rates of depression is that more recent generations have much higher rates of depression than previous ones (Klerman et al., 1985). In addition, the sex differences in rates of depression are narrowing as more men are becoming depressed than in the past. Seligman (1988) argued that this cohort effect in depression is the result of a growing obsession with the self; the needs of others and one's obligations to society or to God are increasingly considered secondary to self-exploration by generations born since 1950. The disadvantage of this trend, Seligman says, is that a person who becomes desolate or depressed has no social network or God to turn to. I would suggest a variation on Seligman's idea: it may be that an increased focus on the self causes a greater tendency for people to ruminate when depressed, to turn inward, and to think a lot about the causes and consequences of their negative emotions. Such focus on emotion is certainly encouraged by much of the popular psychology found in the contemporary media. And although many people benefit from a greater understanding of their own emotional life, some people—including perhaps increasing numbers of men—may develop a ruminative response style as a result of this encouragement to focus on emotion. Thus at least one source of the increases in rates of depression in recent generations, particularly among men, may be an increase in ruminative response style.

This idea that the generations who grew up with pop psychology are more prone to ruminate when depressed may also help to explain why we see much lower levels of unipolar depression and no sex differences in depression in some nonmodern cultures. The Old Order Amish live as though they were still in the nineteenth century, with few modern conveniences and certainly no television or radio. More important, their religion requires a commitment to the community rather than to the self: self-centeredness in any form is considered a sin. The evidence of much lower rates of unipolar depression—and of a complete lack of sex differences in unipolar depression—among the Amish (Egeland & Hostetter, 1983) may be explained partly as follows: perhaps ruminative responses to depression are uncommon among the Amish because such responses would be considered ungodly and would interfere with each person's duties to the community.

What Stops Depression?

How does a ruminator who is depressed recover from her depression? First it is necessary for her to be distracted from her rumination long enough that the mood is substantially relieved. This distraction can be generated by the ruminator herself, by increasing work or physical activity, consciously talking with another person about anything but her mood, doing something she enjoys, or purposely focusing on positive aspects of her life. Simply increasing the number of pleasant activities a depressed person engages in may not relieve depression, however. That is, one can go jogging to distract oneself from one's mood, or one can go jogging and ruminate while jogging. Our studies have found only a weak relationship between simple increases in activity and relief of depression. But subjects who engage in activities specifically to distract themselves do show decreases in depression (Morrow & Nolen-Hoeksema, 1989; Needles, 1987).

Friends can also provide distraction from ruminations. Some studies find that people with few social supports tend to have more difficulty recovering from depression than do those with social supports (Cohen & Willis, 1985). This tendency may occur because the isolation that results from having few friends and relatives makes it easy to ruminate. By contrast, depressed people with many friends and relatives may be more likely to be drawn out of isolated ruminating and forced to engage in activity, or perhaps to square their ruminations against reality. When friends and relatives become either ruminating partners or the source of stress that leads to further rumination, however, they may actually contribute to the depressed person's negative mood.

Two caveats should accompany the hypothesis that ruminators who begin to or are induced to distract themselves will show relief from depression. The first, discussed earlier, is that inherently maladaptive distracting activities, such as excessive alcohol or drug consumption, violence against others, or reckless activities, will in the long run only contribute to more depression because of their negative consequences on a person's social relationships and occupational functioning. Although such activities may distract a depressed individual from her mood in the short run, they may be associated in the long run with increased levels of depression. The second caveat is related to the first. Distraction may help to relieve the symptoms of a current depressive episode, but if the onset of such episodes is frequent and the depressed person never makes an attempt to understand the causes of the episodes once symptoms have abated, she may be at increased risk for future—and potentially severe—episodes. The implied prescription is that once one's depressed mood has abated somewhat, it is wise to consider the sources of that mood. Sometimes the cause will be clear—"I became depressed because a colleague made a snide remark about my work and I began to worry about my chances for tenure"—and understanding the cause may help reduce the risk of depression in similar situations in the future. But searching for the causes of one's depression should wait until the depressed mood has lifted somewhat, lest the mood bias one's search. In the case of the colleague's remark, for example, searching for causes before the depressed mood has passed might lead one to attribute depression incorrectly to one's own incompetence or lack of ability. The causes of a depressive episode or a series of depressive episodes will not always be clear, however. It may be particularly important for people not to ruminate about the causes of their depression while still depressed if the causes are ambiguous. Without a focal point for rumination, depressed people may be able to find many "problems" in life to which to attribute their depression, when in fact these areas of their lives do not appear problematic unless depressed mood is influencing their thinking.

Another tactic that can lead a ruminator to stop ruminating, and thus to become less depressed, is to change the content of the ruminations. Changes in the environment can change the content of ruminations. For example, consider a man who is depressed and ruminating about the fact that he does not have a job and cannot support his family. If he finds a job, the change in his situation may remove his focus of rumination and lead to the remission of his depression. The role of simple changes in daily life—getting a new boss, a difficult child leaving home for college, a spouse offering to take on additional household duties—has often been overlooked in the alleviation of depression. Such changes may challenge the ruminations of a depressed person—forcing him, for example, to reconsider the idea that he is incompetent in light of the realization that there may have been a mismatch between him and his boss.

The content of ruminations may also change when friends or therapists challenge the ruminator's ideas directly or provide explanatory schemes for the problems the ruminator is ruminating about. Indeed, the specific foci and techniques of different types of therapies for depression may be less important than the extent to which these therapies give the ruminator a sense of control over her ruminations. Cognitive therapy teaches the client how to control her ruminations by writing them down and challenging them with evidence. More insight-oriented therapies such as interpersonal therapy may give the client a sense of control over her ruminations by offering her both a cogent explanation of why she may become depressed and new skills for dealing with the sources of depression. Similarly, clients who receive drug therapy are given a biochemical explanation for their depression that may prevent them from ruminatively searching for other explanations. These three therapies have proven nearly equally effective in alleviating depression (Elkin et al., 1986), perhaps because they all give clients an understanding of their depression that helps to resolve their ruminations. Although this hypothesis has not been tested directly, Simons, Garfield, and Murphy (1984) found that depressed patients who responded well to treatment showed greater reductions in negative cognitions than patients who did not respond to treatment, regardless of whether they received antidepressant drugs or cognitive therapy.

Conclusions

I have argued that one determinant of the duration of a depressive episode is the type of responses people engage in when depressed. People who ruminate when depressed tend to remain depressed and may become more severely so than people who try to distract themselves from their depressive symptoms. Laboratory and field tests of this theory have supported the theory. In addition, the response styles theory appears to explain at some least of the sex differences and epidemiological trends in depression. Women tend to have a more ruminative response style than men and in turn are more likely to be depressed and to report longer periods of depression than men. But men's tendency to distract themselves from their depressed moods, when taken to extremes, may contribute to their greater vulnerability to other disorders, such as alcoholism.

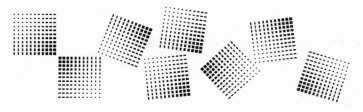

CHAPTER EIGHT

Sex Differences in Depression During Childhood and Adolescence

One of the most striking trends in the epidemiology of sex differences in depression is the switch in the direction of sex differences during adolescence. Before adolescence, boys are somewhat more likely than girls to be depressed, but by age 14 or 15, girls are much more likely than boys to be depressed. This chapter addresses two questions: why are preadolescent boys more vulnerable than preadolescent girls to depression? and what accounts for the appearance of a greater vulnerability to depression in girls than in boys during adolescence?

Boys' Greater Vulnerability to Depression Before Adolescence

Before adolescence boys show more of almost every type of psychopathology than girls, including adjustment reactions, antisocial disorders, anxiety disorders, gender identity disorders, learning disorders, psychotic disorders, and affective disorders (Eme, 1979). Only with anxiety disorders and affective disorders, however, do we see a switch in the ratio of boys to girls with the disorder during adolescence. Several explanations have been offered for boys' greater vulnerability to psychopathology, particularly depression, during childhood. First, boys may be constitutionally weaker than girls and thus more susceptible both to physical and psychological illness (Eme, 1979). There is ample evidence that boys are more vulnerable than girls to physical illness (Garai & Scheinfeld, 1968). Males suffer more birth defects than females do, 37 percent more males than females die in infancy, and boys are afflicted more by major diseases than girls are during childhood. It may be that boys' greater vulnerability to psychological disorders results from the same physiological weaknesses that cause them to be more vulnerable to physical disease.

A different biological explanation is that boys tend to have more irritable temperaments than girls and that this irritability puts them at risk for psychological disorder (Eme, 1979). In a review covering both his own ten years of work on temperament in infants and several other studies, Moss (1974) concluded that males are generally more irritable than females. It also appears that children who are emotionally tense, whose behavior is difficult to change, who have irregular eating, sleeping, and bowel habits, or who tend to be irritable and negative in mood are at relatively high risk for psychological disturbance. Thus if boys have more irritable temperaments than girls, they may also be at higher risk for psychopathology.

Another explanation of boys' greater vulnerability to depression and other psychopathology is that boys are more reactive to environmental stress (Eme, 1979). Several studies have shown that boys are more likely than girls to exhibit depression or behavior disturbances following parental discord or divorce (Hetherington, Cox & Cox, 1979; Nolen-Hoeksema, Girgus & Seligman, 1989; Rutter, 1970). Similarly, males are more likely than females to show psychiatric disorder when they discover they have been adopted or when they experience a change in the location of their home (Hersov, 1977). Thus boys appear to have more negative reactions to environmental stressors than girls, sometimes to the point of developing a psychological disorder.

This greater reactivity to stress in boys may result from their weaker physiology or from their greater irritability. Thus psychological stress may have greater impact on boys than girls for the same reasons that physical hazards such as birth traumas have greater impact on boys than girls—namely because boys are physiologically weaker and more immature than girls. An alternate explanation for boys' greater reactivity to psychological stress is that boys receive less support and more responsibility from adults during times of stress than girls receive (Rutter, 1970). For example, boys are sometimes asked to be "the man of the house" when parents separate and custody of the children is granted to the mother. Boys are also told to be "strong" and "act like a man" rather than cry and ask for reassurance "like a girl" in times of stress. This lack of support for boys may have important consequences for their ability to adapt to stressful changes in their early lives. Although this is an important hypothesis, it remains largely untested (Eme, 1979).

In our study of elementary school children, my colleagues and I found that boys consistently show a much more maladaptive explanatory style than girls (Nolen-Hoeksema, Girgus & Seligman, in press). That is, boys are more likely than girls to say that bad events were their fault and were caused by factors that are stable in time and affect many areas of their lives. This trend is associated with a somewhat greater general tendency toward depression in boys than in girls, and with a much greater tendency for boys to react to their parents' divorce with depression. Thus boys' greater reactivity to stress may result in part from a more maladaptive explanatory style.

Yet another explanation for boys' greater rates of depression and other psychopathology is that adults' tolerance of deviance in boys is lower than their tolerance of deviance in girls. As a result, parents more often bring a son's psychopathology to the attention of clinicians than they do a daughter's psychopathology (Eme, 1979). Parents are less tolerant of a lack of persistence in their sons than in their daughters (Chess & Thomas, 1972). A study of hyperactivity in 74 children found that mothers of highly active boys were critical, disapproving, unaffectionate, and severe in their punishment (Battle & Lacey, 1972). Mothers of hyperactive girls, on the other hand, did not show more intolerance of their daughters than did mothers of girls who were not hyperactive. Although I know of no study of differences in adults' tolerance of boys' and girls' depressive behaviors, it may be that adults are less tolerant of behaviors such as passivity, crying, and self-reproach in boys than in girls because such behaviors violate the sex-role for boys (see Fagot, 1978). Yet studies of sex differences in depression among children in the general population, which do not rely on data from children being treated for depression, also show that boys are more likely than girls to be depressed (Nolen-Hoeksema, Girgus & Seligman, 1989). Thus adults may be less tolerant of depressive symptoms in boys than in girls, but this difference in tolerance does not explain why boys report more depression than girls on questionnaires.

Finally, parents' tendency to put more pressure on boys than on girls to achieve and to be assertive, while at the same time threatening boys with punishment for overstepping boundaries, may create stress for boys that predisposes them to neurotic disorders during childhood (Bardwick, 1971; Gove & Herb, 1974). There is evidence that parents put somewhat more pressure on boys to achieve than they put on girls, at least in the areas of math and science (Hoffman, 1977; Eccles, Adler & Meece, 1984). Parents also report that they have greater expectations of hard work and achievement from their sons than from their daughters.

In summary, various theorists have suggested that boys' greater vulnerability to depression and other psychopathology during childhood can be attributed to their weaker constitution, to a greater intolerance in adults of male deviance than of female deviance, to boys' greater reactivity to psychological stress, to their more maladaptive explanatory styles, and perhaps to a greater pressure by parents for boys to succeed. Each explanation deserves more research, but none of these explanations can account for the dramatic switch in sex differences in depression and anxiety during adolescence. There is no reason why these factors would not operate for adolescent boys as much as for preadolescent boys. Thus there must be additional influences causing females to begin to show so much more depression than males during adolescence.

The Changes of Adolescence

Adolescence is a period of rapid and often simultaneous physiological, environmental, and psychological changes, the most observable and researched of which are the physiological changes. The onset of puberty is difficult to determine for both boys and girls, and puberty can last for six to seven years. During puberty girls experience a rapid growth in height of approximately 10 inches and a gain in body fat of approximately 24 pounds (Warren, 1983). About age 9 or 10, girls experience a dramatic increase in estrogen and progesterone production. Menarche (the first menstrual period) occurs quite a bit later in girls' pubertal development: the average age of menarche in the United States is 12.8 years (National Center for Health Statistics, 1973), but age at onset varies in girls from about 10 to 15 (Faust, 1983). Menstrual cycles often are not regularized for two years following menarche (Faust, 1983). The timing of menarche and the regularity of menstrual cycles appear to be influenced by a number of biological and environmental factors, one of the most important of which is weight. Underweight, poorly nourished girls are at high risk for delay of menarche or cessation of menstruation once it occurs (Warren, 1983). Boys begin puberty an average of two years after girls (Warren, 1983). Boys' weight gain is in lean body mass and skeletal mass rather than in body fat. Mature males have 1.5 times as much muscle and skeletal mass as mature females and half as much body fat (Warren, 1983). There is considerable variation in boys' rates of development. For example, while maturation of the penis may be complete in some boys by age 14, for many boys it is not complete until age 17 or older (Warren, 1983).

Adolescence is also a period of substantial change in children's cognitive abilities. During middle childhood, children are in what Piaget (1954) called the stage of *concrete operational thought*. During this period, children tend to think in concrete terms about the world and themselves. For example, if you ask children age 8 to 10 to describe themselves, they will often mention their likes and dislikes, the activities they enjoy, the number of siblings they have, and so on (see Harter, 1983). Similarly, children of this age tend to accept without much question the values and explanations parents give them. In adolescence children move into what Piaget called the period of *formal operations*. During this period children's ability to think in abstract terms increases substantially: they shift from thinking about the real to thinking about the possible. As a consequence of this increased power of abstract reasoning, adolescents become very sensitive to the arbitrary nature of many of the beliefs they formerly held about the world and about themselves. They begin to think of themselves in terms of abstract psychological constructs, such as traits, rather than in terms of the more concrete characteristics they focused on in childhood (Harter, 1983). Adolescents' infamous obsession with questioning their parents' values and rules and questioning social and religious norms can also be attributed in part to their increase in abstract reasoning ability. In addition, adolescents tend to be quite introspective, becoming much more able to think about their own thinking (a process that Flavell [1979] has termed *metacognition*). Some developmentalists argue that this introspection results in great egocentrism in adolescents (Elkind, 1967). Adolescents often report feeling as though everyone is interested in what they are thinking.

There are substantial changes in the environment for many children as they reach adolescence. Most children move from a relatively structured elementary school where the teacher-to-student ratio is low to a less structured, often very large middle school or high school early in adolescence. Often many of a child's friends from elementary school will go to the same middle school or high school, but the child must still adapt to a new structure, more difficult courses that require increased self-discipline, and many new children. In addition, some children begin working for wages during adolescence, usually in mid- or late adolescence. They may work at a fast food store, for one of their parents, as a delivery person, or, in rural areas, doing field work. Taking on a job means large increases in self-discipline and decreases in time with friends, the responsibility of having money, and new opportunities for succeeding or failing. Finally, some children begin to date and to have sexual encounters early in adolescence. In a study conducted in 1979, the average age of first intercourse among girls was 16, and that age is presumed to have decreased over the last few years (Zelnik & Kantner, 1977). This study also found that among girls age 15 to 19, 50 percent reported having engaged in premarital intercourse. Among the boys in this survey, 56 percent had had intercourse by age 17, and over 40 percent had had intercourse before age 15. Thus sexual encounters are part of heterosexual relationships for at least half of adolescent males and females.

The many biological, cognitive, and environmental changes that occur during adolescence have been said to lead to great emotional turmoil for most adolescents. Erikson (1968) argued that adolescents go through an identity crisis during which they seek a satisfactory and stable self-concept. Anna Freud (1958) stated that during puberty boys experience a resurgence of Oedipal conflicts over their attraction to their mother and their fear of their father, and girls relive the conflict between their need for autonomy and their identification with their mother that they originally experienced during the pre-Oedipal period. Sociologists have argued that adolescents reach physical maturity (including the ability to procreate) before they are psychologically mature enough to cope with the pressures of physical maturity, and that this situation causes distress for many adolescents (Davis, 1940). In addition, parents respond to the adolescent's desire to break away from them by being overly protective, for they perceive the child as not being capable of handling the pressures of newfound sexuality. According to these theorists, this parent-child conflict results in rebellion and distress for most adolescents. Most of these theorists argue that it is natural for adolescents to experience emotional turmoil and distress and thus that we should worry about an adolescent who seems to be *un*disturbed.

Most empirical studies, however, find little evidence that adolescence is typically a time of great turmoil (Coleman, 1961; Douvan & Adelson, 1966; Offer, Ostrov & Howard, 1981; Rutter, 1979). Observational studies of actual interactions between parents and adolescents indicate that the frequency of conflicts and emotional distance does increase as adolescents go through puberty (Hill & Holmbeck, 1987; Steinberg, 1981). These increases tend to be small, however, and the conflicts tend to be over minor issues. In fact, adolescents themselves do not tend to view these conflicts as very serious. For example, Rutter and his colleagues (Rutter, Tizard & Whitmore, 1970) asked parents and teachers to provide behavioral ratings for all 2,303 adolescents on the Isle of Wight. From this total group, 200 adolescents were chosen randomly for interviews. The information obtained from these interviews suggests that for most adolescents, neither their relationship with their parents nor their self-concept was disturbed. About two-thirds of the adolescents reported that they *never* disagreed with their parents. Most of the disagreements that did occur between adolescents and parents were minor ones over clothes, hair, or going out. Similarly, a more recent study found that about 86 percent of 13- to 16-year-olds interviewed said that they felt their parents were happy with them most of the time (Offer, Ostrov & Howard, 1981). Thus only a small percentage of children seem to experience large increases in serious conflict with their parents during adolescence. Similarly, only a minority of children show substantial emotional instability during early adolescence. That is, although the rate of depression clearly increases from childhood to adolescence, depression seems to be a problem for a minority of adolescents. For those adolescents who are depressed, however, the depression appears to be much more stable than earlier theorists suggested. Kandel and Davies (1986) found a strong relationship between depression scores in a group of 14-year-olds and depression scores in the same subjects nine years later. This finding indicates that depression, when it does happen during adolescence, does not simply pass within a short time. It is clear, however, that there tend to be more girls than boys among children who do become depressed during adolescence.

The Impact of Biological Changes

As discussed in Chapter 3, the increase in production of ovarian hormones in girls at puberty does not directly account for increases in rates of depression in girls. Girls show somewhat elevated levels of depression during the initial activation of the endocrine system in the early stages of puberty, but levels of depression decline once hormonal production stabilizes (Brooks-Gunn & Warren, 1987). In searching for possible causes of the increases in depression in girls at puberty, we should not expect that these causes will be common to *all* girls at puberty, for not all girls become depressed. Instead, we need to look for factors that differentiate boys and girls and on which girls show substantial individual differences.

One such factor is the timing of the physical changes of puberty, especially the development of secondary sex characteristics. The development of breasts and pubic hair in girls begins, on average, a few years before the development of genitals and growth in muscle mass in boys. In addition, it appears that boys and girls respond differently to the physical changes of puberty. Girls tend to dislike the changes in their bodies that come with puberty, particularly their weight gain in fat and the loss of the long, lithe, prepubescent look that is idealized in modern fashion. By contrast, boys tend to like the changes in their bodies (Simmons et al., 1979; Tobin-Richards, Boxer & Petersen, 1983). Simmons and colleagues explain:

Girls develop a figure which makes them look qualitatively different from themselves as children. Boys, on the other hand, primarily become taller and more muscular and athletic-looking, a change less dramatically different and a change in line with previous values placed on athletics and body strength. . . . For pubertal boys, then, who are becoming more muscular-looking, the improvement in their own appearance is probably obvious. In contrast, for pubertal girls, it may not be clear whether their particular future develop-ment makes them better or worse looking than their peers, many of whom are also developing figures. [1979, pp. 963–64]

In line with this argument, Dornbusch and colleagues (1984) found that the normal physical changes of puberty decreased girls' satisfac-tion with their bodies, whereas pubertal physical changes increased boys' satisfaction (see also Simmons et al., 1979; Tobin-Richards et al., 1983). In turn, satisfaction with one's own body appears to be more closely related to self-esteem and well-being in girls than in boys (Lerner & Karabenick, 1974).

McCarthy (1989) has argued that this pattern of sex differences in body dissatisfaction and its association with self-esteem may account for the emergence of sex differences in depression in early adoles-cence. Girls' dissatisfaction with their bodies comes from a real-ization of the discrepency between society's ideal of a thin, pre-pubescent body shape for women and the fact that they are gaining fat as their bodies mature. In an attempt to conform to this ideal body shape, girls begin to diet. If they fail in their diet, which they usually do, they feel helpless and may become depressed. If they succeed in their dieting, they may become malnourished, and this malnourishment can also lead to depression. A subset of girls may develop an eating disorder, instead of depression, if their concerns with body image and self-control are particularly strong. McCarthy reviews the literatures on cultural differences in images of the ideal female body shape, sex differences in depression, and rates of eat-ing disorders, and finds that cultures that idealize an extremely thin body shape for females tend also to have high rates of eating dis-orders and higher rates of depression in women than in men. This hypothesis is intriguing and deserves more research.

In addition to the different timing of pubertal changes in boys and girls, there is great variability among girls in the timing of pubertal changes. A number of researchers have suggested that being off-time in pubertal changes compared to peers—particularly maturing early —creates stress for girls (Brooks-Gunn & Ruble, 1982; Clausen, 1975; Faust, 1960; Tobin-Richards et al., 1983). Girls who mature early begin to gain body fat and must deal with the inconvenience and discomfort of menarche before their peers. Some studies find that girls who mature early show less satisfaction with their bodies, are more concerned about their appearance, and have lower self-esteem than other girls (Simmons & Blyth, 1987; Simmons et al., 1979; Tobin-Richards et al., 1983). Simmons and Blyth (1987) found that the dissatisfaction that girls who matured early felt about their bodies persisted at least into ninth grade. On the other hand, early-maturing girls tend to report increased independence from their parents and to perceive themselves as more popular with their peers (Simmons & Blyth, 1987). Older studies have also found that early-maturing girls have higher prestige (Faust, 1960) and more self-confidence (Clausen, 1975) than late-maturing girls. Thus the effects of early maturation on girls' well-being are ambiguous.

It may be that early maturation does not directly affect girls' well-being but sensitizes them to the effects of other stressors. That is, girls whose bodies are undergoing the changes of puberty at a particularly young age, when they are emotionally immature and do not have the social support of peers undergoing the same changes, may find it more difficult to cope well with other stressors they encounter. A study by Simmons and colleagues (reported in Simmons & Blyth, 1987) supports this hypothesis. These researchers assessed pubertal status, self-esteem, and a number of social variables in 237 sixth-grade girls, then reassessed these same variables periodically until the girls were in tenth grade. Neither pubertal status nor the timing of menarche in a girl relative to her peers was related to depressed mood. But girls who matured earlier than their peers and who simultaneously experienced significant changes in their social lives and environments did show significantly lower self-esteem and more depression than other girls. For example, among the early-maturing girls who had already begun dating, 50 percent had low self-esteem scores, compared to 36 to 40 percent of the girls who were either not menstruating or not dating. The early-maturing, dating girls were also doing more poorly in school, as measured by their grades, and showed more behavior problems at school than other girls and boys in the study. There was no effect of dating status on boys' self-esteem. Simmons and colleagues have anecdotal evidence that pubertal girls who were dating showed more problems in self-esteem and school behavior in part because they were under pressure to be sexually active, which they found distressing.

Another environmental change that appears to put early-maturing girls at risk for low self-esteem is the move from a small, intimate elementary school to a large, impersonal high school at nearly the same time the girl reaches menarche. Simmons and colleagues (1979) compared the self-esteem scores of seventh-grade children who had to move to a new high school with those of seventh-graders who remained in their elementary school. They found that girls who moved into high school showed significant declines in self-esteem scores from sixth to seventh grade, whereas girls who remained in the same school showed increases in self-esteem from sixth to seventh grade. This finding suggests that something about moving to a new, large, more impersonal school in early adolescence is detrimental to the self-esteem of girls. By contrast, boys' self-esteem scores increased from sixth to seventh grade regardless of what type of school they attended. The subgroup in this study who showed the lowest self-esteem and the most behavioral problems were early-maturing girls who were dating and who had to move to a new school in seventh grade.

The study by Brooks-Gunn and Warren (1987) suggests that it is more difficult for girls to adjust to negative life events if they are simultaneously undergoing the physical changes of puberty than if they are not, regardless of whether they mature earlier than their peers. These researchers found that girls in the early stages of pubertal change were more likely to become depressed following a negative life event than were girls whose pubertal changes were nearly complete. For example, a girl whose parents divorced during the early stages of the girl's puberty is more likely to become depressed than a girl whose parents divorced when she was prepubescent or had completed puberty. In such a case, the increased risk of depression may occur not only because a girl in the early stages of puberty must adjust to multiple stressors simultaneously, but also because her parents are distracted by the divorce from helping her to adjust to those stressors and changes.

Taken collectively, these studies suggest an increased sensitivity to both normative and nonnormative events in girls experiencing the first physical changes of puberty, and perhaps particularly in girls experiencing these changes before their peers. Having to adapt to multiple, simultaneous changes or stressors may be so difficult for some adolescents that lowered self-confidence and even depression can result. Although both boys and girls face such changes and stressors during adolescence, the period may be more difficult for girls because they tend to be less satisfied with the physical changes of puberty and because these changes come at an earlier age for girls than boys (see Simmons et al., 1987).

A recent study suggests that girls who experience a period of depressed mood and lowered self-esteem in early adolescence may be at risk for depression later. Gjerde, Block, and Block (1988) report data from a longitudinal study of adolescent sex differences in personality and behavioral variables that predict depression in young adulthood. At the beginning of the study, 88 adolescents, age 14, completed a battery of personality inventories and were rated by clinical examiners on behavioral and personality styles. At age 18 the same subjects completed the Center for Epidemiological Studies Depression Scale (Radloff, 1977), a well-validated self-report scale for depression. The researchers found that for girls, but not for boys, low self-esteem scores and high self-consciousness scores at age 14 were both associated with high depression scores at age 18. Given that the early-maturing girls who were dating or had moved into a new school in the Simmons studies were low in self-esteem and high in self-consciousness, this study suggests that such girls would be at risk for depression in early adulthood.

The Impact of Psychosocial Changes

Several theorists have argued that there are substantial divergences in boys' and girls' personality development in early adolescence as boys and girls begin to adopt the personality characteristics deemed appropriate for their sex (see Hill & Lynch, 1983). Particularly when girls and boys become able to procreate, parental pressure for them to assume gender-appropriate attitudes and behavior patterns supposedly increases. According to these theorists, parents will increasingly encourage independence and achievement in boys and nurturance and nonassertiveness in girls as children enter adolescence. In turn, children increasingly adopt attitudes and patterns consistent with their sex role. Hill and Lynch (1983) referred to this increase in sex-role socialization and adoption as *gender intensification.*

Gove and Herb (1974) argued that this increase in pressure to assume the feminine sex role, together with the actual adoption of behaviors consonant with the sex role, causes girls to become more vulnerable to depression and anxiety in adolescence. According to Gove and Herb, girls are expected to begin to base their self-esteem on their relationships with boys and to narrow their aspirations and range of activities to those concordant with their eventual roles as mothers and wives. Such expectations cause conflict in girls because they can no longer value their own achievements or pursue their own interests and abilities, but instead must rely on others for their self-esteem. In addition, girls who reject the pressure to conform to the feminine sex role face rejection by their peers. By contrast, boys continue to face the same expectations in adolescence that they did in childhood: to be assertive and independent and to achieve as much as they can. Thus, Gove and Herb argued, girls face much more stress in adolescence than boys: if they accept the feminine sex role, their nonassertiveness and dependence on others will predispose them to depression and anxiety; if they reject the feminine sex role, they will be rejected. This greater level of stress leads to the increases in rates of depression and anxiety in girls, relative to boys.

There is very little evidence that girls and boys actually conform more to sex-role stereotypes during adolescence. Most studies that have assessed changes during adolescence in the extent to which children describe themselves in terms of sex-stereotyped characteristics have found no tendency for increased sex-typing (e.g., Petersen & Kennedy, 1988). In fact, one study showed that girls increasingly endorsed *male*-stereotyped characteristics—competence, independence, activity—during adolescence (Leahy & Eiter, 1980). These data contradict the hypothesis of gender intensification.

Given the lack of evidence for substantial sex differences among adults in most personality traits said to lead to depression (see Chapter 6), we should not expect substantial divergences in male and female personality development during adolescence. The few sex differences in personality characteristics seen before adolescence do not appear to increase during adolescence. For example, both before and after puberty, girls are less aggressive than boys (Maccoby & Jacklin, 1974), are more modest than boys in their statements of confidence about their abilities (Huston, 1983), are more likely than boys to conform to adult demands and to prefer interaction with adults (Huston, 1983), and are more concerned than boys about same-sex popularity (Simmons & Blyth, 1987). These kinds of sex differences have been said to cause sex differences in depression (see Chapter 6). But the fact that these sex differences in personality are just as large before puberty, when boys are more depressed than girls, calls into question any notion of a straightforward effect of personality differences on girls' increasing vulnerability to depression during adolescence.

Nevertheless, girls may be increasingly pressured by parents and others to assume feminine-typed characteristics and increasingly restricted in their choices for the future. Studies of parents' attitudes toward their children show that parents, especially fathers, have increasingly sex-stereotyped attitudes toward their children (see Block, 1979b). For example, as children enter secondary school, many parents develop sex-differentiated expectations for their children's academic interests, abilities, and levels of achievement (Parsons, Adler & Kaczala, 1982). That is, parents expect boys to be good at math and sports and girls to be good at English and the arts. They consider completion of college and having a career more important for sons than for daughters (Barnett, 1979; Hoffman, 1977). Fathers appear to be particularly likely to see major sex differences in the abilities and personalities in their children. As children enter adolescence, parents report that they allow boys but not girls increasing degrees of independence (Block, 1979b).

Male and female adolescents report differences in their parents' expectations and how their parents treat them. In their study of sixth- through tenth-grade students, Simmons and Blyth (1987) found that boys were more likely than girls to report that their parents' permission was not needed for going places after dark, that they were left at home alone, and that their parents expected them to act older. Girls said they valued independence more than boys did, perhaps because they were not given the independence they wanted. Although girls were more likely than boys to want to go to college and have a high-status job, boys were more likely than girls to report that their parents expected them to have a career. This finding suggests that parents' expectations and encouragements were lower than girls' aspirations, at least from the girls' point of view.

Parents' messages about girls' abilities may affect girls' choices of subjects to study and careers to pursue. In high school the percentage of girls in math courses declines precipitously, whereas girls make up nearly the entire class in feminine-typed courses such as home economics. In addition, girls' performance in math decreases relative to boys' in high school (Grant & Eiden, 1982). In college the percentage of women majoring in math and science is quite small. For example, in 1978 women received only 6 percent of the BS degrees awarded in engineering, 23 percent in architecture, 26 percent in computer science, and 22 percent in the physical sciences (National Center for Educational Statistics, 1980). By contrast, women received 73 percent of the BAs in education, 76 percent in foreign languages, and 88 percent in library science. Although women may be entering these female-dominated fields voluntarily (Eccles, 1985), they may be setting themselves up for low-paying, low-status, and perhaps frustrating jobs (see Chapter 4).

There is evidence that girls sometimes perceive their own competence as a liability in their relationships with peers, especially boys. An early study found that during adolescence girls increasingly want to conceal their intelligence, whereas boys increasingly want to be recognized for their intelligence (Coleman, 1961). Rosen and Aneshensel (1976) surveyed 3,049 children in seventh through twelfth grade, asking about the children's expectations for the consequences of sex-role violations. Girls were more likely than boys to say that they would be liked less by a member of the opposite sex if they were assertive, pursued their own interests, or beat a boy in a competition. Girls were also more likely than boys to say that they tried to conceal their competence, behaved in dependent and compliant ways, and worried about the reactions of others to their appearance and behavior. Girls may be correct in expecting to be rejected if they violate their sex role and act competently and assertively. Early studies found that eleventh-grade girls who received high grades were less popular with boys than were girls with lower grades (Keisler, 1955). There was no association between grades and popularity for boys, however. More recently, studies of assertiveness in college-age women have found that assertive women are rated more negatively and are considered more aberrant than assertive men (see Chapter 4).

The social consequences of showing one's competence and otherwise violating feminine stereotypes may lead to depression in females. Block and Gjerde (in press) find that in adolescent girls there is a significant positive correlation between intelligence and depression, whereas there is a small negative correlation between intelligence and depression in adolescent boys. In other words, intelligence is associated with depression in girls but with lack of depression in boys. In addition, the girls in Block and Gjerde's study who rejected the feminine sex role had higher depression scores than girls who endorsed the feminine sex role. These data support the suggestion that girls who are intelligent and who reject demands to conceal their competence and assertiveness are at increased risk for depression (Gove & Herb, 1974).

These trends are in contrast to several studies of college students showing higher rates of helplessness and depression in women who endorse feminine stereotypes than in women who do not (e.g., Baucom & Weiss, 1986; Ray & Bristow, 1978). Gove and Herb (1974) also argued that girls who accept the feminine sex role, and the narrowing of activities and interests it prescribes, are at risk for depression. How can we reconcile evidence that rejecting the feminine sex role and displaying one's intelligence is associated with depression in high school girls with evidence that accepting the feminine sex role is associated with depression in college women? Perhaps adhering to the feminine sex role in high school is associated with popularity and thus with positive self-esteem and low levels of depression. But in college and as adults, the same young women may find their lack of background in masculine-typed, more highly valued courses backfiring as they find themselves in low-paying jobs and with few occupational choices. They may also have married relatively early and become financially dependent on their husbands. By contrast, intelligent, assertive girls may not be as popular in high school and thus may show somewhat higher levels of depression then, but may find satisfaction and acceptance of their talents in college and thus may show relatively low levels of depression there. This interpretation is speculative and calls for a longitudinal study of the long-term vulnerability to depression of adolescents who do and do not endorse feminine stereotypes.

Increases in Sexual Abuse of Females During Adolescence

One additional explanation for the increase in rates of depression in girls in adolescence cannot be ignored: rates of sexual abuse of girls increase substantially in early adolescence, and many abuse victims continue to be abused throughout their adolescent years (Russell, 1984). In a random sample of 930 adult women, Russell (1984) found that 12 percent had experienced some type of serious intrafamilial sexual abuse (such as an incestuous relationship with a father, stepfather, or uncle) before age 17; 26 percent had experienced serious abuse from someone outside the family before age 17. The greatest increase in the experience of abuse occurred during the period between age 10 and 14. Several other researchers have found that girls age 14 to 15 have the highest risk of being raped of all age groups (Hayman et al., 1968; Hursch & Selkin, 1974; Katz & Mazur, 1979; Schiff, 1969). Girls are two to three times more likely than boys to be the victims of sexual abuse (Finkelhor, 1979). As discussed in Chapter 4, victims of rape and sexual abuse show high levels of depression just after an assault (Burgess & Holmstrom, 1974; Kilpatrick, Veronen & Resick, 1979; Wirtz & Harrell, 1987) and perhaps for many months later (Kilpatrick, Resick & Veronen, 1981). One study found that over half the women who sought therapy for depression as adults in one clinic had been sexually abused as children (Carmen, Rieker & Mills, 1984). It seems plausible, then, that at least some of the increase in rates of depression in adolescent girls can be attributed to increases in the fear of abuse and in actual rates of abuse.

Conclusions

This chapter has examined explanations for the greater degree of depression in boys than in girls before puberty and for the increase in girls' vulnerability to depression during adolescence. Among the hypotheses about boys' vulnerability to depression and other psychopathology before puberty are that boys are constitutionally weaker than girls and are thus more susceptible to physical and psychological illness; that boys have more irritable temperaments than girls and are thus more vulnerable to psychopathology; and that adults tolerate less deviance in boys than in girls and thus bring disturbed boys to the attention of mental health professionals more than they do disturbed girls. Studies of children in the general population also show that boys are more likely than girls to become depressed, and these studies do not depend on data from children undergoing psychiatric treatment. Yet another explanation is that boys are more reactive than girls to environmental stress, perhaps because they have more maladaptive explanatory styles. Finally, it has been suggested that parents put more pressure on boys to be aggressive and to achieve, at the same time threatening boys with punishment for transgressions, and that these pressures cause conflict in boys. There are two problems with these explanations of boys' greater vulnerability to depression and other psychopathology during childhood: none of the explanations has been researched sufficiently, and it is not clear why any of these factors would change at adolescence, as would seem to be necessary to explain why boys begin to show less depression than girls do.

This chapter also examined the impact of the biological and psychosocial changes of adolescence on girls' and boys' relative vulnerability to depression. The development of secondary sex characteristics in girls appears to have an indirect effect on their emotional well-being. Girls do not like the physical changes of puberty, and they have poorer body images than do boys. In addition, there appears to be some increased vulnerability to negative life events in girls during some period of pubertal change, although it is unclear exactly when this period of sensitivity occurs.

In opposition to the gender intensification hypothesis, boys and girls do not show diverging patterns of personality development in adolescence. The few sex differences in self-concept seen in prepubescent children appear to be maintained in adolescents. Because these sex differences are apparent both before and after the switch in sex differences in depression, they cannot explain this switch in any straightforward way. It may be that pressures from adults to conform to sex roles lead some girls to choose less than optimal life plans for themselves. In addition, there is evidence that girls may become increasingly concerned with the possible consequences of violating their sex roles. They worry that showing their intelligence and being assertive will result in social rejection, and they may be correct. Girls who describe themselves in terms of male characteristics and are intelligent appear to have higher levels of depression in high school, but women who endorse the feminine stereotype are most prone to depression at college age. The adoption of the feminine sex role may contribute to popularity and thus to positive well-being in high school but may backfire in college and adulthood because women who adopt the feminine sex role may choose low-paying or unfulfilling occupations. Finally, rates of sexual abuse of females increase substantially with puberty and are very high in adolescents, and girls who have been abused are at risk for depression. The hypothesis that this increase in abuse accounts to a significant extent for girls' increased depression remains to be tested empirically, but it seems plausible.

There are far too few relevant studies to draw any conclusions about why the rates of depression rise so greatly during adolescence in females compared to males. No single biological, psychological, or social factor is likely to account entirely for the switch. We need a longitudinal study in which depression and a number of biological factors (such as hormonal changes and pubertal development), psychological factors (such as self-concept and personal goals), and social factors (such as restrictions on freedom and choice, expectations of others, life events, and victimization) are assessed periodically in a large group of males and females from age 10 to at least early adulthood. Only with such a study can the contribution of these factors to sex differences in depression be adequately assessed.

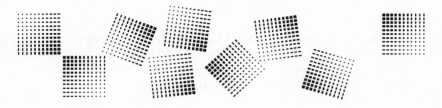

CHAPTER NINE

Priorities for Future Research, and What We Can Do Now

Many more questions about sex differences in depression have been raised than answered in this book. Many of the plausible hypotheses about the causes of women's greater rates of depression either have not been supported by evidence or have been so underresearched that we cannot assess them conclusively. Recognizing how much remains to be studied is the first step toward establishing a more accurate understanding of the greater rates of depression in women than in men. In this chapter I describe ten important questions or sets of questions that need to be researched further before we will understand much about sex differences in depression. Then I suggest some tactics we can use to reduce women's vulnerability to depression even before we have a full understanding of it.

Ten Questions to Guide Future Research

Question 1: Why is there such a great rise in the rates of depression in females compared to males during adolescence? We have hardly begun to understand the increase in depression in females during adolescence. Chapter 8 described the small contribution of hormonal changes during early adolescence to depression levels in girls, but there is little evidence that hormones continue to play a role in the increase in depression in females later in adolescence. There really are far too few data on the relationship between hormones and moods to draw any conclusions, however. Similarly, there have been very few studies of the effects of the psychosocial changes of adolescence on depression in females.

I suggested in Chapter 8 that we need a longitudinal study of depression in adolescent males and females to begin to understand the emergence of sex differences in depression. Several variables should be examined in such a study. Hormone levels should be tracked from before puberty through late adolescence to determine whether the increase in depression in girls during the activation of the hormonal system in early adolescence is a transient or a long-term effect. It is possible that girls who become depressed during this period will be at risk for depression in other periods in which hormonal levels change precipitously, such as the postpartum period or perhaps the premenstrual period. Such a finding would suggest that a subset of females have problems with the hormonal system that cause them to become depressed when they experience precipitous changes in hormone levels. Alternatively, an episode of depression during the early adolescent period may negatively affect a girl's developing self-image and self-esteem, putting her at increased risk for depression later in life regardless of biological changes. The only way to test such hypotheses is through a prospective longitudinal study.

Such a study should also examine the effects of the development of secondary sex characteristics on girls' self-image and vulnerability to depression. The studies described in Chapter 8 provided complex and sometimes contradictory data about the effects of pubertal change on girls' self-esteem. Some girls seem to like looking "grown up," whereas others seem to dislike the body fat they gain during puberty. Some studies described in Chapter 8 suggested that a combination of pubertal change and life events lead to poor self-esteem in some girls, but it is unclear during what stages of pubertal development girls are more sensitive to life events. It is also unclear from these studies how pubertal changes and life events affect girls' self-concepts. Future studies should use better measures of what pubertal development means to girls, what girls think about the changes in their bodies, and what it is like to be going through puberty concurrently with a negative event such as the divorce of one's parents. These studies should also follow adolescents for a long enough period to determine whether being depressed or having low self-esteem in early adolescence leads to an increased rate of depression in late adolescence and adulthood.

Further research is also needed on the possible changes during adolescence in males' and females' levels of self-confidence, sense of efficacy in obtaining desired lifestyles and careers, and ways of handling periods of distress. There have been only a few longitudinal studies of psychological change during adolescence (e.g., Simmons & Blyth, 1987). These studies suggest that there is not a large divergence in the personality development of males and females during adolescence. Nevertheless, males and females take different paths in higher education and careers, and females become more likely than males to be depressed by late adolescence. Perhaps an increasingly large subset of females do not feel they have adequate career choices and are uncomfortable with new pressures to date and to compete with other females in the social domain. These females may be likely to be depressed in late adolescence. A study testing this hypothesis should also examine whether boys' self-concepts remain stable and how boys handle the stress of social comparison and the pressure to achieve in college or in a new job. We should not assume that boys experience less stress than girls or that their ways of coping with stress are necessarily effective. There may be an increasingly large subset of males who are distressed by the pressure to succeed and whose attempts to cope with this pressure lead them to develop problems other than depression, such as alcoholism or drug addiction.

The kind of support adolescents receive from their families is likely to influence their adaptation to the changes of adolescence. Longitudinal studies should assess the kinds of family atmosphere that make it most difficult for females and males to come through adolescence successfully, as well as the differences between the family support of females who develop depression by late adolescence and those who do not. Studies investigating these questions should examine the actual behavior of families and not rely on self-reports of parents and adolescents. We currently have very little observational data on interactions between parents and adolescents, let alone data distinguishing between such interactions for adolescents who develop depression and for those who do not. Large longitudinal studies such as the ones suggested here are extremely costly but would be extremely valuable if they helped us to understand the development of sex differences in depression during adolescence, for such an understanding might help us reduce or even prevent the increase in depression in females.

Question 2: Is there a direct effect of certain biological factors on women's moods? What is the relative contribution of biological and psychological factors to depression in women? As discussed in Chapter 3, there is mixed evidence for a direct effect of hormones on women's moods. Even among studies that have claimed to show a direct effect of hormones on moods, the results have shown only a *correlation* between hormone levels and moods: even when there is evidence of parallel fluctuation in levels of hormones and moods, there is no evidence of a causal effect of hormones on moods. We need more prospective studies in which a biological marker such as a tendency toward abnormal or shifting hormone levels is used to *predict* which women will be most likely to become depressed during a given period such as the postpartum period. Additional evidence for a role of hormones or hormonal change in women's depression comes from studies showing an increased risk of depression in women during certain reproductive events, although such an increase usually occurs only in women who have a history of depression. We need to determine whether depression associated with reproductive events results from a direct effect of hormones on mood or whether the physical stress of massive hormonal shifts leads to a sensitivity to external stress and sometimes to depression. It could be useful to examine whether women who undergo physical stressors other than hormonal shifts during these periods are also at increased risk for depression.

We may have more success in determining the relative influence of biological and psychological factors on women's vulnerability to depression. Future studies could extend the work of O'Hara and colleagues (1984), seeking to determine whether biological factors (such as the normality of a woman's hormonal system) or psychosocial factors (such as a woman's explanatory style or social supports) best predict depression in women, perhaps especially during reproductive events such as the postpartum period. Determining the relative influence of biological and psychological factors on women's depression is not important merely to settle the debate between proponents of the two views. The outcome of such research could have important implications for treatment. If psychosocial factors are the primary cause of depression in women, then it may not be advisable to put women on antidepressant drugs, which can have negative side effects. On the other hand, if the causes of depression in women are often biological, we would not want to suggest to a depressed woman that she needs to undergo therapy to change her personality or environment. Even assuming that depression is caused by a combination of biological and psychological factors, research clarifying the relative roles of these factors could help in the design of an appropriately balanced approach to therapy.

Question 3: Will recent changes in sex roles result in changes in sex differences in depression? There is some evidence that sex differences in depression have narrowed over the last decade (Klerman et al., 1985), perhaps because changes in women's social roles make women less prone to depression or perhaps merely because the rates of depression in men are increasing. It is not yet clear whether there is a straightforward effect of changes in the social roles of women on their vulnerability to depression. It may be that there is no universal effect of a given role on the emotional health of women but rather that a woman's emotional health depends on whether she is in the role she wants to be in and is valued in that role. Some women thrive on the multiple challenges of a profession, motherhood, and keeping a home; others are overwhelmed by these multiple roles. Some women love raising their children full time; others would be frustrated by this single role. Future research should investigate the characteristics that make certain roles a better match for certain women. Such research could help us to identify when a woman's depression results from a mismatch between her goals or individual characteristics and the particular role she is filling.

Question 4: To what extent is women's higher vulnerability to depression explained by the high numbers of women who are physically or sexually victimized? As discussed in Chapter 4, the rates of victimization of women are very high, and many victims of domestic violence, rape, and other types of assault are depressed after the assault, sometimes for long periods. But what we know about victims comes largely from the subset of victims who seek help. We need a more complete picture of the effects of severe victimization on the emotional health of women who do not seek help or who never tell a therapist that they have been victimized. Given the very high rates of victimization, a causal relationship between victimization and depression could account in large part for the higher numbers of females than males who are depressed. A related question is why some women are able to recuperate emotionally from victimization in a shorter period and to a greater extent than other women. Research on how people recuperate from trauma suggests that having strong social supports is an important facilitator of recuperation (Windholz, Marmar & Horowitz, 1985). People who have close friends or family members in whom they can confide appear better able to cope with trauma than people who do not have such support. This finding suggests that victims of rape and other forms of violence who have good support networks are better able to recover from their trauma than those who do not (see Wirtz & Harrell, 1987). Thus future studies need to determine the effects of victimization on the rates of depression in women and to explore why some women are able to cope with victimization without becoming severely depressed for a long time.

Question 5: Does the experience of job discrimination affect women's emotional health? Crosby's (1982) study showed no relationship between pay discrimination and depression or satisfaction in women. This finding seems to suggest that discrimination does not affect emotional health in women. But there may be other forms of discrimination, such as sexual harassment or difficulty being promoted, that contribute to a sense of helplessness and depression in women. A study comparing the emotional health of women in different work environments—for example, comparing a male-dominated environment in which sexual harassment of women is common with an environment in which men and women are given equal opportunities and fair treatment—would offer important insights into the role of discrimination in women's depressions. Such insights could inform theories of depression in women and provide additional justification for laws against discrimination.

Question 6: Are women who are aware of discrimination and the threat of victimization more vulnerable to depression? As discussed under Question 4, being victimized or discriminated against may lead to a sense of helplessness and depression. Perhaps the mere *awareness* of the high probability of victimization or discrimination leads some women to feel helpless. Crosby (1982) and others have argued that women shut out any awareness rather than cope with the helplessness that discrimination engenders. Similarly, Basow (1986)

noted that a woman's degree of professional success correlates negatively with the likelihood of her saying there is discrimination against
women in her field. Basow suggested that women maintain their
motivation to fight their way to the top by denying the possibility of
discrimination. In another line of research, Hodell (1988) has shown
that women and men sometimes blame the victim of a rape for her
victimization. For women, one explanation of this phenomenon is
that blaming the victim allows them to believe that they can avoid
being raped if they never do what the victim did. The fact that most
women underestimate the probability of being raped may result from
lack of information, but it may also reflect a defensive denial of the
threat.

Further study of this question can help to determine whether
making a woman more aware of the obstacles and threats she faces
will make her feel more helpless and perhaps more depressed. Assuming that it will, one obvious solution is to give women both information about their condition and the tools for combating obstacles
and threats so that they feel powerful and efficacious. For example,
rape education should be combined with self-defense training, and
consciousness-raising should be combined with assertiveness training.

*Question 7: Are there larger sex differences in the personality
characteristics said to lead to depression in people in the general
population than in college students?* There are few if any sex differences in assertiveness, dependency, and other personality characteristics in college students, just as there are no differences in depression
in this group. We might obtain stronger evidence for personality
explanations of the sex differences in depression if we examined
adults of various ages who are not in college. Such a study should
also compare the effects of personality on sex differences in depression with the effects of other factors that differentiate men and
women, such as social status, family and work roles, and biology.
Even though we might see bigger sex differences in personality in
non-college students, these differences would not necessarily be the
cause of women's greater vulnerability to depression.

Indeed, throughout the literature on the causes of sex differences in
depression, often the only evidence given for a theory is data showing a sex difference in a certain variable. For example, supporters
of the theory that social orientation makes women more vulnerable

to depression often settle for evidence that women are more socially oriented than men, without showing that this orientation is a cause of greater depression in women. Women are usually shorter than men, too, but this sex difference is probably not a cause of sex differences in depression. Just because we find a sex difference in some characteristic, we cannot necessarily claim that this is what leads to sex differences in depression.

To establish that a sex difference in a given variable causes sex differences in depression, a program of research must meet three criteria. First, it must show that whenever the variable is present, sex differences in depression are present. For example, if we think women's lack of assertiveness relative to men causes their greater rates of depression, then every time we find a difference in assertiveness between a group of men and a group of women, we should also find that the women are more depressed than the men. Second, studies must show that eliminating the sex difference in the variable causes the sex differences in depression to disappear. If we give the group of women in the previous example assertiveness training, we would expect their rates of depression to decline to the same level as the men's. Third, if at all possible, studies should manipulate the extent to which one group exhibits the variable to see whether this experimental group becomes more depressed than a control group. None of the proposed explanations for the sex differences in depression has met all three of these criteria yet, largely because the relevant studies simply have not been done.

Question 8: Are there differences in the way women and men respond to stress and their own moods that lead the two sexes to be vulnerable to different disorders? As discussed in Chapter 7, women are more likely to be ruminative and men more likely to distract themselves in response to feelings of depression. This difference may be one reason women are more prone to depression than men are. Likewise, men's ways of dealing with emotions may lead to other disorders, such as alcoholism and sociopathy. Indeed, it may be that men and women are equally likely to experience stress but that differences in how the sexes handle stress lead to sex differences in several psychological disorders. To test this hypothesis, we need to design prospective studies that seek to predict rates of several types of disorders in men and women according to the types of responses they tend to show to stress. A virtue of this type of study is that it goes beyond the simple notion that women are pathological and men are not, asking instead whether both sexes have functional and dysfunctional patterns that we should understand. To focus narrowly on women's depression is to miss the larger picture of sex differences in vulnerability to many types of disorders.

Question 9: What types of therapy are more effective for depression in women and what types for men? There are many types of psychological and biological therapies for depression. The psychological therapy currently most used in the treatment of depression is cognitive therapy (see Beck et al., 1979), which is based on the premise that thinking in irrational ways about oneself, the world, and the future makes one depressed. In cognitive therapy the therapist helps the client recognize his irrational thoughts and consider alternative, more adaptive ways of thinking about events. Another psychological therapy for depression that is gaining recognition is interpersonal therapy (Klerman et al., 1985), which is based on the premise that problems in interpersonal relationships are often the source of depression. In interpersonal therapy the therapist helps the client identify patterns in his relationships. (For example, the client may always take the role of the sacrificial nurturer.) Through insight into such patterns and the discussion of alternate patterns of relating to others, the client may become able to have more satisfying relationships. Drug therapies are also commonly used in the treatment of depression. Two classes of drugs are used: tricyclic antidepressants and monoamine oxidase inhibitors (MAOIs). Tricyclic antidepressants are thought to relieve depression by increasing the levels of the neurotransmitter norepinephrine in the synapses of the brain. Common types of tricyclics are imipramine, amitriptyline, and doxepin. MAOIs inhibit the breakdown of the neurotransmitters implicated in depression, thereby increasing their availability in the synapses of the brain. Sometimes these drugs are prescribed alone for a depressed person, and sometimes a combination of drug therapy and psychotherapy is prescribed.

In the last decade there have been a few studies comparing the effectiveness of these types of therapy in the treatment of depression. All three therapies have been found to be effective, but several studies have shown cognitive therapy and interpersonal therapy to be more effective than drug therapy (Kovacs et al., 1981; Weissman et al., 1981). One very large study, conducted by the National Institute of

Mental Health, found interpersonal therapy, cognitive therapy, and imipramine to be equally effective in relieving a depressive episode (Elkin et al., 1986).

We do not know whether there are any sex differences in the effectiveness of these therapies, for none of the published studies of therapy outcomes has tested for sex differences. Because women are somewhat more likely to think of themselves as socially oriented and men are somewhat more likely to think of themselves as rational and analytic, interpersonal therapy might appeal more to women and cognitive therapy might appeal more to men, but this hypothesis has not been tested. There is some evidence that women's hormonal fluctuations can interfere with the effectiveness of drug therapies (Hamilton, 1986). This evidence suggests that, on the whole, drug therapies may be less effective for women than for men and perhaps should be supplemented by psychotherapy for women.

We need studies that assess the relative effectiveness of different therapies for women and men. Because no single type of therapy is likely to be effective for all women, or for all men, studies of therapy outcomes should try to assess the individual characteristics that make one type of therapy more helpful than another for a given man or woman.

Question 10: How should we interpret the fact that there are apparently no sex differences in depression in some cultures, such as the Amish? I have referred to the lack of sex differences in depression among the Amish several times in passing, indicating whether the finding does or does not fit with a particular theory of sex differences in depression. For example, I speculated in Chapter 4 that the Amish show no sex differences in depression because men's and women's sex roles are valued equally by the society and that Amish women are thus no more likely than Amish men to become depressed. But my comments have been only speculations. We need studies in which researchers actually go into different cultures and investigate the experience and causes of depression in men and women in an attempt to understand the presence or absence of sex differences in depression in that culture. For example, it may be that Amish women's sex role is not as highly valued as that of Amish men, but that women are not more depressed than men because both sexes have deep religious beliefs that help them to deal with life circumstances without succumbing to depression. We will not be able to assess any explanation of the absence of sex differences in depression among the Amish unless we can somehow ask the Amish to inform us about themselves.

What We Can Do Now

With an awareness of the increase in vulnerability to depression in females as they go through adolescence, we can begin to design programs that attempt to halt this rise. Some programs should provide information about the dramatic increase in depression in females during adolescence so that individual adolescent females know they are not the only ones who are depressed. Programs should also provide adolescents with information on how and where they can receive help if they are distressed. Such help should be available through school counselors and other sources. Programs should also be designed to help adolescents, particularly females, realize that they have many options for defining themselves, their futures, their careers, and so on. The goal of such programs would be to help prevent a sense of helplessness and hopelessness about the future and to promote a sense of choice and efficacy.

The second action we can take immediately to decrease women's vulnerability to depression is to try to reduce the threat of rape, domestic violence, and sexual harassment. Simply reducing the number of women that are victimized should reduce the number of women who are depressed. We can also provide the best support possible to help women escape ongoing victimization and to recuperate from victimization.

Finally, we can call into question notions that women have inherently biological and psychological weaknesses that make them more prone to depression than men are. This kind of questioning may lead to new theorizing and research on the sources of depression in women and may also have a strong effect on how women think about their own depression. It is possible that the prevailing ideas about why women become depressed affect women's understandings of their own depressive episodes. The following pages expand on this argument.

Searching for Explanations and Solutions When Depressed

Each person may have his or her own set of beliefs about why men and women become depressed. We might call these beliefs "gender beliefs about depression" (see Deaux & Major, 1987). Such beliefs will be more conscious and well formed in some people than in others. For many people, these beliefs will be influenced by the popular culture's prevailing beliefs about the causes of depression. The figure on page 209 presents a model of how gender beliefs can lead to different experiences of depression in men and women. The first assumption in this model is that people who become depressed search for reasons why they are depressed and for appropriate responses to their state. Several theorists have argued that when a person's current state or condition differs from his desired state, he will initiate a self-regulatory process involving an analysis of the causes of the current state and ways of reattaining the desired state (Carver & Scheier, 1981; Duval & Wicklund, 1972; Pyszczynski & Greenberg, 1987). Clinical observations and empirical studies suggest that people who are depressed initiate this self-regulatory process. Clinicians have frequently described depression as a state characterized by heightened self-preoccupation and evaluation of one's own condition (Abraham, 1960; Arieti & Bemporad, 1980; Beck, 1976). Correlational studies also find that the more depressed a person is, the more he will report engaging in self-directed thought and evaluation by endorsing such statements as "I am trying to figure myself out" (Fenigstein, Scheier & Buss, 1975; Scheier & Carver, 1977; Smith, Ingram & Roth, 1985). In addition, laboratory studies have found that self-directed attention increases significantly among people who are frustrated or who have just failed at a task (Greenberg & Pyszczynski, 1986; Pyszczynski & Greenberg, 1986). This trend is particularly true of people who are already in a state of depression. Depressed subjects show greater base levels of self-directed attention than nondepressed subjects, and the degree of self-focus among depressed subjects increases significantly more in the face of frustration than does that among nondepressed subjects.

If the intended function of self-directed attention in depression is to reduce the discrepancy between a desired state (positive mood) and a current state (depression), this process can be aided by two

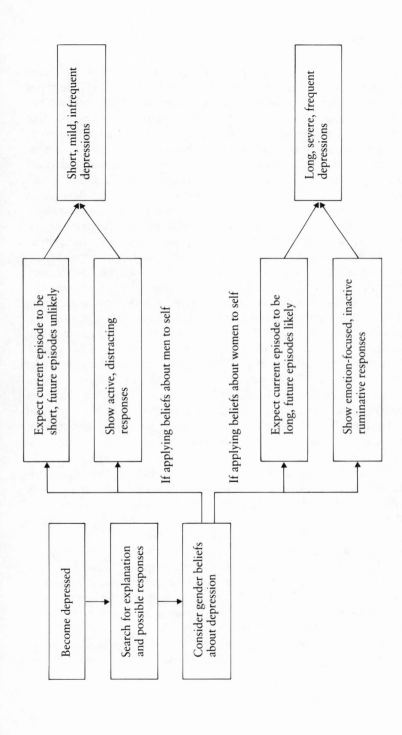

The effects of gender beliefs on interpretations of and responses to depression

types of analysis. First, people can assess the causes of their current state; that is, they can ask, "Why am I depressed?" The types of causes a person considers will be influenced by her existing beliefs about the causes of depression in most people, in people like her, and in her specifically. Different types of causes imply different expectations about the duration of the mood, the likelihood of its recurrence, and the effectiveness of actions the person might undertake to control the mood (see Abramson, Seligman & Teasdale, 1978). For example, if the person believes that the cause of her depression is a stable factor such as a personality trait ("I am always nonassertive"), this belief implies a high likelihood of recurrence of the conditions leading to the depressive episode, perhaps a long duration of the episode, and difficulties in overcoming the episode. By contrast, if the person believes the cause of the current episode is an unstable factor such as not having had enough sleep, this belief implies a low likelihood of recurrence of the episode, a short duration of the current episode, and little difficulty overcoming the current episode. The other type of analysis a person can engage in when depressed is an analysis of the appropriate responses to her mood. That is, she can ask herself, "What should I do, can I do, to make myself feel better?" The responses to this question may be implied by the causes to which the mood has been attributed, but responses to depression can also be considered separately from the causes of depression. Indeed, people may think more frequently about what they should do to relieve their depression than about the causes of their depression.

This model assumes that people also have beliefs about appropriate and effective responses to depression. Adult subjects are certainly willing to offer beliefs about appropriate responses to depression (Rippere, 1977). Friends and loved ones are also often willing—sometimes too willing—to provide advice about what a depressed person should do to bring herself out of the depression (Coyne, 1976). Survey studies indicate that the responses believed to be appropriate for depression include "do something physical to distract yourself," "talk with others," "go off by yourself and get in touch with your feelings," and "just live through it until it goes away" (Nolen-Hoeksema, 1987; Rippere, 1977).

For some people, beliefs about the causes of depression and appropriate responses to depression will be well formed and often conscious. For others, these beliefs may not be well formed and may only be brought to conscious consideration when the person is depressed. In both of these cases, however, cultural beliefs about the causes of and appropriate responses to depression may influence the beliefs of at least some people. According to this model, one cultural influence on individual beliefs about the causes of and responses to depression is cultural gender beliefs about depression.

Gender Beliefs and Judgments About the Causes of and Responses to Depression

Gender beliefs influence many types of judgments. As discussed in Chapter 4, people's judgments about other people's successes and failures, their capabilities, and traits are influenced by gender stereotypes. Further, people's judgments of their own values, traits, and capabilities are sometimes affected by gender stereotypes. The influence of gender beliefs on people's assessments of themselves and others varies greatly in different situations, however. Deaux and Major (1987) have described several conditions that influence the extent to which gender beliefs determine a person's assessments of a situation. In situations where there are many cues that gender is a determinant, gender beliefs will affect more strongly the judgments people make. For example, when subjects are explicitly told that a certain task is performed better by males or by females, their own performance will conform to the expectations for their gender (e.g., Deaux & Farris, 1977). Similarly, when a given task is strongly linked to cultural stereotypes about gender, subjects will use these gender beliefs to make judgments about their own and others' abilities to learn the task. In addition, gender beliefs are more likely to influence judgments of one's own behavior when other people indicate that they are interpreting one's situation or behavior in terms of gender beliefs. Deaux and Major (1987) cite the example of a player on a men's softball team who turns to his colleague and says, "You throw just like a woman." Such a cue might prompt the hearer to think about his own behavior in terms of his own and the culture's beliefs about the athletic abilities of women.

Depression is a situation in which gender beliefs may frequently be used to guide a person's thinking about the situation. The symptoms of depression in themselves may prompt many people to consider the role of gender. For men the symptoms of depression (such as passivity and low self-confidence) are the opposite of the character-istics stereotypically assigned to their gender, whereas for women the symptoms of depression coincide with the characteristics stereo-typically assigned to their gender (Radloff & Monroe, 1978). This similarity between the symptoms of depression and gender stereo-types about women may suggest to the depressive person that gender plays a role in the development of depression and that certain re-sponses to depression are typical to and appropriate for one's gender. By contrast, the symptoms of schizophrenia, which include delu-sions, hallucinations, and bizarre behaviors, do not resemble any of the characteristics in either gender stereotype and thus would prob-ably not prompt a person to consider the role of gender in their development.

Other people in a depressed person's environment may explicitly or implicitly indicate that gender is a factor relevant to the causes of and solutions to his or her depression. Passivity and self-derision are unacceptable characteristics in males, and men who are depressed may be explicitly told by their friends to "act like a man and pull yourself together." Laboratory studies show that men who act non-assertively and emotionally are "punished" by others even more than are women who act assertively and confidently (see Basow, 1986). Thus even if a man is not explicitly told that his depressive behavior is unacceptable in light of the male stereotype and that he is expected to bring himself out of his depression, the punishments and rewards he receives from others for his behaviors may indicate that gender beliefs set up definite expectations for his behavior.

Women are also told by the popular media that depression is a condition associated with gender and interpretable through gender beliefs. In the last ten to twenty years hundreds of articles and tele-vision shows have presented anecdotal and empirical evidence that depression is a woman's disease, attributable to women's person-alities, social status, or biology. The belief that women's hormones and nonassertive, emotional personalities cause them to suffer more depressions has been accepted by clinicians and the laity for many years (see Shields, 1975). In addition, in the last twenty years popular conceptions of how one should respond to emotion have empha-sized sex differences in those responses: women are said to be more attuned to their emotions, whereas men are said to avoid dealing with their emotions. Many of the popular conceptions of depression hold that women's responses may be more adaptive.

Thus the symptoms of depression themselves, together with explicit indications from other people that gender is salient in understanding depression, may lead a depressed person to think of his or her state in terms of gender beliefs. The extent to which these beliefs lead the depressed person to think of his or her depression in terms of gender will be influenced by the degree of his or her concern with conforming to gender stereotypes and tendency to interpret many situations in terms of gender (see Bem, 1985; Deaux & Major, 1987). Because a given man or woman will be exposed to different beliefs about the salience of gender to depression from one episode of depression to another, there will be substantial differences both from person to person and within a person across time regarding the influence of gender beliefs on people's thoughts about their own depressive episodes (see Deaux & Major, 1987). But according to this model, gender beliefs will often influence men's and women's thoughts about their depression and will lead to different explanations for these episodes, different expectations for current and future levels of depression, and sex differences in the responses to episodes of depression.

Gender Beliefs, Expectations, and Responses to Depression

If a depressed woman uses the common gender beliefs about depression to interpret her own episode of depression, she might say to herself, "Women are vulnerable to depression because they are dependent, nonassertive, oppressed, or influenced by hormones. Presumably I am depressed because I am dependent, nonassertive, oppressed, or influenced by my hormones." Such an explanation for one's own depression leads to certain expectations about the duration and controllability of depressive episodes. Specifically, if depression is caused by relatively immutable factors, such as personality, society, or biology, then one's ability to control current and future episodes of depression appears low. Based on such beliefs, one would expect that a current depressive episode will not be short and that future episodes of depression cannot be prevented.

If a depressed man uses the common gender beliefs about depression to interpret his own episode of depression, he might say to himself, "Men seldom get depressed. Women get depressed because they are dependent, nonassertive, oppressed, or influenced by hormones. Because men don't have these problems, my depression probably isn't caused by such factors. Men's depressions are usually caused by problems in their jobs, so something at work must be the cause of my depression." There are not as many well-specified gender beliefs about the causes of depression in men as there are about the causes of depression in women. Further, gender beliefs rule out some of the most immutable factors as possible causes of depression in men, and the one factor often said to contribute to men's depressions—job difficulties—is a relatively mutable one. Thus a man using gender beliefs to interpret his depression might be led to expect that he can change the circumstances leading to his depression, thereby relieving his current depression and preventing future episodes.

Evidence that men and women have different beliefs about the causes of depression comes from a survey study of 65 women and 83 men (Nolen-Hoeksema & Morrow, 1988). We asked subjects to rate their level of agreement with eight beliefs about the typical causes of depression. As predicted by this model, men tended to agree more than women with statements such as, "Depression is just like any other problem that comes up—you just have to find ways to solve it." By contrast, women agreed more strongly than men with statements that depression often has biological causes and that it comes on uncontrollably.

In Chapter 7 I discussed the sex differences in the ways men and women typically respond to their symptoms of depression. Men tend to try to distract themselves from those feelings, especially with physical activities such as sports. Women tend not to distract themselves from their emotion, trying instead to "get in touch" with their feelings as a way of understanding them. Women's approach often involves talking with friends about feelings. Men's and women's choices of responses may be influenced in part by gender beliefs about the appropriate responses to depression. Whatever the source of these responses, however, the data presented in Chapter 7 indicate that men's distracting style serves to dampen depressive episodes, whereas women's ruminative style serves to amplify such episodes.

Implications for Therapy and Intervention

The gender belief model suggests that the prevailing beliefs about the causes of depression in men and women may lead women to attribute their depressions to relatively uncontrollable factors and to choose maladaptive responses to their depressions. If this hypothesis is true, then informing women that many of the prevailing beliefs about the causes of their depression may be untrue might lead to a greater ability among women to control their depressions. The model also suggests that therapists and others should be careful not to be unduly influenced by the prevailing gender beliefs about depression when dealing with depressed women. If an individual woman's depression is indeed linked to hormonal balances, nonassertiveness, dependency, being discriminated against, or being in an oppressive relationship, then therapy should of course focus on correcting these circumstances—just as it should if such circumstances are the cause of an individual man's depression. But therapists should keep in mind that clients' interpretations and presentations of their depressions may be shaped by gender beliefs and should help clients explore the several possible causes of their distress.

Conclusions

The more we understand about why women are at higher risk for depression than men, the more we can prevent women from becoming depressed and intervene effectively with women who are depressed to help them recover. Greater understanding of women's depressions begins with an assessment of what we currently know. The primary goal of this book has been to assess the current state of knowledge about why women are more likely than men to be depressed. I must conclude that we know much less than we need to know. The topic of depression in women has interested many clinicians and researchers, but too little research has been done on most of the possible explanations of women's depressions to allow firm conclusions about their validity. Meanwhile, decisions must be made by psychologists, psychiatrists, and other interested parties about what types of therapy would be most helpful to depressed women, and how women should be advised to change their lives so as to make them more fulfilling and healthy. Such advice to women should be tempered with a caution that currently there are no definitive answers to the question "Why are women so much more likely than men to be depressed?"

The conclusion that we do not know enough about why women are prone to depression should challenge researchers to test existing explanations more thoroughly. It should also free researchers to consider new explanations for women's depressions, rather than assume that the well-known explanations have been proven correct. When the talents of more good researchers are directed toward the question why women are at increased risk for depression, we may begin to understand the "gray fog" that afflicts many women.

References

References

Abplanap, J. M., Haskett, R. F., & Rose, R. M. (1979). Psychoendocrinology of the menstrual cycle: 1. Enjoyment of daily activities and moods. *Psychosomatic Medicine, 41*, 587–604.

Abraham, G. E., Elsner, C. W., & Lucas, L. A. (1978). Hormonal and behavioral changes during the menstrual cycle. *Senologia, 3*, 33–38.

Abraham, K. (1960). Notes on the psychoanalytic treatment of manic depressive insanity and allied conditions. In *Selected papers on psychoanalysis*. New York: Basic Books. (Original work published 1911.)

Abramson, L. Y., Seligman, M. E. P., & Teasdale, J. (1978). Learned helplessness in humans: Critique and reformulation. *Journal of Abnormal Psychology, 87*, 49–74.

Achenbach, T. M., & Edelbrock, C. (1983). *Manual for the child behavior checklist and revised child behavior profile*. Burlington, VT: Queen City Printers.

Alagna, S. W., & Hamilton, J. A. (in press). On a premenstrual psychiatric diagnosis: What's in a name? *Professional Psychology*.

Albert, N., & Beck, A. T. (1975). Incidence of depression in early adolescence: A preliminary study. *Journal of Youth and Adolescence, 4*, 301–307.

Allen, M. G. (1976). Twin studies of affective illness. *Archives of General Psychiatry, 33*, 1476–1478.

Alloy, L. B., & Abramson, L. Y. (1982). Learned helplessness, depression, and the illusion of control. *Journal of Personality and Social Psychology, 42*, 1114–1126.

Amenson, C. S., & Lewinsohn, P. M. (1981). An investigation into the observed sex differences in prevalence of unipolar depression. *Journal of Abnormal Psychology, 90*, 1–13.

American Psychiatric Association. (1968). *Diagnostic and statistical manual of mental disorders* (2nd ed.). Washington, DC: Author.

American Psychiatric Association. (1980). *Diagnostic and statistical manual of mental disorders* (3rd ed.). Washington, DC: Author.

American Psychiatric Association. (1987). *Diagnostic and statistical manual of mental disorders* (3rd ed., revised). Washington, DC: Author.

American Psychological Association. (1989). *Task force on women and depression: Final report.* Washington, DC: Author.

Andersch, B., Hahn, L., Andersson, M., & Isaksson, B. (1978). Body water and weight in patients with premenstrual tension. *British Journal of Obstetrics and Gynaecology, 85*, 546–551.

Andersen, A. N., Larsen, J. F., Steenstrup, O. R., Svendstrup, B., & Nielson, J. (1977). Effect of bromocriptine on the premenstrual syndrome. *British Journal of Obstetrics and Gynaecology, 84*, 370–374.

Anderson, J. C., Williams, S., McGee, R., & Silva, P. A. (1987). DSM-III disorders in preadolescent children. *Archives of General Psychiatry, 44*, 69–76.

Andreasen, N. C., Rice, J., Endicott, J., Coryell, W., Grove, W. M., & Reich, T. (1987). Familial rates of affective disorder. *Archives of General Psychiatry, 44*, 461–469.

Aneshensel, C. S. (1986). Marital and employment role-strain, social support, and depression among adult women. In S. E. Hobfoll (Ed.), *Stress, social support, and women* (pp. 99–114). New York: Hemisphere.

Aneshensel, C. S., Frerichs, R. R., & Clark, V. A. (1981). Family roles and sex differences in depression. *Journal of Health and Social Behavior, 22*, 379–393.

Arieti, S., & Bemporad, J. R. (1980). The psychological organization of depression. *American Journal of Psychiatry, 137*, 1360–1365.

Atkin, C. (1975). *Effects of television advertising on children* (second-year experimental evidence). Michigan State University, Department of Communication.

Backstrom, T., & Cartensen, H. (1974). Estrogen and progesterone in plasma in relation to premenstrual tension. *Journal of Steroid Biochemistry, 5*, 257–260.

Backstrom, T., & Mattsson, B. (1975). Correlations of symptoms in premenstrual tension to oestrogen and progesterone concentration in blood plasma. *Neuropsychobiology, 1*, 80–86.

Backstrom, T., Sanders, D., & Leask, R. (1983). Mood, sexuality, hormones and the menstrual cycle: 2. Hormone levels and their relationship to the premenstrual syndrome. *Psychosomatic Medicine, 45*, 503–507.

Baldessarini, R. J. (1986). A summary of biomedical aspects of mood disorders. In J. C. Coyne (Ed.), *Essential papers on depression* (pp. 459–492). New York: New York University Press.

Baldwin, J. A. (1971). *The mental hospital in the psychiatric service: A case register study.* New York: Oxford University Press.

Ballinger, C. G., Buckley, D. E., Naylor, G. J., & Stansfield, D. A. (1979). Emotional disturbance following childbirth: Clinical findings and urinary excretion of cyclic AMP. *Psychological Medicine, 9,* 293–300.

Bandura, A. (1973). *Aggression: A social learning analysis.* Englewood Cliffs, NJ: Prentice-Hall.

Bandura, A. (1977). Self-efficacy: Toward a unifying theory of behavioral change. *Psychological Review, 84,* 191–215.

Bandura, A. (1986). *Social foundations of thought and action.* Englewood Cliffs, NJ: Prentice-Hall.

Bandura, A., & Cervone, D. (1983). Self-evaluative and self-efficacy mechanisms governing the motivational effects of goal systems. *Journal of Personality and Social Psychology, 45,* 1017–1028.

Bar-Tal, D., & Frieze, I. H. (1977). Achievement motivation for males and females as a determinant of attributions for success and failure. *Sex Roles, 3,* 301–313.

Bardwick, J. M. (1971). *The psychology of women: A study of bio-cultural conflicts.* New York: Harper & Row.

Barnett, R. C. (1979, March). *Parent child-rearing attitudes: Today and yesterday.* Paper presented at the meeting of the Society for Research in Child Development, San Francisco.

Barthol, K. M. (1978). The sex structuring of organizations: A search for possible causes. *Academy of Management Review, 3,* 805–815.

Baruch, G., Barnett, R., & Rivers, C. (1983). *Life prints.* New York: McGraw-Hill.

Bash, K. W., & Bash-Liechti, J. (1969). Studies on the epidemiology of neuro-psychiatric disorders among the rural population of the province of Khuzestan, Iran. *Social Psychiatry, 4,* 137–143.

Bash, K. W., & Bash-Liechti, J. (1974). Studies on the epidemiology of neuro-psychiatric disorders among the population of the city of Shiraz, Iran. *Social Psychiatry, 9,* 163–171.

Basow, S. A. (1986). *Gender stereotypes: Traditions and alternatives* (2nd ed.). Monterey, CA: Brooks/Cole.

Battle, E., & Lacey, B. A. (1972). Context for hyperactivity in children over time. *Child Development, 43,* 757–772.

Baucom, D. H., & Weiss, B. (1986). Peers' granting of control to women with different sex role identities: Implications for depression. *Journal of Personality and Social Psychology, 51,* 1075–1080.

Bazzoui, W. (1970). Affective disorders in Iraq. *British Journal of Psychiatry,* *117*, 185–203.

Beck, A. T. (1967). *Depression: Clinical, experimental and theoretical aspects.* Philadelphia: University of Pennsylvania Press.

Beck, A. T. (1976). *Cognitive therapy and the emotional disorders.* New York: International Universities Press.

Beck, A. T., Rush, A. J., Shaw, B. F., & Emery, G. (1979). *Cognitive therapy of depression.* New York: Guilford.

Beck, J. A. L. (1977). Locus of control, task expectancies, and children's performance following failure. *Journal of Educational Psychology, 71,* 207–210.

Bem, S. L. (1974). The measurement of psychological androgyny. *Journal of Consulting and Clinical Psychology, 42,* 155–162.

Bem, S. L. (1985). Androgyny and gender schema theory: A conceptual and empirical integration. In T. B. Sonderegger (Ed.), *Psychology and gender: Nebraska symposium on motivation, 1984* (Vol. 32, pp. 179–226). Lincoln: University of Nebraska Press.

Berah, E. F. (1983). Sex differences in psychiatric morbidity: An analysis of Victorian data. *Australian and New Zealand Journal of Psychology, 17,* 266–273.

Bernadt, M. W., & Murray, R. M. (1986). Psychiatric disorder, drinking and alcoholism: What are the links? *British Journal of Psychiatry, 148,* 393–400.

Bernard, J. (1972). *The future of marriage.* New York: Bantam Books.

Bernardy, R. (1987). An important new family issue. *Gray Panther Network, 11,* 4–5.

Berndt, S. M., Berndt, D. J., & Kaiser, C. F. (1982). Attributional styles for helplessness and depression: The importance of sex and situational context. *Sex Roles, 8*(4), 433–441.

Bibring, E. (1953). The mechanism of depression. In P. Greenacre (Ed.), *Affective disorders* (pp. 13–48). New York: International Universities Press.

Blaney, P. H. (1986). Affect and memory: A review. *Psychological Bulletin, 99,* 229–246.

Blatt, S. J., Wein, S. J., Chevron, E., & Quinlan, D. M. (1979). Parental representations and depression in normal young adults. *Journal of Abnormal Psychology, 88,* 388–397.

Blazer, D., & Williams, C. D. (1980). Epidemiology of dysphoria and depression in an elderly population. *American Journal of Psychiatry, 137,* 439–444.

Block, J. H. (1976). Issues, problems, and pitfalls in assessing sex differences: A critical review of *The psychology of sex differences. Merrill-Palmer Quarterly, 22,* 283–308.

Block, J. H. (1979a). Another look at sex differentiation in the socialization behaviors of mothers and fathers. In J. Sherman & F. L. Denmark (Eds.), *The psychology of women: Future directions of research* (pp. 31–87). New York: Psychological Dimensions.

Block, J. H. (1979b, September). *Personality development in males and females: The influence of differential socialization.* Paper presented as part of the Master Lecture Series at the meeting of the American Psychological Association, New York.

Block, J., & Gjerde, P. F. (in press). Depressive symptomatology in late adolescence: A longitudinal perspective on personality antecedents. In J. E. Rolf, A. Masten, D. Cicchetti, K. Neuchterlein, & S. Weintraub (Eds.), *Risk and protective factors in the development of psychopathology.* New York: Cambridge University Press.

Blood, R. O., & Wolfe, D. M. (1960). *Husbands and wives: The dynamics of married living.* New York: Free Press.

Bloom, L. Z., Coburn, K., & Pearlman, J. (1975). *The new assertive woman.* New York: Dell.

Blos, P. (1962). *On adolescence: A psychoanalytic interpretation.* New York: Free Press.

Blumberg, N. J. (1980). Effects of neonatal risk, maternal attitude, and cognitive style on early postpartum adjustment. *Journal of Abnormal Psychology, 89,* 139–150.

Bornstein, P. E., Clayton, P. J., Halikas, J. A., Maurice, W. L., & Robins, E. (1973). The depression of widowhood after thirteen months. *British Journal of Psychiatry, 122,* 561–566.

Bower, G. H. (1981). Mood and memory. *American Psychologist, 36,* 129–148.

Boyd, J. H., & Weissman, M. M. (1981). Epidemiology of affective disorders: A re-examination and future directions. *Archives of General Psychiatry, 38,* 1039–1046.

Braverman, J., & Roux, J. F. (1978). Screening for the patient at risk for postpartum depression. *Obstetrics and Gynecology, 52,* 731–736.

Brockner, J., & Hulton, A. J. B. (1978). How to reverse the vicious cycle of low self-esteem: The importance of attentional focus. *Journal of Experimental Social Psychology, 14,* 564–578.

Brody, E. M. (1985). Parent care as a normative family stress. *The Gerontologist, 25,* 19–29.

Brooks-Gunn, J., & Ruble, D. N. (1982). Developmental processes in the experience of menarche. In A. Baum & J. E. Singer (Eds.), *Handbook of medical psychology: Issues in child health and illness* (Vol. 2, pp. 117–147). Hillsdale, NJ: Erlbaum.

Brooks-Gunn, J., & Warren, M. P. (1987, April). *Biological and social con-*

tributions to negative affect in young adolescent girls. Paper presented to the Society for Research in Child Development, Baltimore, MD.

Broverman, I. K., Broverman, D. M., Clarkson, F. E., & Rosenkrantz, P. S. (1972). Sex-role stereotypes: A current appraisal. *Journal of Social Issues, 28,* 59–78.

Brown, D. G. (1956). Sex-role preference in young children. *Psychological Monographs, 70* (Whole No. 421).

Brown, L. K. (1979). Women and business management. *Signs, 5,* 266–288.

Brown, L. S. (1988, September). *Victimization as a risk factor in depressive symptomatology in women.* Paper presented to the APA Task Force on Women and Depression, Boston, MA.

Brown, S. M. (1979). Male versus female leaders: A comparison of empirical studies. *Sex Roles, 5,* 595–611.

Bryson, R., Bryson, J. B., & Johnson, M. F. (1978). Family size, satisfaction, and productivity in dual-career couples. *Psychology of Women Quarterly, 3,* 67–77.

Bryson, S. E., & Pilon, D. J. (1984). Sex differences in depression and the method of administering the Beck Depression Inventory. *Journal of Clinical Psychology, 40,* 529–534.

Buchan, T. (1969). Depression in South African patients. *South African Medical Journal, 43,* 1055–1058.

Bunney, Jr., W. E., & Davis, J. M. (1982). Norepinephrine in depressive reactions: A review. *Archives of General Psychiatry, 13,* 483–494.

Burgess, A. W., & Holmstrom, L. (1974). Rape trauma syndrome. *American Journal of Psychiatry, 131,* 981–986.

Burke, R. J., & Weir, T. (1976). Relationship of wives' employment status to husband, wife, and pair satisfaction and performance. *Journal of Marriage and the Family, 38,* 279–288.

Burnam, M. A., Stein, J. A., Golding, J. M., Siegel, J. M., Sorenson, S. B., Forsythe, A. B., & Telles, C. A. (1988). Sexual assault and mental disorders in a community population. *Journal of Consulting and Clinical Psychology, 56,* 843–850.

Buss, A. H. (1961). *The psychology of aggression.* New York: Wiley.

Buss, A., & Scheier, M. (1976). Self-consciousness, self-awareness and self-attribution. *Journal of Research in Personality, 10,* 463–468.

Buss, D. M. (1988). The evolution of human intrasexual competition: The tactics of mate attraction. *Journal of Personality & Social Psychology, 54,* 616–628.

Butler, L. D., & Nolen-Hoeksema, S. (1988). *Sex differences in choices of responses to depression.* Unpublished data, Stanford University, Stanford, CA.

Byrne, D. G. (1980). The prevalence of symptoms of depression in an Australian general population. *Australian and New Zealand Journal of Psychiatry, 14*, 65–71.

Cadoret, R., & Winokur, G. (1974). Depression in alcoholism. *Annals of the New York Academy of Sciences, 23*, 34–39.

Canadian Bureau of Statistics. (1970). *Mental health statistics: 1. Institutional admissions and separation, 1967.* Ottawa: The Queen's Printer.

Cantor, M. H. (1983). Strain among caregivers: A study of the experience in the United States. *The Gerontologist, 23*, 597–604.

Carlson, G. A., & Cantwell, D. P. (1980). Unmasking masked depression in children and adolescents. *American Journal of Psychiatry, 137*, 445–449.

Carmen, E., Rieker, P. P., & Mills, T. (1984). Victims of violence and psychiatric illness. *American Journal of Psychiatry, 141*, 378–383.

Carstensen, L. L., Morrow, J., & Roberts, T. (1988, May). *Emotional responses to interpersonal conflicts: A field study of couples.* Paper presented at the Stanford-Berkeley Conference, Stanford, CA.

Carver, C. S., Blaney, P. H., & Scheier, M. F. (1979). Reassertion and giving up: The interactive role of self-directed attention and outcome expectancy. *Journal of Personality and Social Psychology, 37*, 1859–1870.

Carver, C. S., & Scheier, M. F. (1981). *Attention and self-regulation: A control-theory approach to human behavior.* New York: Springer.

Centers, R., Raven, B. H., & Rodrigues, A. (1971). Conjugal power structure: A re-examination. *American Sociological Review, 36*, 264–278.

Chapman, L. J., & Chapman, D. T. (1969). Illusory correlations as an obstacle to the use of valid psychodiagnostic signs. *Journal of Abnormal Psychology, 74*, 271–280.

Cherry, L. (1975). The preschool teacher-child dyad: Sex differences in verbal interaction. *Child Development, 46*, 532–535.

Chess, S., & Thomas, C. (1972). Differences in outcome with early intervention in children with behavior disorders. In M. Roff, L. Robins, & M. Pollack (Eds.), *Life history research in psychopathology* (Vol. 2, pp. 35–46). Minneapolis: University of Minnesota Press.

Chevron, E. S., Quinlan, D. M., & Blatt, S. J. (1978). Sex roles and gender differences in the expression of depression. *Journal of Abnormal Psychology, 87*, 680–683.

Chino, A. F., & Funabiki, D. (1984). A cross-validation of sex differences in the expression of depression. *Sex Roles, 11*, 175–187.

Chodoff, P. (1972). The depressive personality: A critical review. *Archives of General Psychiatry, 27*, 666–673.

Chodorow, N. (1978). *The reproduction of mothering.* Berkeley, CA: University of California Press.

Christie, K. M. (1968). *A first assessment of costs and benefits associated with drug usage in New Zealand mental hospitals.* Auckland: New Zealand Institute of Economic Research.

Clancy, K., & Gove, W. (1974). Sex differences in mental illness: An analysis of response bias in self-reports. *American Journal of Sociology, 80,* 205–216.

Clark, D. M., & Teasdale, J. D. (1982). Diurnal variation in clinical depression and accessibility of memories of positive and negative experiences. *Journal of Abnormal Psychology, 91,* 87–95.

Clark, M. S., & Isen, A. M. (1982). Towards understanding the relationship between feeling states and social behavior. In A. Hastorf & A. M. Isen (Eds.), *Cognitive social psychology* (pp. 72–108). New York: Elsevier.

Clarke, A. E., & Ruble, D. N. (1978). Young adolescents' beliefs concerning menstruation. *Child Development, 49,* 231–234.

Clausen, J. A. (1975). The social meaning of differential physical and sexual maturation. In S. E. Dragaster & G. H. Elder, Jr. (Eds.), *Adolescence in the life cycle* (pp. 25–48). New York: Halstead.

Clayton, P. J. (1981). The epidemiology of bipolar affective disorder. *Comprehensive Psychiatry, 22,* 31–43.

Cleary, P. D., & Mechanic, D. (1983). Sex differences in psychological distress among married people. *Journal of Health and Social Behavior, 24,* 111–121.

Cloninger, C. R., Christiansen, K. O., Reich, T., & Gottesman, I. (1978). Implications of sex differences in the prevalence of antisocial personality, alcoholism, and criminality for familial transmission. *Archives of General Psychiatry, 35,* 941–951.

Cohen, S., & Willis, T. A. (1985). Stress, social support, and the buffering hypothesis. *Psychological Bulletin, 98,* 310–357.

Coleman, J. S. (1961). *The adolescent society: The social life of the teenager and its impact on education.* New York: Free Press.

Comstock, G. W., & Helsing, K. J. (1976). Symptoms of depression in two communities. *Psychological Medicine, 6,* 551–563.

Cone, R. I., Davis, G. A., & Coy, R. W. (1981). Effects of ovarian steroids on serotonin metabolism within grossly dissected and microdissected brain regions of the ovariectomized rat. *Brain Research Bulletin, 7,* 639–644.

Cooper, C. (1988, April). *Individuality and connectedness in families of early adolescents.* Talk given at Center for Studies of Families, Children and Youth, Stanford University.

Cooper, J. E., Kendell, R. E., Gurland, B. J., Sartorius, N., & Farkas, T. (1969). Cross-national study of diagnosis of the mental disorders: Some results from the first comparative investigation. *American Journal of Psychiatry, 125* (Suppl.), 21–29.

Cooper, M. L., Russell, M., & George, W. H. (1988). Coping, expectancies, and alcohol abuse: A test of social learning formulations. *Journal of Abnormal Psychology, 97,* 218–230.

Cotton, N. S. (1979). The familial incidence of alcoholism: A review. *Journal of Studies on Alcohol, 40*, 89–116.

Coyne, J. C. (1976). Depression and the response of others. *Journal of Abnormal Psychology, 85*, 186–193.

Coyne, J. C., Metalsky, G. I., & Lavelle, T. L. (1980). Learned helplessness as experimenter-induced failure and its alleviation with attentional redeployment. *Journal of Abnormal Psychology, 89*, 350–357.

Crosby, F. J. (1982). *Relative deprivation and working women*. Oxford: Oxford University Press.

Crull, P. (1984). Sexual harassment and women's health. In W. Chavkin (Ed.), *Double exposure* (pp. 100–120). New York: Monthly Review Press.

Culberg, J. (1972). Mood changes and menstrual symptoms with different gestagen-estrogen combinations. *Acta Psychiatrica Scandinavica, 40*, 89–116.

Cutrona, C. E. (1982). Nonpsychotic postpartum depression: A review of recent research. *Clinical Psychology Review, 2*, 487–503.

Cutrona, C. E. (1983). Causal attributions and perinatal depression. *Journal of Abnormal Psychology, 92*(2), 161–172.

Dalton, K. (1964). *Premenstrual syndrome*. Springfield, IL: Charles C. Thomas.

Dauber, R. B. (1984). Subliminal psychodynamic activation in depression: On the role of autonomy issues in depressed college women. *Journal of Abnormal Psychology, 93*, 9–18.

Davidson, J., & Robertson, E. (1985). A follow-up study of postpartum illness, 1946–1978. *Acta Psychiatrica Scandinavica, 71*, 451–457.

Davis, K. (1940). The sociology of parent-youth conflict. *American Sociological Review, 5*, 523–536.

Davison, G. C., & Neale, J. M. (1982). *Abnormal psychology: An experimental clinical approach* (3rd ed.). New York: Wiley.

Dean, G., Walsh, D., Downing, H., & Shelley, E. (1981). First admissions of native-born and immigrants to psychiatric hospitals in south-east England, 1976. *British Journal of Psychiatry, 139*, 506–512.

Deaux, K. (1979). Self evaluations of male and female managers. *Sex Roles, 5*, 571–580.

Deaux, K., & Farris, E. (1977). Attributing causes for one's own performance: The effects of sex, norms, and outcome. *Journal of Research in Personality, 11*, 59–72.

Deaux, K., & Major, B. (1987). Putting gender into context: An interactive model of gender-related behavior. *Psychological Review, 94*, 369–389.

Deaux, K., & Taynor, J. (1973). Evaluation of male and female ability: Bias works two ways. *Psychological Reports, 32*, 261–262.

Demarchi, G. W., & Tong, J. E. (1972). Menstrual, diurnal, and activation effects on the resolution of temporally paired flashes. *Psychophysiology, 9,* 362–367.

Deutsch, H. (1944). *The psychology of women.* New York: Grune & Stratton.

Diener, C. I., & Dweck, C. S. (1978). Analysis of learned helplessness: Continuous changes in performance, strategy, and achievement cognitions following failure. *Journal of Personality and Social Psychology, 36,* 451–462.

Dornbusch, S. M., Carlsmith, J. M., Duncan, P. D., Gross, R. T., Martin, J. A., Ritter, P. L., & Siegel-Gorelick, B. (1984). Sexual maturation, social class, and the desire to be thin among adolescent females. *Developmental and Behavioral Pediatrics, 5,* 308–314.

Douvan, E., & Adelson, J. (1966). *The adolescent experience.* New York: Wiley.

Duval, S., & Wicklund, R. (1972). *A theory of objective self-awareness.* New York: Academic Press.

Dweck, C. S. (1975). The role of expectations and attributions in the alleviation of learned helplessness. *Journal of Personality and Social Psychology, 31,* 451–462.

Dweck, C. S., & Bush, E. S. (1976). Sex differences in learned helplessness: 1. Differential debilitation with peer and adult evaluators. *Developmental Psychology, 12,* 147–156.

Dweck, C. S., Davidson, W., Nelson, S., & Enna, B. (1978). Sex differences in learned helplessness: 2. The contingencies of evaluative feedback in the classroom. 3. An experimental analysis. *Developmental Psychology, 14,* 268–276.

Dweck, C. S., & Elliott, E. S. (1983). Achievement motivation. In P. Mussen & E. M. Hetherington (Eds.), *Handbook of Child Psychology* (Vol. 4, pp. 643–691). New York: Wiley.

Dweck, C. S., & Licht, B. G. (1980). *Human helplessness: Theory and applications.* New York: Academic Press.

Dweck, C. S., & Repucci, D. (1973). Learned helplessness and reinforcement responsibility in children. *Journal of Personality and Social Psychology, 25,* 109–116.

Eagly, A. H. (1978). Sex differences in influenceability. *Psychological Bulletin, 85,* 86–116.

Eagly, A. H. (1983). Gender and social influence: A social psychological analysis. *American Psychologist, 38,* 971–981.

Eagly, A. H., & Carli, L. L. (1981). Sex of researchers and sex-typed communications as determinants of sex differences in influenceability: A meta-analysis of social influence studies. *Psychological Bulletin, 90,* 1–20.

Eagly, A. H., & Crowley, M. (1986). Gender and helping behavior: A meta-analytic review of the social psychological literature. *Psychological Bulletin, 100,* 283–308.

Eagly, A. H., & Steffen, V. J. (1986). Gender and aggressive behavior: A meta-analytic review of the social psychological literature. *Psychological Bulletin, 100,* 309–330.

Eaton, W. W., & Kessler, L. G. (1981). Rates of symptoms of depression in a national sample. *American Journal of Epidemiology, 114,* 528–538.

Ebeling, J., King, M., & Rogers, M. (1977). Hierarchical position in the work organization and job satisfaction: Findings in national survey data. *Human Relations, 32,* 387–394.

Eccles, J. (1985). Sex differences in achievement patterns. In T. B. Sonderegger (Ed.), *Psychology and gender: Nebraska symposium on motivation, 1984* (Vol. 32, pp. 97–132). Lincoln: University of Nebraska Press.

Eccles, J., Adler, T., & Meece, J. L. (1984). Sex differences in achievement: A test of alternate theories. *Journal of Personality and Social Psychology, 46,* 26–43.

Eccles, J. S., Miller, C., Tucker, M. L., Becker, J., Schramm, W., Midgley, R., Holmes, W., Pasch, L., & Miller, M. (1988, March). *Hormones and affect at early adolescence.* Paper presented at the biannual meeting of the Society for Research on Adolescence, Alexandria, VA.

Egeland, J. A., & Hostetter, S. M. (1983). Amish study: 1. Affective disorders among the Amish, 1976–1980. *American Journal of Psychiatry, 140,* 56–61.

Ehrenreich, B., & English, D. (1978). *For her own good.* New York: Anchor Press.

El-Islam, M. F. (1969). Depression and guilt: A study at an Arab psychiatric clinic. *Social Psychiatry, 4,* 56–58.

Elkin, I., Shea, T., Imber, S., Pilkonis, P., Sotsky, S., Glass, D., Watkins, J., Leber, W., & Collins, J. (1986, May). *NIMH treatment of depression collaborative research program: Initial outcome findings.* Paper presented to the American Association for the Advancement of Science, Philadelphia, PA.

Elkind, D. (1967). Egocentrism in adolescence. *Child Development, 38,* 1025–1034.

Ellis, E. M., Atkeson, B. M., & Calhoun, K. S. (1981). Short reports. *Journal of Abnormal Psychology, 90,* 263–266.

Eme, R. F. (1979). Sex differences in childhood psychopathology: A review. *Psychological Bulletin, 86,* 574–595.

Ensel, W. M. (1982). The role of age in the relationship of gender and marital status to depression. *Journal of Nervous & Mental Disease, 170,* 536–543.

Epstein, L. J. (1976). Symposium on age differentiation in depressive illness. *Journal of Gerontology, 31,* 278–282.

Erikson, E. H. (1968). *Identity: Youth and crisis.* New York: Norton.

Essen-Moeller, E. (1956). Individual traits and morbidity in a Swedish rural population. *Acta Psychiatrica Neurologica Scandinavica, 100,* 1–160.

Essen-Moeller, E., & Hagnell, O. (1961). The frequency and risk of depression within a rural population group in Scania. *Acta Psychiatrica Scandinavica, 162,* 28–32.

Etaugh, C., & Hughes, V. (1975). Teachers' evaluations of sex-typed behaviors in children: The role of teacher sex and school setting. *Developmental Psychology, 11,* 394–395.

Ezeilo, B. N., & Onyeama, W. (1980). Marital status and psychiatric illness: A Nigerian perspective. *Psychopathologie Africaine, 16,* 309–319.

Faden, V. B. (1977). *Primary diagnoses of discharges from nonfederal general hospital psychiatric inpatient units, U.S., 1975 (Mental Health Statistical Note 137).* Rockville, MD: Department of Health, Education, and Welfare Publications.

Fagot, B. I. (1974). Sex differences in toddlers' behavior and parental reaction. *Developmental Psychology, 10,* 554–558.

Fagot, B. I. (1977). Consequences of moderate cross-gender behavior in preschool children. *Child Development, 48,* 902–907.

Fagot, B. I. (1978). The influence of sex of child on parental reactions to toddler children. *Child Development, 49,* 459–465.

Farber, P. D., Khavari, K. A., & Douglass, IV, F. M. (1980). A factor analytic study of reasons for drinking: Empirical validation of positive and negative reinforcement dimensions. *Journal of Consulting and Clinical Psychology, 48,* 780–781.

Faust, M. S. (1960). Developmental maturity as a determinant in prestige of adolescent girls. *Child Development, 31,* 173–184.

Faust, M. S. (1983). Alternate constructions of adolescent growth. In J. Brooks-Gunn & A. C. Petersen (Eds.), *Girls at puberty: Biological and psychosocial perspectives* (pp. 29–50). New York: Plenum Press.

Feather, N. T. (1969). Attribution of responsibility and valence of success and failure in relation to initial confidence and task performance. *Journal of Personality and Social Psychology, 13,* 129–144.

Feather, N. T., & Simon, J. G. (1971). Attribution of responsibility and valence of outcome in relation to initial confidence and success and failure of self and other. *Journal of Personality and Social Psychology, 18,* 173–188.

Feather, N. T., & Simon, J. G. (1975). Reactions to male and female success and failure in sex-linked cultures. *Journal of Personality and Social Psychology, 31,* 20–31.

Federal Bureau of Investigation. (1986). *Crime in the United States: Uniform crime report.* Washington, DC: U.S. Department of Justice.

Feighner, J. P., Robins, E., Guze, S. B., Woodruff, R. A., Winokur, G., & Munoz, R. (1972). Diagnostic criteria for use in psychiatric research. *Archives of General Psychiatry, 26,* 57–63.

Feldman-Summers, S., & Kiesler, S. B. (1974). Those who are number two try harder: The effects of sex on attributions of causality. *Journal of Personality and Social Psychology, 30* (6), 846–855.

Fenichel, O. (1945). *The psychoanalytic theory of neurosis.* New York: Norton.

Fenigstein, A. (1979). Self-consciousness, self-attention, and social interaction. *Journal of Personality and Social Psychology, 37,* 75–78.

Fenigstein, A., & Levine, M. P. (1984). Self-attention, concept activation, and the causal self. *Journal of Experimental Social Psychology, 20,* 231–245.

Fenigstein, A., Scheier, M. F., & Buss, A. H. (1975). Public and private self-consciousness: Assessment and theory. *Journal of Consulting and Clinical Psychology, 43,* 522–527.

Fidell, L. S. (1976). Empirical verification of sex discrimination in hiring practices in psychology. In R. Unger & F. Denmark (Eds.), *Woman: Dependent or independent variable?* (pp. 779–782). New York: Psychological Dimensions.

Fieve, R. R., Go, R., Dunner, D. L., & Elston, R. (1984). Search for biological/genetic markers in a long-term epidemiological and morbid risk study of affective disorders. *Journal of Psychiatric Research, 18,* 425–445.

Finkelhor, D. (1979). *Sexually victimized children.* New York: Free Press.

Firth, M. (1982). Sex discrimination in job opportunities for women. *Sex Roles, 8,* 891–901.

Flavell, J. H. (1979). Metacognition and cognitive monitoring: A new area of cognitive-developmental inquiry. *American Psychologist, 34,* 906–911.

Forgas, J. P., & Bower, G. H. (1987). Mood effects on person-perception judgments. *Journal of Personality and Social Psychology, 53,* 53–60.

Forgas, J. P., Bower, G. H., & Krantz, S. E. (1984). The influence of mood on perception of social interactions. *Journal of Experimental Social Psychology, 20,* 497–513.

Foucault, M. (1965). *Madness and civilization.* New York: Mentor Books.

Frank, R. T. (1931). The hormonal causes of premenstrual tension. *Archives of Neurological Psychiatry, 26,* 1053.

Freud, A. (1958). Adolescence. *Psychoanalytic Study of the Child, 13,* 255–278.

Freud, S. (1905/1964). Three essays on the theory of sexuality. In *Collected works* (Vol. 7, pp. 125–245). London: Hogarth Press.

Freud, S. (1917/1964). Mourning and melancholia. In *Collected works* (Vol. 14, pp. 243–258). London: Hogarth Press.

Freud, S. (1925/1964). Some psychical consequences of the anatomical distinctions between the sexes. In J. Strachey (Ed.), *The standard edition of the complete psychological works of Sigmund Freud* (Vol. 19, pp. 248–258). London: Hogarth Press.

Freud, S. (1931/1964). Female sexuality. In J. Strachey (Ed.), *The standard edition of the complete psychological works of Sigmund Freud* (Vol. 21, pp. 225–243). London: Hogarth Press.

Friedan, B. (1963). *The feminine mystique.* New York: Norton.

Frieze, I. H., Parsons, J. E., Johnson, P. B., Ruble, D. N., & Zellman, G. L. (1978). *Women and sex roles: A social psychological perspective.* New York: Norton.

Frieze, I. H., & Snyder, H. N. (1980). Children's beliefs about the causes of success and failure in school settings. *Journal of Educational Psychology, 72*, 186–196.

Frieze, I. H., Whitley, B., Hanusa, B., & McHugh, M. (1982). Assessing the theoretical models for sex differences in causal attributions for success and failure. *Sex Roles, 3*, 333–343.

Frodi, A., Macaulay, J., & Thome, P. R. (1977). Are women always less aggressive than men? A review of the experimental literature. *Psychological Review, 84*, 634–660.

Frost, W. D., & Averill, J. R. (1982). Differences between men and women in the everyday experience of anger. In J. R. Averill (Ed.), *Anger and aggression: An essay on emotion* (pp. 281–316). New York: Springer-Verlag.

Fuchs, V. R. (1986). Sex differences in economic well-being. *Science, 232*, 459–464.

Funabiki, D., Bologna, N. C., Pepping, M., & Fitzgerald, K. C. (1980). Revisiting sex differences in the expression of depression. *Journal of Abnormal Psychology, 89*, 194–202.

Garai, J., & Scheinfeld, A. (1968). Sex differences in mental and behavioral traits. *Genetic Psychology Monographs, 77*, 169–299.

Gayford, J. J. (1975). Wife battering: A preliminary survey of 100 cases. *British Medical Journal, 1*, 194–197.

Gelder, M. (1978). Hormones and postpartum depression. In M. Sandler (Ed.), *Mental illness in pregnancy and the puerperium* (pp. 80–90). Oxford: Oxford University Press.

Gentemann, K. M. (1984). Wife beating: Attitudes of a non-clinical population. *Victimology, 9*, 109–119.

Gershon, E. S. (1983). The genetics of affective disorders. In L. Grinspoon (Ed.), *Psychiatry update* (pp. 434–457). Washington, DC: American Psychiatric Press.

Gershon, E. S., & Bunney, W. E. (1976). The question of X-linkage in bipolar manic-depressive illness. *Journal of Psychiatric Research, 13*, 99–117.

References   233

Gershon, E. S., & Liebowitz, J. H. (1975). Sociocultural and demographic correlates of affective disorders in Jerusalem. *Journal of Psychiatric Research, 12*, 37–50.

Gerson, K. (1985). *Hard choices: How women decide about work, career and motherhood.* Berkeley, CA: University of California Press.

Gibbons, F. X., Smith, T. W., Ingram, R. E., Pearce, K., Brehm, S. S., & Schroeder, D. (1985). Self-awareness and self-confrontation: Effects of self-focused attention on members of a clinical population. *Journal of Personality and Social Psychology, 48*, 662–675.

Gilligan, C. (1982). *In a different voice: Psychological theory and women's development.* Cambridge, MA: Harvard University Press.

Gilman, C. P. (1975). *The living of Charlotte Perkins Gilman.* New York: Harper & Row.

Gitelson, B., Petersen, A. C., & Tobin-Richards, M. H. (1982). Adolescents' expectancies of success, self-evaluations, and attributions about performance on spatial and verbal tasks. *Sex Roles, 8*, 411–419.

Gjerde, P. F., Block, J., & Block, J. H. (1988). Depressive symptoms and personality during late adolescence: Gender differences in the externalization-internalization of symptom expression. *Journal of Abnormal Psychology, 97*, 475–486.

Glass, G. V., McGraw, B., & Smith, M. L. (1981). *Meta-analysis in social research.* Beverly Hills, CA: Sage.

Goldberg, S. (1968). Are women prejudiced against women? *Transactions, 5*, 28–30.

Golden, M., & Birns, B. (1975). Social class and infant intelligence. In M. Lewis (Ed.), *Origins of intelligence: Infancy and early childhood* (pp. 299–351). New York: Plenum.

Golin, S., Terrell, T., Weitz, J., & Drost, P. L. (1979). The illusion of control among depressed patients. *Journal of Abnormal Psychology, 88*, 454–457.

Goodenough, E. W. (1957). Interest in persons as an aspect of sex differences in the early years. *Genetic Psychology Monographs, 55*, 287–323.

Gordon, R. E., Kapostins, E. E., & Gordon, K. K. (1965). Factors in postpartum emotional adjustment. *Obstetrics and Gynecology, 25*, 158–166.

Gore, S., & Mangione, T. W. (1983). Social roles, sex roles and psychological distress: Additive and interactive models of sex differences. *Journal of Health and Social Behavior, 24*, 300–312.

Gottman, J. (1979). *Marital interaction: Experimental investigations.* New York: Academic Press.

Gottman, J. M., & Levenson, R. W. (in press). The social psychophysiology of marriage. In P. Noller & M. A. Fitzpatrick (Eds.), *Perspectives on marital interaction.* San Diego: College Hill Press.

Gove, W. (1972). The relationship between sex roles, marital status, and mental illness. *Social Forces, 51*, 34–44.

Gove, W., & Herb, T. (1974). Stress and mental illness among the young: A comparison of the sexes. *Social Forces, 53*, 256–265.

Gove, W. R., & Geerken, M. R. (1976). Response bias in survey of mental health: An empirical investigation. *American Journal of Sociology, 82*, 1289–1317.

Gove, W. R., McCorkel, J., Fain, T., & Hughes, M. (1976). Response bias in community surveys of mental health: Systematic bias or random noise? *Social Science and Medicine, 10*, 497–502.

Gove, W. R., & Tudor, J. F. (1973). Adult sex roles and mental illness. *American Journal of Sociology, 78*, 812–835.

Grant, E. C. G., & Pryse-Davies, J. (1968). Effect of oral contraceptives on depressive mood changes and endometrial monoamine oxidase and phosphates. *British Medical Journal, 3*, 777–780.

Grant, W. F., & Eiden, L. J. (1982). *Digest of educational statistics*. Washington, DC: National Center for Educational Statistics, U.S. Department of Education.

Green, R., Goetze, V., Whybrow, P., & Jackson, R. (1973). X-linked transmission of manic-depressive illness. *Journal of the American Medical Association, 223*, 1289.

Greenberg, J., & Pyszczynski, T. (1986). Persistent high self-focus after failure and low self-focus after success: The depressive self-focusing style. *Journal of Personality and Social Psychology, 50*, 1039–1044.

Greer, L. D. (1980). *Children's comprehension of formal features with masculine and feminine connotations*. Unpublished master's thesis, Department of Human Development, University of Kansas.

Gruber, K. J., & Gaebelein, J. (1979). Sex differences in listening comprehension. *Sex Roles, 5*, 299–310.

Hackman, E., Wirz-Justice, A., & Lichsteiner, M. (1972). The uptake of dopamine and serotonin in the rat brain during progesterone decline. *Psychopharmacologia, 32*, 182–191.

Halbreich, U., Ben-David, M., Assael, M., & Bornstein, R. (1976). Serum-prolactin in women with premenstrual syndrome. *Lancet, 2*, 654.

Halbreich, U., Endicott, J., & Nee, J. (1983). Premenstrual depressive changes. *Archives of General Psychiatry, 40*, 535–542.

Halevi, H. S., Naor, E., & Cochavy, Z. (1969). *Census of mental inpatients, 1964*. Jerusalem: Ministry of Health.

Hall, G. S. (1904). *Adolescence: Its psychology and its relations to physiology, anthropology, sociology, sex, crime, religion and education*. Englewood Cliffs, NJ: Prentice-Hall.

Hamilton, J. A. (1986). An overview of the clinical rationale for advancing gender-related psychopharmacology and drug abuse research. In B. A. Ray & M. C. Braude (Eds.), *Women and drugs: A new era for research* (NIDA Research Monograph 65, pp. 14–20). Rockville, MD: National Institute on Drug Abuse.

Hamilton, J. A., Alagna, S. W., King, L. S., & Lloyd, C. (1987). The emotional consequences of gender-based abuse in the workplace: New counseling programs for sex discrimination. *Women and Therapy, 6*, 155–182.

Hamilton, J. A., & Conrad, C. D. (1987). Toward a developmental psychopharmacology: The physiological basis of age, gender, and hormonal effects on drug responsivity. In J. D. Call, R. L. Cohen, S. I. Harrison, I. N. Berlin, & L. A. Stone (Eds.), *Basic handbook of child psychiatry* (Vol. 5, pp. 66–81). New York: Basic Books.

Hamilton, J. A., Gallant, S., & Lloyd, C. (in press). Evidence for a menstrual-linked artifact in determining rates of depression. *Journal of Nervous and Mental Diseases.*

Hammen, C. L., & Padesky, C. A. (1977). Sex differences in the expression of depressive responses on the Beck Depression Inventory. *Journal of Abnormal Psychology, 86*, 609–614.

Hammen, C. L., & Peters, S. D. (1977). Differential responses to male and female depressive reactions. *Journal of Consulting and Clinical Psychology, 45*, 994–1001.

Handley, S. L., Dunn, T. L., Baker, J. M., Cockshott, C., & Gould, S. (1977). Mood changes in puerperium, and plasma tryptophan and cortisol concentrations. *British Medical Journal, 2*, 18–22.

Handley, S. L., Dunn, T. L., Waldron, G., & Baker, J. M. (1980). Tryptophan, cortisol, and puerperal mood. *British Journal of Psychiatry, 136*, 498–508.

Hankin, J. R., & Oktay, J. S. (1979). *Mental disorder and primary care: An analytic review of the literature* (NIMH Series D, No. 5, DHEW Publication No. 78-661). Washington, DC: U.S. Government Printing Office.

Harris, B. (1980). Prospective trial of L-tryptophan in maternity blues. *British Journal of Psychiatry, 137*, 233–235.

Harter, S. (1983). Developmental perspectives on the self-system. In P. H. Mussen (Ed.), *Handbook of Child Development* (Vol. 4, pp. 275–385). New York: Wiley.

Hartup, W. W., & Keller, E. D. (1960). Nurturance in preschool children and its relation to dependency. *Child Development, 31*, 681–689.

Haward, L. R. C. (1977). Cognition in dementia presenilis. In W. L. Smith & M. Kinsbourne (Eds.), *Aging and dementia* (pp. 189–202). New York: Spectrum.

Hayman, C. R., Stewart, W. F., Lewis, F. R., & Grant, M. (1968). Sexual assault on women and children in the District of Columbia. *Public Health Reports, 83,* 12.

Heckhausen, H. (1980). Task-irrelevant cognitions during an exam: Incidence and effects. In H. W. Krohne & L. Laux (Eds.), *Achievement, stress, and anxiety.* Washington, DC: Hemisphere.

Heiby, E. M. (1983). Depression as a function of the interaction of self and environmentally controlled reinforcement. *Behavior Therapy, 14,* 430–433.

Heilman, M. E., & Guzzo, R. A. (1978). The perceived cause of work success as a mediator of sex discrimination in organizations. *Organizational Behavior and Human Performance, 21,* 346–357.

Helgason, T. (1961). The frequency of depressive states in Iceland as compared with other Scandinavian countries. *Acta Psychiatrica Scandinavica, 162,* 81–90.

Helgason, T. (1977). Psychiatric services and mental illness in Iceland: Incidence study (1966–1967) with a 6–7 year follow-up. *Acta Psychiatrica Scandinavica, 268,* 1–140.

Henderson, S., Duncan-Jones, P., Byrne, D. G., Scott, R., & Adcock, S. (1979). Psychiatric disorder in Canberra: A standardized study of prevalence. *Acta Psychiatrica Scandinavica, 60,* 355–374.

Henton, J., Cate, R., Koval, J., Lloyd, S., & Christopher, S. (1983). Romance and violence in dating relationships. *Journal of Family Issues, 4,* 467–482.

Hersov, L. (1977). Emotional disorders. In M. Rutter & L. Hersov (Eds.), *Child psychiatry* (pp. 428–454). Oxford: Blackwell Scientific.

Herzog, A., & Detre, T. (1976). Psychotic reactions associated with childbirth. *Diseases of the Nervous System, 37,* 229–235.

Hetherington, E. M., Cox, M., & Cox, R. (1979). Play and social interaction in children following divorce. *Journal of Social Issues, 35,* 26–49.

Hill, J. P., & Holmbeck, G. N. (1987). Familial adaptation to biological change during adolescence. In R. M. Lerner & T. T. Foch (Eds.), *Biological-psychosocial interactions in early adolescence: A life-span perspective* (pp. 207–224). Hillsdale, NJ: Erlbaum.

Hill, J. P., & Lynch, M. E. (1983). The intensification of gender-related role expectations during early adolescence. In J. Brooks-Gunn & A. C. Petersen (Eds.), *Girls at puberty* (pp. 201–228). New York: Plenum.

Hirschfeld, R. M. A., & Cross, C. K. (1982). Epidemiology of affective disorders: Psychosocial risk factors. *Archives of General Psychiatry, 39,* 35–46.

Hodell, M. (1988). *Blaming the victim.* Unpublished data, Stanford University, Stanford, CA.

Hoffman, L. W. (1977). Changes in family roles, socialization, and sex differences. *American Psychologist, 32,* 644–657.

Hollick, F. (1849). *The diseases of women, their cause and cure familiarly explained.* New York: T. W. Strog.

Holmes, T. H., & Rahe, R. H. (1967). The social readjustment rating scale. *Journal of Psychosomatic Research, 11,* 213–218.

Horney, K. (1930/1967). The distrust between the sexes. In H. Kelman (Ed.), *Feminine psychology* (pp. 107–118). New York: Norton.

Horney, K. (1934/1967). The overvaluation of love: A study of a present-day feminine type. In H. Kelman (Ed.), *Feminine psychology* (pp. 182–213). New York: Norton.

Horney, K. (1935). The problem of feminine masochism. *Psychoanalytic Review, 22,* 241–257.

Horney, K. (1935/1967). Personality changes in female adolescents. In H. Kelman (Ed.), *Feminine psychology* (pp. 234–244). New York: Norton.

Hull, J. G., & Levy, A. S. (1979). The organizational functioning of the self: An alternative to the Duval and Wicklund model of self-awareness. *Personality and Social Psychology, 37,* 756–768.

Hursch, C. J., & Selkin, J. (1974). *Rape prevention research project.* Annual report of the Violence Research Unit, Division of Psychiatric Services, Department of Health and Hospitals, Denver. (Mimeographed.)

Huston, A. C. (1983). Sex-typing. In E. M. Hetherington (Ed.), *Handbook of child psychology: 4. Socialization, personality, and social development.* New York: Wiley.

Ingram, R. E. (1984). Toward an information-processing analysis of depression. *Cognitive Therapy and Research, 8,* 443–478.

Jacklin, C. N., & Maccoby, E. E. (1978). Social behavior at 33 months in same-sex and mixed-sex dyads. *Child Development, 49,* 557–569.

Jacobson, A., & Richardson, B. (1987). Assault experiences of 100 psychiatric inpatients: Evidence of the need for routine inquiry. *American Journal of Psychiatry, 144,* 908–913.

Jacobson, E. (1971). *Depression.* New York: International Universities Press.

Jacobson, S., Fasman, J., & DiMascio, A. (1975). Deprivation in the childhood of depressed women. *Journal of Nervous and Mental Disease, 160,* 5–14.

Janowsky, D. S., Berens, S. C., & Davis, J. M. (1973). Correlations between mood, weight, and electrolytes during the menstrual cycle: A renin-angiotensin-aldosterone hypothesis of premenstrual tension. *Psychosomatic Medicine, 35,* 143–154.

Janowsky, D. S., Fann, W. E., & Davis, J. M. (1971). Monoamines and ovarian hormone-linked sexual and emotional changes: A review. *Archives of Sexual Behavior, 1,* 205–218.

Janowsky, D. S., Gorney, R., & Mandell, A. J. (1967). The menstrual cycle.

Psychiatric and ovarian-adrenocortical hormone correlates: Case study and literature review. *Archives of General Psychiatry, 17*, 459–469.

Janowsky, D. S., & Rausch, J. (1985). Biochemical hypotheses of premenstrual tension syndrome. *Psychological Medicine, 15*, 3–8.

Jarrahi-Zadeh, A., Kane, Jr., F. J., van de Castle, R. L., Lachenbruch, P. A., & Ewing, J. A. (1969). Emotional and cognitive changes in pregnancy and early puerperium. *British Journal of Psychiatry, 115*, 797–805.

Johnson, P. (1976). Women and power: Toward a theory of effectiveness. *Journal of Social Issues, 32*, 99–110.

Kandel, D. B., & Davies, M. (1986). Adult sequelae of adolescent depressive symptoms. *Archives of General Psychiatry, 43*, 255–262.

Kandel, D. B., Davies, M., & Raveis, V. H. (1985). The stressfulness of daily social roles for women: Marital, occupational and household roles. *Journal of Health and Social Behavior, 26*, 64–78.

Kanter, R. M. (1977). *Men and women of the corporation.* New York: Basic Books.

Kaplan, A. (1986). The "self-in-relation": Implications for depression in women. *Psychotherapy, 23* (2), 234–242.

Kaplan, S. L., Hong, G. K., & Weinhold, C. (1984). Epidemiology of depressive symptomatology in adolescents. *Journal of the American Academy of Child Psychiatry, 23*, 91–98.

Kashani, J. H., Beck, N. C., Hoeper, E. W., Fallahi, C., Corcoran, C. M., McAllister, J. A., Rosenberg, T. K., & Reid, J. C. (1987). Psychiatric disorders in a community sample of adolescents. *American Journal of Psychiatry, 144*, 584–589.

Kashani, J. H., Cantwell, D. P., Shekim, W. O., & Reid, J. C. (1982). Major depressive disorder in children admitted to an inpatient community mental health center. *American Journal of Psychiatry, 139*, 5.

Kashani, J. H., & Carlson, G. A. (1987). Seriously depressed preschoolers. *American Journal of Psychiatry, 144*, 3.

Kashani, J. H., Holcomb, W. R., & Orvaschel, H. (1986). Depression and depressive symptoms in preschool children from the general population. *American Journal of Psychiatry, 143*, 9.

Katz, S., & Mazur, M. (1979). *Understanding the rape victim: A synthesis of research findings.* New York: Wiley.

Kazdin, A. E., French, N. H., Unis, A. S., & Esveldt-Dawson, K. (1983). Assessment of childhood depression: Correspondence of child and parent ratings. *Journal of the American Academy of Child Psychiatry, 22*, 157–164.

Keislar, E. R. (1955). Peer group ratings of high school pupils with high and low school marks. *Journal of Experimental Education, 23*, 375–378.

Kelley, H. H., Cunningham, J. D., Grisham, J. A., Lefebvre, L. M., Sink,

C. R., & Yablon, G. (1978). Sex differences in comments made during conflict within close heterosexual pairs. *Sex Roles, 4*, 473–492.

Kessler, R. C., Price, R. H., & Wortman, C. B. (1985). Social factors in psychopathology: Stress, social support, and coping processes. *Annual Review of Psychology, 36*, 531–572.

Kilpatrick, D. G., Best, C. L., Veronen, L. J., Amick, A. E., Villeponteaux, L. A., & Ruff, G. A. (1985). Mental health correlates of criminal victimization: A random community survey. *Journal of Consulting and Clinical Psychology, 53*, 866–873.

Kilpatrick, D., Resick, P., & Veronen, L. (1981). Effects of a rape experience: A longitudinal study. *Journal of Social Issues, 37*, 105–122.

Kilpatrick, D., Veronen, L., & Resick, P. (1979). The aftermath of rape: Recent empirical findings. *American Journal of Orthopsychiatry, 49*, 658–669.

King, D. A., & Buchwald, A. M. (1982). Sex differences in subclinical depression: Administration of the Beck Depression Inventory in public and private disclosure situations. *Journal of Personality and Social Psychology, 42*, 963–969.

Klaiber, E. L., Broverman, D. M., Vogel, W., & Kobayshi, V. (1979). Estrogen therapy for severe persistent depressions in women. *Archives of General Psychiatry, 6*, 550–554.

Kleinke, C. L., Staneski, R. A., & Mason, J. K. (1982). Sex differences in coping with depression. *Sex Roles, 8*, 877–889.

Klerman, G. L., Lavori, P. W., Rice, J., Reich, T., Endicott, J., Andreasen, N. C., Keller, M. B., & Hirschfield, R. M. A. (1985). Birth-cohort trends in rates of major depressive disorder among relatives of patients with affective disorder. *Archives of General Psychiatry, 42*, 689–693.

Kohlberg, L. (1966). A cognitive-developmental analysis of children's sex-role concepts and attitudes. In E. Maccoby (Ed.), *The development of sex differences* (pp. 82–173). Stanford, CA: Stanford University Press.

Kohn, R. L., Wolfe, D. M., Quinn, R. P., & Snoek, J. D. (1965). *Organizational stress: Studies in role conflict and ambiguity.* New York: Wiley.

Koss, M. P., Gidyez, C. A., & Wisniewski, N. (1987). The scope of rape: Incidence and prevalence of sexual aggression and victimization in a national sample of higher education students. *Journal of Consulting and Clinical Psychology, 55*(2), 162–170.

Kovacs, M. (1980). Rating scales to assess depression in school-aged children. *Acta Paedopsychiatrica, 46*, 305–315.

Kovacs, M., & Beck, A. T. (1977). An empirical-clinical approach toward a definition of childhood depression. In J. G. Schulterbrandt & A. Askin (Eds.), *Depression in childhood* (pp. 1–27). New York: Raven Press.

Kovacs, M., Rush, A. J., Beck, A. T., & Hollon, S. D. (1981). Depressed outpatients treated with cognitive therapy or pharmacotherapy: A one-year follow-up. *Archives of General Psychiatry, 38*, 33–39.

Krebs, D. L., & Miller, D. T. (1985). Altruism and aggression. In G. Lindzey & E. Aronson (Eds.), *Handbook of social psychology* (3rd ed., Vol. 2, pp. 1–71). New York: Random House.

Krupinski, J., & Stoller, A. (1962). Survey of institutionalized mental patients in Victoria, Australia, 1882–1959: 2. Analyses in terms of diagnoses. *Medical Journal of Australia, 1*, 1314–1315.

Kuhl, J. (1981). Motivational and functional helplessness: The moderating effect of state versus action orientation. *Journal of Personality and Social Psychology, 40*, 155–170.

Kutner, S. J., & Brown, W. L., (1972). Types of oral contraceptives, depression and premenstrual symptoms. *Journal of Nervous & Mental Disease, 55*, 153–162.

Ladisich, W. (1977). Influence of progesterone on serotonin metabolism: A possible causal factor for mood changes. *Psychoneuroendocrinology, 2*, 257–266.

Lamb, M. E., & Roopnarine, J. L. (1979). Peer influences on sex-role development in preschoolers. *Child Development, 50*, 1219–1222.

Lamont, J., Fischhoff, J., & Gottlieb, H. (1976). Recall of parental behaviors in female neurotic depressives. *Journal of Clinical Psychology, 32*, 762–765.

Langlois, J. H., & Downs, A. C. (1980). Mothers, fathers and peers as socialization agents of sex-typed play behaviors in young children. *Child Development, 51*, 1237–1247.

Langner, T. (1962). A twenty-two item screening score of psychiatric symptoms indicating impairment. *Journal of Health and Human Behavior, 3*, 269–276.

Leahy, R. L., & Eiter, M. (1980). Moral judgment and the development of real and ideal androgynous self-image during adolescence and young adulthood. *Developmental Psychology, 16*, 362–370.

Lee, D., & Hertzberg, J. (1978). Theories of feminine personality. In I. H. Frieze, J. E. Parsons, P. B. Johnson, D. N. Rube & G. L. Zellman (Eds.), *Women and sex roles: A social psychological perspective* (pp. 28–44). New York: Norton.

Leighton, A. H., Lambo, T. A., Hughes, C. C., Leighton, D. C., Murphy, J. M., & Macklin, D. B. (1963). *Psychiatric disorder among the Yoruba*. Ithaca, NY: Cornell University Press.

Lenny, E. (1977). Women's self confidence in achievement settings. *Psychological Bulletin, 84*, 1–13.

Lerner, R. M., & Karabenick, S. A. (1974). Physical attractiveness, body attitudes, and self-concept in late adolescents. *Journal of Youth and Adolescence, 3* (4), 307–316.

LeUnes, A. D., Nation, J. R., & Turley, N. M. (1980). Male-female performance in learned helplessness. *Journal of Psychology, 104*, 255–258.

Lewinsohn, P. M. (1974). A behavioral approach to depression. In R. J. Friedman & M. M. Katz (Eds.), *The psychology of depression: Contemporary theory and research*. Washington, DC: Winston-Wiley.

Lewinsohn, P. M., Hoberman, H., Teri, L., & Hautzinger, M. (1985). An integrative theory of depression. In S. Reiss & R. Bootzin (Eds.), *Theoretical issues in behavior therapy* (pp. 331–359). New York: Academic Press.

Lloyd, C. (1980). Life events and depressive disorder reviewed. *Archives of General Psychiatry, 37*, 529–548.

Lobitz, W. C., & Post, R. D. (1979). Parameters of self-reinforcement and depression. *Journal of Abnormal Psychology, 88*, 33–41.

Lockheed, M. E., & Hall, K. P. (1976). Conceptualizing sex as a status characteristic: Applications to leadership training strategies. *Journal of Social Issues, 32*, 111–124.

Maccoby, E. E., & Jacklin, C. N. (1974). *The psychology of sex differences*. Stanford, CA: Stanford University Press.

Maccoby, E. E., & Jacklin, C. N. (1980). Sex differences in aggression: A rejoinder and reprise. *Child Development, 51*, 964–980.

Maccoby, E. E., & Jacklin, C. N. (1987). Gender segregation in childhood. In E. H. Reese (Ed.), *Advances in child development and behavior* (Vol. 20, pp. 239–288). New York: Academic Press.

Manly, P. C., McMahon, R. B., Bradley, C. F., & Davidson, P. O. (1982). Depressive attributional style and depression following childbirth. *Journal of Abnormal Psychology, 91*, 245–254.

Martin, D. J., Abramson, L. Y., & Alloy, L. B. (1984). Illusion of control for self and others in depressed and nondepressed college students. *Journal of Personality and Social Psychology, 46*, 125–136.

Martin, F. M., Brotherson, J. H. F., & Chave, S. P. W. (1957). Incidence of neurosis in a new housing estate. *British Journal of Preventative and Social Medicine, 11*, 196–202.

Martin, M. E. (1977). A maternity hospital study of psychiatric illness associated with childbirth. *Irish Journal of Medical Science, 146*, 239–244.

Masters, J. C., Barden, C., & Ford, M. E. (1979). Affective states, expressive behaviors, and learning in children. *Journal of Personality and Social Psychology, 37*, 370–380.

Mazer, M. (1967). Psychiatric disorders in general practice: The experience of an island community. *American Journal of Psychiatry, 124*, 609–615.

McBride, A. B. (1988, August). *Multiple roles, intimate relationships, and depression*. Paper presented at the 96th annual convention of the American Psychological Association, Atlanta, GA.

McCarthy, M. (1989). *Greater depression in women and a greater concern for thinness: Is there a relationship?* Unpublished manuscript.

McDougall, M. M. (1921). *Psychology of the other-one.* Columbia: Missouri Books.

McHugh, M. C., Frieze, I. H., & Hanusa, B. (1982). Attributions and sex differences in achievement: Problems and new perspectives. *Sex Roles, 8*(4), 467–479.

Mead, M. (1974). On Freud's view of female psychology. In J. Strouse (Ed.), *Women and analysis* (pp. 95–106). New York: Grossman.

Mendlewicz, J., Fleiss, J. L., & Fieve, R. R. (1972). Evidence for X-linkage in the transmission of manic-depressive illness. *Journal of the American Medical Association, 222,* 1624.

Merikangas, K. R., Weissman, M. M., & Pauls, D. L. (1985). Genetic factors in the sex ratio of major depression. *Psychological Medicine, 15,* 63–69.

Miller, J. B. (1976). *Toward a new psychology of women.* Boston: Beacon Press.

Millet, K. (1970). *Sexual politics.* New York: Doubleday.

Miranda, J., & Persons, J. B. (1988). Dysfunctional attitudes are mood-state dependent. *Journal of Abnormal Psychology, 97,* 76–79.

Mischel, W. (1968). *Personality and assessment.* New York: Wiley.

Mischel, W. (1973). Toward a cognitive social learning theory reconceptualization of personality. *Psychological Review, 80,* 252–283.

Mitchell, J. (1974). *Psychoanalysis and feminism: Freud, Reich, Laing and women.* New York: Random House.

Mohan, B. (1972). *Social psychiatry in India: A treatise on the mentally ill.* Calcutta: The Minerva Association.

Moos, R. H. (1968). The development of a menstrual distress questionnaire. *Psychosomatic Medicine, 30,* 853–867.

Moos, R. H. (1969). Typology of menstrual cycle symptoms. *American Journal of Obstetrics & Gynecology, 103*(3), 390–402.

Moos, R. H., Kopell, B. S., Melges, F. T., Yalom, I. D., Lunde, D. T., Clayton, R. B., & Hamburg, D. A. (1969). Fluctuations in symptoms and moods during the menstrual cycle. *Journal of Psychosomatic Research, 13,* 37–44.

Moretti, M. M., Fine, S., Haley, G., & Marriage, K. (1985). Childhood and adolescent depression: Child-report versus parent-report information. *Journal of the American Academy of Child Psychiatry, 24,* 298–302.

Morrow, J., & Nolen-Hoeksema, S. (1989). The effects of response sets for depression: The remediation of depressive affect. *Journal of Personality and Social Psychology.*

Moss, H. (1974). Early sex differences and mother-infant interaction. In R. Friedman, R. Richard, & R. Vande Wiele (Eds.), *Sex differences in behavior* (pp. 149–163). New York: Wiley.

Munday, M., Brush, M. G., & Taylor, R. W. (1981). Correlations between progesterone, oestradiol and aldosterone levels in the premenstrual syndrome. *Clinical Endocrinology, 14,* 1–9.

Myers, J. K., & Weissman, M. M. (1980). Use of a self-report symptom scale to detect depression in a community sample. *American Journal of Psychiatry, 137,* 1081–1084.

Myers, J. K., Weissman, M. M., Tischler, G. L., Holzer, C. E., Leaf, P. J., Orvaschel, H., Anthony, J. C., Boyd, J. H., Burke, J. D., Kramer, M., & Stoltzman, R. (1984). Six-month prevalence of psychiatric disorders in three communities: 1980 to 1982. *Archives of General Psychiatry, 41,* 959–967.

Nadelman, L. (1974). Sex identity in American children: Memory, knowledge, and preference tests. *Developmental Psychology, 10,* 413–417.

Natale, M., & Hantas, M. (1982). Effect of temporary mood states on selective memory about the self. *Journal of Personality and Social Psychology, 42,* 927–934.

National Center for Educational Statistics. (1980, January). Degrees awarded in 1978. Reported in *Chronicle of Higher Education.*

National Center for Health Statistics. (1973). *Age at menarche.* United States Vital and Health Statistics, Series 2, No. 133. Washington, DC: Public Health Service.

National Institute of Mental Health. (1987). *Psychiatric hospitalizations in 1980.* Unpublished data, Survey and Reports Branch, Division of Biometry and Applied Sciences.

Needles, D. J. (1987). *Coping styles and their effects on depressed mood.* Unpublished manuscript, Stanford University, Department of Psychology, Stanford.

Nicholls, J. G. (1975). Causal attributions and other achievement-related cognitions: Effects of task outcome, attainment value, and sex. *Journal of Personality and Social Psychology, 31,* 379–389.

Nolen-Hoeksema, S. (1987). Sex differences in unipolar depression: Evidence and theory. *Psychological Bulletin, 101,* 259–282.

Nolen-Hoeksema, S. (1988). Life-span views on depression. In P. B. Baltes, D. L. Featherman & R. M. Lerner (Eds.), *Life-span development and behavior* (Vol. 9, pp. 203–241). Hillsdale, NJ: Erlbaum.

Nolen-Hoeksema, S. (1989). *Responses to depression: The maintenance of depressive affects through rumination.* (Under review.)

Nolen-Hoeksema, S., Girgus, J. S., & Seligman, M. E. P. (1989). *Individual differences in the course of depression in children of divorce.* (Under review.)

Nolen-Hoeksema, S., Girgus, J. S., & Seligman, M. E. P. (in press). Sex differences in explanatory style and depression in children. *Journal of Youth and Adolescence.*

Nolen-Hoeksema, S., & Morrow, J. (1988). *Beliefs about depression.* Unpublished data.

Nolen-Hoeksema, S., Morrow, J., & Fredrickson, B. L. (1989a). *The effects of response sets on the daily experience of depressive mood: A diary study.* Unpublished manuscript.

Nolen-Hoeksema, S., Morrow, J., & Fredrickson, B. L. (1989b). *Responses to depression.* Unpublished data, Stanford University.

Notman, M., & Nadelson, C. C. (1973). Medicine: A career conflict for women. *American Journal of Psychiatry, 130,* 1123–1127.

Nott, P. N., Franklin, M., Armitage, C., & Gelder, M. G. (1976). Hormonal change and mood in the puerperium. *British Journal of Psychiatry, 128,* 279–283.

Nott, R. N., & Fleminger, J. J. (1975). Presenile dementia: The difficulties of early diagnosis. *Acta Psychiatrica Scandinavica, 51,* 210–217.

O'Brien, P. M. S., Craven, D., Selby, C., & Symonds, E. M. (1979). Treatment of premenstrual syndrome by spironolactone. *British Journal of Obstetrics and Gynaecology, 86,* 142–147.

Offer, D., Ostrov, E., & Howard, K. I. (1981). *The adolescent: A psychological self portrait.* New York: Basic Books.

O'Hara, M. W., Neunaber, D. J., & Zekoski, E. M. (1984). Prospective study of postpartum depression: Prevalence, course, and predictive factors. *Journal of Abnormal Psychology, 93* (2), 158–171.

O'Hara, M., Rehm, L. P., & Campbell, S. B. (1982). Predicting depressive symptomatology: Cognitive-behavioral models and postpartum depression. *Journal of Abnormal Psychology, 91,* 457–461.

Olasov, B., & Jackson, J. (1987). Effects of expectancies on women's reports of moods during the menstrual cycle. *Psychosomatic Medicine, 49* (1), 65–78.

Orley, J., & Wing, J. K. (1979). Psychiatric disorders in two African villages. *Archives of General Psychiatry, 36,* 513–520.

Osborn, R. N., & Vicars, W. M. (1976). Sex stereotypes: An artifact in leader behavior and subordinate satisfaction analysis? *Academy of Management Journal, 19,* 439–449.

Overmier, J. B., & Seligman, M. E. P. (1967). Effects of inescapable shock upon subsequent escape and avoidance learning. *Journal of Comparative and Physiological Psychology, 63,* 28–33.

Padesky, C., & Hammen, C. (1977). *Help-seeking for depression: Sex differences in college students.* Unpublished manuscript, University of California, Los Angeles.

Paige, K. E. (1973, September). Women learn to sing the menstrual blues. *Psychology Today, 7,* 41–46.

Parachini, A. (1985, May 9). Study: Turnover of women in "men's" jobs isn't high. *Easton Express,* p. C10.

Parelman, A. (1983). *Emotional intimacy in marriage: A sex-roles perspective.* Ann Arbor, MI: UMI Research Press.

Parke, R. D., & Suomi, S. J. (1980). Adult male-infant relationships: Human and nonprimate evidence. In K. Immelmann, G. Barlow, M. Main & L. Petrinovitch (Eds.), *Behavioral development: The Bielefeld interdisciplinary project* (pp. 100–725). New York: Cambridge University Press.

Parker, G. (1979). Parental characteristics related to depressive disorders. *British Journal of Psychiatry, 134,* 138–147.

Parlee, M. (1982). Changes in moods and activation levels during the menstrual cycle in experimentally naive subjects. *Psychology of Women Quarterly, 7,* 119–131.

Parlee, M. B. (1973). The premenstrual syndrome. *Psychological Bulletin, 80*(6), 454–465.

Parlee, M. B. (1974). Stereotypic beliefs about menstruation: A methodological note on the Moos menstrual distress questionnaire and some new data. *Psychosomatic Medicine, 36*(3), 229–240.

Parsons, J. E., Adler, T. F., & Kaczala, C. M. (1982). Socialization of achievement attitudes and beliefs: Parental influences. *Child Development, 53,* 310–321.

Parsons, J. E., Meece, J. L., Adler, T. F., & Kaczala, C. M. (1982). Sex differences in attributional patterns and learned helplessness. *Sex Roles, 8,* 421–432.

Patrick, G. T. W. (1895/1979). The psychology of woman. In J. H. Williams (Ed.), *Psychology of women: Selected readings* (pp. 3–11). New York: Norton.

Paykel, E. S., Emms, E. M., Fletcher, J., & Rassaby, E. S. (1980). Life events and social support in puerperal depression. *British Journal of Psychiatry, 136,* 339–346.

Pearce, J. (1978). The recognition of depressive disorder in children. *Journal of the Royal Society of Medicine, 71,* 494–500.

Peplau, L. A. (1983). Roles and gender. In H. H. Kelley, E. Berscheid, A. Christensen, J. H. Harvey, T. L. Huston, G. Levinger, E. McClintock, L. A. Peplau & D. R. Peterson (Eds.), *Close relationships* (pp. 220–264). New York: Freeman.

Peplau, L. A. (1984). Power in dating relationships. In J. Freeman (Ed.), *Women: A feminist perspective* (3rd ed., pp. 106–121). Palo Alto, CA: Mayfield.

Peplau, L. A., & Gordon, S. L. (1985). Women and men in love: Gender differences in close heterosexual relationships. In V. E. O'Leary, R. K. Unger & B. S. Wallston (Eds.), *Women, gender, and social psychology* (pp. 257–291). Hillsdale, NJ: Erlbaum.

Perlick, D., & Atkins, A. (1984). Variations in the reported age of a patient:

A source of bias in the diagnosis of depression and dementia. *Journal of Consulting and Clinical Psychology, 52*, 812–820.

Perloff, R. M. (1977). Some antecedents of children's sex-role stereotypes. *Psychological Reports, 40*, 463–466.

Petersen, A. C., & Kennedy, R. (1988, April). *The development of depression: Is adolescence depressogenic for girls?* Paper presented at the meeting of the Society for Research on Adolescence, Alexandria, VA.

Peterson, C., & Seligman, M. E. P. (1984). Causal explanations as a risk factor for depression: Theory and evidence. *Psychological Review, 91*, 347–374.

Petty, F., & Nasrallah, H. A. (1981). Secondary depression in alcoholism: Implications for future research. *Comprehensive Psychiatry, 22*, 587–595.

Phillips, D. L., & Segal, B. E. (1969). Sexual status and psychiatric symptoms. *American Sociological Review, 34*, 58–72.

Piaget, J. (1954). *The construction of reality in the child.* New York: Basic Books.

Pietromonaco, P. R., & Markus, H. (1985). The nature of negative thoughts in depression. *Journal of Personality and Social Psychology, 48*, 799–807.

Post, F. (1975). Dementia, depression and pseudodementia. In D. F. Benson & D. Blumer (Eds.), *Psychiatric aspects of neurologic disease* (pp. 99–120). New York: Grune & Stratton.

Protheroe, C. (1969). Puerperal psychoses: A long-term study, 1927–1961. *British Journal of Psychiatry, 115*, 9–30.

Pugh, T. F., Jerath, B. K., Schmidt, W. M., & Reed, R. B. (1963). Rates of mental disease related to childbearing. *The New England Journal of Medicine, 268*(22), 1224–1228.

Puig-Antich, J. (1986). Psychobiological markers: Effects of age and puberty. In M. Rutter, C. E. Izard & P. B. Read (Eds.), *Depression in young people.* New York: Guilford Press.

Pyszczynski, T., & Greenberg, J. (1986). Evidence for a depressive self-focusing style. *Journal of Personality, 20*, 95–106.

Pyszczynski, T., & Greenberg, J. (1987). Self-regulatory perseveration and the depressive self-focusing style: A self-awareness theory of reactive depression. *Psychological Bulletin, 201*, 122–138.

Pyszczynski, T., Holt, K., & Greenberg, J. (1987). Depression, self-focused attention, and expectancies for positive and negative future life events for self and others. *Journal of Personality and Social Psychology, 52*, 994–1001.

Radloff, L. S. (1975). Sex differences in depression: The effects of occupation and marital status. *Sex Roles, 1*, 249–267.

Radloff, L. S. (1977). The CES-D scale: A self-report depression scale for research in the general population. *Journal of Applied Psychological Measurement, 1*, 385–401.

Radloff, L. S., & Monroe, M. K. (1978). Sex differences in helplessness with implications for depression. In L. S. Hansen & R. S. Rapoza (Eds.), *Career development and the counseling of women* (pp. 199–221). Springfield, IL: Thomas.

Rado, S. (1928). The problem of melancholia. *International Journal of Psychoanalysis, 9*, 420–438.

Randour, M., Strasburg, G., & Lipman-Blumen, J. (1982). Women in higher education: Trends in enrollment and degrees earned. *Harvard Education Review, 52*, 189–202.

Rao, A. V. (1970). A study of depression as prevalent in south India. *Transcultural Psychiatric Research Review, 7*, 166–167.

Raush, H. L., Barry, W. A., Hertel, R. K., & Swain, M. A. (1974). *Communication conflict and marriage.* San Francisco: Jossey-Bass.

Ray, E. P., & Bristow, A. R. (1978, April). *Sex role identities in depressed women.* Paper presented at the meeting of the Southwestern Psychological Association, New Orleans, LA.

Rees, W. D., & Lutkins, S. G. (1971). Parental depression before and after childbirth: An assessment with the Beck Depression Inventory. *Journal of the Royal College of General Practitioners, 21*, 26–31.

Rehm, L. P. (1977). A self-control model of depression. *Behavior Therapy, 8*, 787–804.

Reich, T., Clayton, P., & Winokur, G. (1969). Family history studies: 5. The genetics of mania. *American Journal of Psychiatry, 125*, 1358–1369.

Reid, R. L., & Yen, S. S. C. (1981). Premenstrual syndrome. *American Journal of Obstetrics and Gynecology, 1*, 85–104.

Repetti, R. L. (in press). Family and occupational roles and women's mental health. In M. Schwartz (Ed.), *Women at work—1987.* Los Angeles: UCLA Institute of Industrial Relations.

Repetti, R. L., & Crosby, F. (1984). Women and depression: Exploring the adult role explanation. *Journal of Social and Clinical Psychology, 2*(1), 57–70.

Rholes, W. S., Blackwell, J., Jordan, C., & Walters, C. (1980). A developmental study of learned helplessness. *Developmental Psychology, 16*, 616–624.

Rich, A. (1976). *Of woman born: Motherhood as experience and institution.* New York: Norton.

Rie, H. E. (1966). Depression in childhood: A survey of some pertinent contributions. *Journal of the American Academy of Child Psychiatry, 5*, 653–683.

Rippere, V. (1977). What's the thing to do when you're feeling depressed: A pilot study. *Behavior Research and Therapy, 15*, 185–191.

Rivera-Tovar, A. D., & Frank, E. (1988, August). *Late luteal phase dysphoric disorder.* Paper presented at American Psychological Association Convention, Atlanta, GA.

Roberts, R. E., & O'Keefe, S. J. (1981). Sex differences in depression reexamined. *Journal of Health and Social Behavior, 22,* 394–400.

Roberts, T. A., & Nolen-Hoeksema, S. (1990). Sex differences in reactions to feedback. *Sex Roles.*

Robins, L. N., Helzer, J. E., Croughan, J., & Ratcliff, K. S. (1981). National Institute of Mental Health Diagnostic Interview Schedule: Its history, characteristics, and validity. *Archives of General Psychiatry, 38,* 381–389.

Robins, L. N., Helzer, J. E., Weissman, M. M., Orvaschel, H., Gruenberg, E., Burke, J. D., & Regier, D. A. (1984). Lifetime prevalence of specific psychiatric disorders in three sites. *Archives of General Psychiatry, 41,* 949–958.

Rosen, B. C., & Aneshensel, C. S. (1976). The chameleon syndrome: A social psychological dimension of the female sex role. *Journal of Marriage and the Family, 38,* 605–617.

Rosenfield, S. L. (1980). Sex differences in depression: Do women always have higher rates? *Journal of Health and Social Behavior, 21,* 33–42.

Ross, C. E., & Mirowsky, J. (1988). Child care and emotional adjustment to wives' employment. *Journal of Health and Social Behavior, 29,* 127–138.

Rothbart, M. K. (1971). Birth order and mother-child interaction in an achievement situation. *Journal of Personality and Social Psychology, 17,* 113–120.

Rounsaville, B. J. (1978). Theories in marital violence: Evidence from a study of battered women. *Victimology, 3,* 11–31.

Rubin, Z., Peplau, L. A., & Hill, C. T. (1981). Loving and leaving: Sex differences in romantic attachments. *Sex Roles, 7,* 821–835.

Rubinow, D. R., & Roy-Byrne, P. (1984). Premenstrual syndromes: Overview from a methodological perspective. *American Journal of Psychiatry, 141,* 163–172.

Rush, A. J., Beck, A. T., Kovacs, M., & Hollon, S. D. (1977). Comparative efficacy of cognitive therapy and pharmacotherapy in the treatment of depressed outpatients. *Cognitive Therapy and Research, 1,* 17–39.

Russell, D. E. H. (1984). *Sexual exploitation.* Beverly Hills, CA: Sage Library of Social Research.

Russell, D. E. H., & Howell, N. (1983). The prevalence of rape in the United States revisited. *Journal of Women in Culture and Society, 8*(4), 688–695.

Rutter, M. (1970). Sex difference in children's responses to family stress. In E. J. Anthony & C. Koupernik (Eds.), *The child in his family* (pp. 165–196). New York: Wiley.

Rutter, M. (1979). *Changing youth in a changing society.* Cambridge, MA: Harvard University Press.

Rutter, M., Tizard, J., & Whitmore, K. (1970/1981). *Education, health and behavior.* Huntington, NY: Krieger.

Saenger, G. (1968). Psychiatric outpatients in America and the Netherlands: A transcultural comparison. *Social Psychiatry, 3,* 149–164.

Sarason, I. G. (1975). Anxiety and self-preoccupation. In I. G. Sarason & C. D. Spielberger (Eds.), *Stress and anxiety* (pp. 27–44). Washington, DC: Hemisphere.

Scarf, M. (1980). *Unfinished business: Pressure points in the lives of women.* New York: Ballantine.

Scheier, M. F., & Carver, C. S. (1977). Self-focused attention and the experience of emotion: Attraction, repulsion, elation, and depression. *Journal of Personality and Social Psychology, 35,* 625–636.

Scheier, M. F., Carver, C. S., & Gibbons, F. X. (1979). Self-directed attention, awareness of bodily states, and suggestibility. *Journal of Personality and Social Psychology, 37,* 1576–1588.

Schiff, A. F. (1969). Statistical features of rape. *Journal of Forensic Sciences, 14,* 1.

Schmidt, J. M. (1981). *The effects of subliminally presented anaclitic and introjective stimuli on normal young adults.* Unpublished doctoral dissertation, University of Southern Mississippi, Hattiesburg.

Schwarz, N., & Clore, G. L. (in press). How do I feel about it? The informative function of affective states. In K. Fiedler & J. Forgas (Eds.), *Affect, cognition, and social behavior.* Toronto: Hogrefe International.

Seligman, M. E. P. (1975). *Helplessness: On depression, development, and death.* San Francisco: Freeman.

Seligman, M. E. P. (1988, August). *Why is there so much depression? The waxing of the individual and the waning of the commons.* Paper presented to the American Psychological Association, Atlanta, GA.

Seligman, M. E. P., & Maier, S. F. (1967). Failure to escape traumatic shock. *Journal of Experimental Psychology, 74,* 1–9.

Serbin, L. A., O'Leary, K. D., Kent, R. N., & Tonick, I. J. (1973). A comparison of teacher response to the preacademic and problem behavior of boys and girls. *Child Development, 44,* 796–804.

Shapiro, S. (1986). Are elders underserved? *Generations, 10,* 14–17.

Shields, S. A. (1975). Functionalism, darwinism, and the psychology of women. *American Psychologist, 30,* 739–754.

Simmons, R. G., & Blyth, D. A. (1987). *Moving into adolescence: The impact of pubertal change and school context.* New York: Aldine DeGruyter.

Simmons, R. G., Blyth, D. A., Van Cleave, E. F., & Bush, D. M. (1979).

Entry into early adolescence: The impact of school structure, puberty, and early dating on self-esteem. *American Sociological Review, 44*, 948–967.

Simmons, R. G., Burgeson, R., Carlton-Ford, S., & Blyth, D. A. (1987). The impact of cumulative change in early adolescence. *Child Development, 58*, 1220–1234.

Simon, J. G., & Feather, N. T. (1973). Causal attributions for success and failure at university examinations. *Journal of Educational Psychology, 64*, 46–56.

Simons, A. D., Garfield, S. L., & Murphy, G. E. (1984). The process of change in cognitive therapy and pharmacotherapy for depression. *Archives of General Psychiatry, 41*, 45–51.

Slade, P. (1984). Premenstrual emotional changes in normal women: Fact or fiction? *Journal of Psychosomatic Research, 28*, 1–7.

Slovic, P. (1966). Risk-taking in children: Age and sex differences. *Child Development, 37*, 169–176.

Smith, P. K., & Daglish, L. (1977). Sex differences in parent and infant behavior in the home. *Child Development, 48*, 1250–1254.

Smith, P. K., & Green, M. (1975). Aggressive behavior in English nurseries and play groups: Sex differences and response of adults. *Child Development, 46*, 211–214.

Smith, S. L. (1976). The menstrual cycle and mood disturbances. *Clinical Obstetrics and Gynecology, 19*, 391–397.

Smith, T. W., Ingram, R. E., & Roth, L. D. (1985). Self-focused attention and depression: Self-evaluation, affect and life stress. *Motivation and Emotion, 9*, 381–389.

Smucker, M. (1982). *The children's depression inventory: Norms and psychometric analysis*. Unpublished doctoral dissertation, Pennsylvania State University, University Park.

Sohn, D. (1982). Sex differences in achievement self-attributions: An effect-size analysis. *Sex Roles, 8*(4), 345–357.

Sommer, B. (1973). The effect of menstruation on cognitive and perceptual-motor behavior: A review. *Psychosomatic Medicine, 33*, 411–428.

Sorenson, A., & Stromgren, E. (1961). The Samso investigation. *Acta Psychiatrica Scandinavica, 162*, 63–68.

Sorenson, S. B., Stein, J. A., Siegel, J. M., Golding, J. M., & Burnam, M. A. (1987). The prevalence of adult sexual assault: The Los Angeles Epidemiological Catchment Area Project. *American Journal of Epidemiology, 126*, 1154–1164.

Spencer, H. (1891). *The study of sociology*. New York: Appleton.

Stangler, R. S., & Printz, A. M. (1980). DSM-III: Psychiatric diagnosis in a university population. *American Journal of Psychiatry, 137*, 937–940.

Stark, E., Flitcraft, A., & Frazier, W. (1979). Medicine and patriarchal violence: The social construction of a "private" event. *International Journal of Health Services, 9*, 461–493.

Stein, G., Milton, F., Bebbington, P., Wood, K., & Copper, A. (1976). Relationship between mood and free and total plasma tryptophan in postpartum women. *British Medical Journal, 2*, 457.

Steinberg, L. (1981). Transformations in family relations at puberty. *Developmental Psychology, 17*, 833–840.

Steiner, M., Haskett, R. F., & Carroll, B. J. (1980). Premenstrual tension syndrome: The development of research diagnostic criteria and new rating scales. *Acta Psychiatrica Scandinavica, 62*, 177–190.

Strack, S., Blaney, P. H., Ganellen, R. J., & Coyne, J. C. (1985). Pessimistic self-preoccupation, performance deficits, and depression. *Journal of Personality and Social Psychology, 49*, 1076–1085.

Stroebe, M. S., & Stroebe, W. (1983). Who suffers more? Sex differences in health risks of the widowed. *Psychological Bulletin, 93*, 279–301.

Sweeney, P. D., Anderson, K., & Bailey, S. (1986). Attributional style in depression: A meta-analytic review. *Journal of Personality and Social Psychology, 50*, 974–991.

Sweeney, P. D., Moreland, R. L., & Gruber, K. L. (1982). Gender differences in performance attributions: Students' explanations for personal success or failure. *Sex Roles, 8*, 359–373.

Taylor, J. W. (1979). The timing of menstruation-related symptoms assessed by a daily symptom rating scale. *Acta Psychiatrica Scandinavica, 60*, 87–105.

Taynor, J., & Deaux, K. (1973). When women are more deserving than men: Equity, attribution and perceived sex differences. *Journal of Personality and Social Psychology, 28*, 360–367.

Teasdale, J. D. (1983). Negative thinking in depression: Cause, effect or reciprocal relationship? *Advances in Behavior Research and Therapy, 5*, 3–26.

Teasdale, J. D. (1985). Psychological treatments for depression: How do they work? *Behavior Research and Therapy, 23*, 157–165.

Teasdale, J. D. (1988). Cognitive vulnerability to persistent depression. *Cognition and Emotion, 2*, 247–274.

Teasdale, J. D., & Fogarty, S. J. (1979). Differential effects of induced mood on retrieval of pleasant and unpleasant events from episodic memory. *Journal of Abnormal Psychology, 88*, 248–257.

Terborg, J. R. (1977). Women in management: A research review. *Journal of Applied Psychology, 62*, 647–664.

Thase, M. E., Frank, E., & Kupfer, D. J. (1985). Biological processes in major depression. In E. E. Beckham & W. R. Leber (Eds.), *Handbook of depression: Treatment, assessment, and research* (pp. 816–913). Home-wood, IL: Dorsey Press.

Thom, M. (Ed.). (1987). *Letters to 'Ms.,' 1972–1987.* New York: Holt.

Thorndike, E. L. (1911). *Individuality.* Boston: Houghton Mifflin.

Tobin-Richards, M., Boxer, A., & Petersen, A. C. (1983). The psychological significance of pubertal change: Sex differences in perceptions of self during early adolescence. In J. Brooks-Gunn & A. C. Petersen (Eds.), *Girls at puberty: Biological and psychosocial perspectives* (pp. 127–154). New York: Plenum Press.

Turner, R. G. (1978). Effects of differential request procedures and self-consciousness on trait attributions. *Journal of Research in Personality, 12,* 431–438.

U.S. Merit Systems Protection Board. (1981). *Sexual harassment in the federal workplace: Is it a problem?* Washington, DC: U.S. Government Printing Office.

Unger, R. K. (1975). *Status, power, and gender: An examination of parallelisms.* Paper presented at the conference on New Directions for Research on Women, Madison, WI.

Vadher, A., & Ndetei, D. M. (1981). Life events and depression in a Kenyan setting. *British Journal of Psychiatry, 139,* 134–137.

Vanfossen, B. E. (1981). Sex differences in the mental health effects of spouse support and equality. *Journal of Health and Social Behavior, 22,* 130–143.

Verbrugge, L. M. (1983). Multiple roles and physical health of women and men. *Journal of Health and Social Behavior, 24,* 16–30.

Vermeulen, A., & Verdonck, L. (1976). Plasma androgen levels during the menstrual cycle. *American Journal of Obstetrics and Gynecology, 125,* 491–494.

Vetter, B. M. (1981). Women scientists and engineers: Trends in participation. *Science, 214,* 1313–1321.

Wahrman, R., & Pugh, M. D. (1974). Sex, non-conformity, and influence. *Sociometry, 37,* 137–147.

Walker, L. (1983). Victimology and the psychological perspectives of battered women. *Victimology, 8,* 82–104.

Walker, M. S., & McGilp, S. (1978). Excretory patterns of urinary free 11-hydroxycorticosteroids and total oestrogens throughout the normal menstrual cycle. *Annals of Clinical Biochemistry, 15,* 201–202.

Wallston, B. S., & O'Leary, V. E. (1981). Sex makes a difference: Differential perceptions of women and men. In L. Wheeler (Ed.), *Review of personality and social psychology* (pp. 9–41). Beverly Hills, CA: Sage.

Walsh, M. R. (1977, February). *Coping strategies of professional women: A comparison of two generations of women physicians.* Paper presented at Research Conference of the Association of Women in Psychology, St. Louis.

Warren, M. P. (1983). Physical and biological aspects of puberty. In J. Brooks-Gunn & A. C. Petersen (Eds.), *Girls at puberty: Biological and psychosocial perspectives* (pp. 3–28). New York: Plenum Press.

Weeke, A., Bille, M., Videbech, T., Dupont, A., & Juel-Nielsen, N. (1975). Incidence of depressive syndromes in a Danish county. *Acta Psychiatrica Scandinavica, 51*, 28–41.

Weinberger, D. A. (in press). The construct validity of the repressive coping style. In J. L. Singer (Ed.), *Repression and dissociation: Defense mechanisms and personality styles.* Chicago: University of Chicago Press.

Weiner, B. (Ed.). (1974). *Achievement motivation and attribution theory.* Morristown, NJ: General Learning Press.

Weiner, E., & Bachtold, L. (1972). *Personality characteristics of women in American politics.* Paper presented at the meeting of the American Political Science Association, Washington, DC.

Weissman, M. M. (1979). The myth of involutional melancholia. *Journal of the American Medical Association, 242*, 742–744.

Weissman, M. M., Kidd, K. K., & Prusoff, B. A. (1982). Variability in rates of affective disorders in relatives of depressed and normal probands. *Archives of General Psychiatry, 39*, 1397–1403.

Weissman, M. M., & Klerman, G. L. (1977). Sex differences in the epidemiology of depression. *Archives of General Psychiatry, 34*, 98–111.

Weissman, M. M., Klerman, G. L., Prusoff, B. A., Sholomskas, D., & Padian, N. (1981). Depressed outpatients: Results one year after treatment with drugs and/or interpersonal psychotherapy. *Archives of General Psychiatry, 38*, 51–55.

Weissman, M. M., & Myers, J. K. (1978). Affective disorders in a United States community: The use of research diagnostic criteria in an epidemiological survey. *Archives of General Psychiatry, 35*, 1304–1311.

Whitehead, R. E. (1934). Women pilots. *Journal of Aviation Medicine, 5*, 47–49.

Whiting, B., & Edwards, C. P. (1973). A cross-cultural analysis of sex differences in the behavior of children aged three through eleven. *Journal of Social Psychology, 91*, 171–188.

Williams, J. B. W., & Spitzer, R. L. (1983). The issue of sex bias in DSM-III. *American Psychologist, 38*, 793–798.

Williams, J. H. (Ed.). (1979). *Psychology of women: Selected readings.* New York: Norton.

Windholz, M. J., Marmar, C. R., & Horowitz, M. J. (1985). A review of the research on conjugal bereavement: Impact on health and efficacy of intervention. *Comprehensive Psychiatry, 26*, 433–447.

Wing, J. K. (1976). A technique for studying psychiatric morbidity in inpatient and outpatient series and general population samples. *Psychological Medicine, 6,* 667–671.

Winokur, G. (1973). Depression in the menopause. *American Journal of Psychiatry, 130,* 92–93.

Winokur, G., & Clayton, P. (1967). Family history studies: 2. Sex differences and alcoholism in primary affective illness. *British Journal of Psychiatry, 113,* 973–979.

Winokur, G., Rimmer, J., & Reich, T. (1971). Alcoholism: 4. Is there more than one type of alcoholism? *British Journal of Psychiatry, 118,* 525–531.

Winokur, G., & Tanna, V. L. (1969). Possible role of X-linked dominant factor in manic-depressive disease. *Diseases of the Nervous System, 30,* 89–93.

Wirtz, P. W., & Harrell, A. V. (1987). Effects of postassault exposure to attack-similar stimuli on long-term recovery of victims. *Journal of Consulting and Clinical Psychology, 55*(1), 10–16.

World Health Organization. (1980). *The international classification of diseases* (9th ed.). Geneva: Author.

Yalom, I. D., Lunde, D. T., Moos, R. H., & Hamburg, D. A. (1968). "Postpartum blues" syndrome: A description and related variables. *Archives of General Psychiatry, 18,* 16–27.

Yap, P. M. (1965). Phenomenology of affective disorders in Chinese and other cultures. In A. V. S. deReuch, & R. Porter (Eds.), *Transcultural psychiatry* (pp. 84–105). Boston: Little, Brown.

Zappert, L. T., & Stansbury, K. (1984). *In the pipeline: A comparative analysis of men and women in graduate programs in science, engineering and medicine at Stanford University* (Working Paper No. 20). Institute for Research on Women and Gender, Stanford University, Stanford, CA.

Zappert, L. T., & Weinstein, H. M. (1985). Sex differences in the impact of work on physical and psychological health. *American Journal of Psychiatry, 142,* 1174–1178.

Zelnick, M., & Kantner, J. F. (1977). Sexual and contraceptive experience of young, unmarried women in the United States, 1976 and 1971. *Family Planning Perspectives, 9,* 55–71.

Zilboorg, G., & Henry, G. W. (1941). *A history of medical psychology.* New York: Norton.

Zullow, H. M. (1984). *The interaction of rumination and explanatory style in depression.* Unpublished master's thesis, University of Pennsylvania, Philadelphia.

Zullow, H. M., Oettingen, G., Peterson, C., & Seligman, M. E. P. (1988). Pessimistic explanatory style in the historical record. *American Psychologist, 43,* 673–682.

Index

Library of Congress Cataloging-in-Publication Data

Nolen-Hoeksema, Susan, 1959–
Sex differences in depression / Susan Nolen-Hoeksema.
    p. cm.
Includes bibliographical references.
ISBN 0-8047-1640-4 (cl.):   ISBN 0-8047-2180-7 (pbk.)
    1. Depression, Mental—Sex factors.   2. Women—Mental health.
3. Women—Social conditions.   I. Title.
RC537.N65 1990   89-27303
616.85'27—dc20   CIP

⊗   This book is printed on acid-free paper